VAJRA HEART REVISITED

Teachings on the Path of Trekchö

Kyabje Tulku Urgyen Rinpoche

RANGJUNG YESHE BOOKS ❧ WWW.RANGJUNG.COM

Padmasambhava • *Treasures from Juniper Ridge* • *Advice from the Lotus-Born, Dakini Teachings* • *Following in Your Footsteps: The Lotus-Born Guru in Nepal*

Padmasambhava and Jamgön Kongtrül • *The Light of Wisdom, Vol. 1, & Vol. 2, Vol. 3, Secret, Vol. 4 & Vol. 5*

Padmasambhava, Chokgyur Lingpa, Jamyang Khyentse Wangpo, Tulku Urgyen Rinpoche, Orgyen Tobgyal Rinpoche, & others • *Dispeller of Obstacles* • *The Tara Compendium* • *Powerful Transformation* • *Dakini Activity*

Yeshe Tsogyal • *The Lotus-Born*

Dakpo Tashi Namgyal • *Clarifying the Natural State*

Tsele Natsok Rangdröl • *Mirror of Mindfulness* • *Heart Lamp*

Chokgyur Lingpa • *Ocean of Amrita* • *The Great Gate* • *Skillful Grace* • *Great Accomplishment* • *Guru Heart Practices*

Traktung Dudjom Lingpa • *A Clear Mirror*

Jamgön Mipham Rinpoche • *Gateway to Knowledge, Vol. 1, Vol. 2, Vol. 3, & Vol. 4*

Tulku Urgyen Rinpoche • *Blazing Splendor* • *Rainbow Painting* • *As It Is, Vol. 1 & Vol. 2* • *Vajra Speech* • *Repeating the Words of the Buddha* • *Dzogchen Deity Practice* • *Vajra Heart Revisited*

Adeu Rinpoche • *Freedom in Bondage*

Khenchen Thrangu Rinpoche • *King of Samadhi* • *Crystal Clear*

Chökyi Nyima Rinpoche • *Present Fresh Wakefulness* • *Bardo Guidebook*

Tulku Thondup • *Enlightened Living*

Orgyen Tobgyal Rinpoche • *Life & Teachings of Chokgyur Lingpa* • *Straight Talk*

Dzigar Kongtrül Rinpoche • *Uncommon Happiness*

Tsoknyi Rinpoche • *Fearless Simplicity* • *Carefree Dignity*

Marcia Binder Schmidt • *Dzogchen Primer* • *Dzogchen Essentials* • *Quintessential Dzogchen* • *Confessions of a Gypsy Yogini* • *Precious Songs of Awakening Compilation*

Erik Pema Kunsang • *Wellsprings of the Great Perfection* • *A Tibetan Buddhist Companion* • *The Rangjung Yeshe Tibetan-English Dictionary of Buddhist Culture & Perfect Clarity*

VAJRA HEART REVISITED

Teachings on the Path of Trekchö

Kyabje Tulku Urgyen Rinpoche

Foreword by Tsoknyi Rinpoche

Rangjung Yeshe PUBLICATIONS

Boudhanath, Hong Kong & Esby
2006

Rangjung Yeshe Publications
55 Mitchell Blvd, Suite 20
San Rafael, CA 94903 USA

Address mail to:
Rangjung Yeshe Publications
C/O Above
www.rangjung.com
www.lotustreasure.com

1 3 5 7 9 8 6 4 2

First paperback edition published in 2020

Printed in the United States of America

Distributed to the book trade by:
Perseus Books/Ingram

Publication data: ISBN13: 978-1-7328717-6-2 (pbk)

Title: *Vajra Heart Revisited: Teachings on the Path of Trekchö*

Kyabje Tulku Urgyen Rinpoche, Padmasambhava, Chokgyur Lingpa, Karmey Khenpo Rinchen Dargye, Longchenpa, Nyoshul Khen Rinpoche & Tsoknyi Rinpoche
Translated by Erik Pema Kunsang & Marcia Binder Schmidt

1. Vajrayana/Yidam—Tradition of Pith Instructions
2. Buddhism—Tibet

Photos courtesy of Marcia Binder Schmidt, Noah Gordon, Greg Rabold
Cover Photo: Oscar Fernandez
First Edition

CONTENTS

SUPPLICATIONS TO
KYABJE TULKU URGYEN RINPOCHE

Peerless holder of the family and teaching lineage
Of Chokgyur Lingpa, the great tertön king of the Dharma,
Bodhisattva vidyadhara, you benefit whoever connects with you,
Urgyen Tsewang Palbar, I supplicate you.

Written by Jigdrel Yeshe Dorje (Kyabje Dudjom Rinpoche)

Siddha son, Karma Urgyen, think of me.
Regard me from the wisdom space of awareness and emptiness.
Having received the mind transmission as your destined child,
May I seize the kingdom of realization.

Composed by Kyabje Dilgo Khyentse Rinpoche

Tulku Urgyen Rinpoche, Osel Ling, 1992

FOREWORD

Tsoknyi Rinpoche

What I remember is that Tulku Urgyen Rinpoche always mentioned that when his guru, Samten Gyatso, gave teachings on mind nature, he made sure that his students understood. Once he held them in his care, untiringly, again and again, he would repeat (the instructions), call them back, and check to make sure that they had understood. I think that influenced Tulku Urgyen Rinpoche, and he also taught that way.

The first time I received the pointing-out instructions was at the age of fourteen, in Rinpoche's small room, not far from where we are now (at Nagi Gompa). At that time, he repeated them again, and again, and again, that day and the next day. He showed by gesture, common language, and examples that were always rooted in quotations by Guru Rinpoche, Vairotsana, and others.

The main thing, nowadays, is that the most important teaching, the heart of Buddhism, is, especially, to find your own nature of mind. No matter what kind of teachings Tulku Urgyen Rinpoche gave, he tried to bring it back so that you would realize your mind nature. Presently looking around, I can see that we were very fortunate, as it is difficult to receive teachings like he gave. Either you will get a fully loaded teaching or just some kind of reading transmission, and you will have to figure it out yourself.

Tulku Urgyen Rinpoche was not like that. He remained in the nature of mind and (when he taught) it was like we were bathing together. Or as another example, it was like we were making wine, pressing the grapes together. Every moment you got something; you knew something. For me, personally, that type of teaching is very important. Mind nature teaching is the root teaching. Then you can get teachings from Nyoshul Khen Rinpoche and Khenpo Namdrol, and somewhere you can connect to it. It does not become only intellectual. But, if you do not have the nature of mind (experience), and you just listen to all those texts, it becomes somewhat heavy. Then it becomes another intellectual (pursuit). You do not know where to connect.

The point is that Tulku Urgyen Rinpoche was inspired by Samten Gyatso and he has that (same style). This was how he transmitted the teachings to me; I saw with my own eyes, and he taught in that way to many students. And those teachings are in this book, *Vajra Heart Revisted.*

PREFACE

Marcia Binder Schmidt

In these times, it is almost embarrassing to speak of one's teacher as being the perfect master that he was. Firstly, current-day masters of that caliber are very few and far between; secondly, there is much talk of abuse and misuse of power; and finally, while exiled Tibetan teachers devote a good deal of time to preserving the Dharma, they unfortunately spend less time practicing or studying it. Additionally, it sounds like one is praising oneself for having the great fortune to connect with such a teacher, thereby elevating one's position and specialness. Comparing my characteristics to my teacher's is easy to do: it is like the example that Kyabje Tulku Urgyen Rinpoche gave in his memoir, *Blazing Splendor,* where he likened his own guru to delicious food and himself to what comes out after digesting it.

Kyabje Tulku Urgyen Rinpoche's impeccable qualities were evident to all who met him and received teachings and empowerments from him. Many great teachers who knew him expressed these sentiments. For example, Tartang Rinpoche said, "Tulku Urgyen was someone with great kindness and a strong sense of loyalty; he never changed his feelings for someone once he had gotten to know them well…Tulku Urgyen was also free of deceit and duplicity. If he said something, you could always trust that his words and his heart were in harmony." Or like Orgyen Tobgyal Rinpoche, "Tulku Urgyen had confidence and utterly pure trust based on his personal, direct understanding that buddha-nature really is present in every sentient being. Just like oil is present in each and every sesame seed, any sentient being can realize the awakened state and thus has the basis for enlightenment. Therefore, Tulku Urgyen showed respect for every sentient being and didn't turn against anyone. He felt this not as mere platitude, but from the core of his heart. The great masters of this time—the Karmapa of incomparable kindness, Kyabje Dudjom Rinpoche, and Dilgo

Khyentse Rinpoche—have all venerated Tulku Urgyen as one of their root gurus and a jewel in their crown ornament."

Similarly, Tarik Tulku stated:

Even though he had the status of someone whom the Karmapa venerated at the crown of his own head, Tulku Urgyen did not become full of self-importance or take advantage of this fame. When in a group of lamas or sitting in a large religious gathering, he always refused to preside as the head, always insisting on taking a lower position. Taking the lower seat is a sign of having tamed one's own mind, and this is how he always acted. Otherwise, since he was the Karmapa's guru, it would have been perfectly fine to maintain a dignified presence, but because of being a tantric practitioner, he would regard himself as lower than any other lama or even than an ordinary, fully ordained monk.

True humility is the sign of having gained experience and realization. Without experience and realization, we become involved in mundane attitudes—conceit towards people below, jealousy towards people above, and competitiveness towards our equals. This is unavoidable, because the five poisonous emotions of attachment, anger, dullness, pride, and envy still remain alive within our stream of being. Even though someone may dress up as a renunciate or a yogi, these negative emotions still become evident from time to time. Tulku Urgyen, however, was not at all like that.

These are not empty praises but clear examples of how my teacher truly was. Please imagine what it is like to meet the person you waited your whole life to meet and to then stay in his presence for many years. In these dark times, it takes an incalculable storehouse of merit, which I pray I have not depleted. Kyabje Tulku Urgyen Rinpoche was one of the best in every way—as a person, a teacher, a tantric practitioner, and a vajra master. He never ceased to amaze me and he never let me down, ever.

Kyabje Tulku Urgyen Rinpoche was in the tradition of a hidden yogi, fully realized but low key and humble. He could keep that secret as long as he did not teach or give empowerments—but when he did, his noble-ness and skill were revealed. The Dharma flowed through him with utmost brilliance, compassion, accomplishment, and attention to detail. He viewed the recognition of mind essence as being inherent and easily acknowledged, and he taught with such confidence that students could feel this in a vivid and viable way. He himself explained how he was authorized to give mind teachings by his guru Samten Gyatso:

> When I was around twenty, Samten Gyatso told me, "You appear to be someone who can give mind teachings. You are the kind of person who finds it all quite easy, not seeing how anyone could have problems understanding the nature of mind. You could end up too blasé; then again, maybe you simply will be very confident … "
>
> "You feel that realizing the nature of mind is simply a mat-ter of course," he continued, "but I want you to understand: some people do not know the nature of mind, and there definitely is a reason for that. There are many people whose practice of 'mind essence' is nothing more than remaining absentminded and unaware in the state of the all-ground.
>
> "Nevertheless, for the time being, you should go ahead and test your confidence on a few old men and women. You might be able to benefit one or two, so it's fine for you to teach them."
>
> In this way, he gave me the go-ahead to begin teaching.

> I started giving people advice on understanding the nature of mind because I was very talkative. I couldn't help it; it would just slip out! When I spent time with Samten Gyatso, I listened in on whatever instructions he gave. Often it would be the pointing-out instruction and advice on how to truly meditate in the simplest way.
>
> Afterward, there might be some people outside his room who couldn't quite understand what he had said. They would ask me, "How can it be that easy?" And I would say, "Why do you think it has to be difficult? It really is so easy." Then they would reply, "But I don't get it." And I'd tell them, "What do you mean, you don't get it? Just let be!" I had that attitude because I'd heard what my uncle had said, and I'd just parrot it.
>
> My uncle would then call me in and repeat, "It seems you are

the talkative type, as well as someone who thinks that recognizing mind nature is totally easy. I think that in the future you will be like this as well—you will be both talkative and somebody who acts like it is really simple!" And he was right.

On one hand, maybe with my teaching style I'm just fooling everybody, making it too simple. But on the other hand, this is really how it is! It is the truth. What is the use of trying to sit and push and struggle, when we can allow the three kayas of buddhahood to be naturally present? Why do we have to strain and contort ourselves into an uncomfortable posture and an uptight meditative state with some hope that in the future, after lots of effort, we may get there? We don't need to go through all that trouble and tension. All we need to do is totally let be and recognize our nature right now.[1]

That is how he transmitted the teachings, in a simple and confident way. From the onset, he unfolded the entire essential path of practice to those in his presence. He guided his students in a way that revealed and unpacked their self-hidden potential and continuously helped them develop the ability to recognize their nature, by providing teachings to stabilize recognition of mind's nature and enhance the practice of it. His wish was to establish his students in the quintessential training of recognizing mind essence, free of any unhealthy dependence upon him. His specialty was guiding students through their own experience, as he skillfully led each one to individually meet his or her nature. For many, the taste of rigpa was undeniable in his presence. He did not give up on people and repeatedly responded to questions from students on how to definitively decide and gain confidence in the practice of Trekchö.

Thus, this book is a collection of teachings on the path of Trekchö. Many of these are presented in the style of Tulku Urgyen Rinpoche, as questions and answers regarding misunderstandings, doubts, pitfalls, vital points, pith instructions, and clarifications. It is built upon an earlier restricted book, *Vajra Heart*. Since much of its content has since been openly shared in other publications, it seemed timely to review and expand upon *Vajra Heart*'s many formidable topics. This book is an unrestricted *Yeshe Lama*[2] for the path of Trekchö, a roadmap for practice that covers all the key points of this path.

In the Great Perfection, there are several approaches to practicing the preliminaries. Here I am following the outline of *Lamrim Yeshe Nyingpo,* a terma text of Guru Rinpoche that varies from the systems in Jigme Lingpa's *Yeshe Lama* and in Dudjom Lingpa's *Neluk Rangjung, (nas lugs byung jung).* *Rushan,* or separation, in this tradition, only applies to Tögal practice, whereas the preliminaries for Trekchö are the vajra body, four speech yogas, resting in the natural state, and remaining in freshness. The two other systems label them as the secret practice within the outer, inner, and secret rushan practices and give various ways to train in them. In all traditions, the instructions contained in the *Three Words Striking the Vital Point* fall under the main part of practice.

The book concludes with enhancement practices as well as bardo teachings, based on a Longchenpa text, and it includes an ultimate guru yoga written by Kyabje Tulku Urgyen Rinpoche himself. Finally, in the appendix, there is a commentary on this guru yoga written by Nyoshul Khen Rinpoche. Khen Rinpoche determined that this profound guru yoga was a mind treasure and inserted terma signs whenever he directly quoted the root text. So, please do not be annoyed that the terma signs are not in the first presentation of the guru yoga, as that was how Kyabje Tulku Urgyen Rinpoche originally dictated it. Terma needs to be verified by someone other than the actual tertön.

Kyabje Tulku Urgyen Rinpoche loved the Dzogchen teachings and had the utmost respect for the lineages and lineage holders of that tradition. Toward the end of his life, he requested the Longchen Nyingtig hearing lineage from Nyoshul Khen Rinpoche, even though he had had it before. His motivation was twofold, as far as I understood: Firstly, the beauty of the teachings, their truth, and the skillful presentation by Khen Rinpoche had tears of joy rolling down his face. Secondly, it was a way to show younger lamas the specialness of Nyoshul Khen Rinpoche, for if an acknowledged Dzogchen master took such teachings from another teacher, then surely that teacher was someone worth flocking to, which is what happened.

There is also an amusing side to this tale. By the time this took place, both masters were advanced in age and not in the best health. For the transmission to take place, Nyoshul Khen Rinpoche, who spoke in a whisper, needed a microphone and Kyabje Tulku Urgyen Rinpoche, who was hard of hearing, needed an earphone. As Rinpoche later remarked,

"The hearing lineage this time was transmitted from one who could barely speak to one who could barely hear!" The unfolding of this event gives a small glimpse into the humor and specialness of my teacher, who embodied the depth and profundity of the Great Perfection with the lightness and joy of a fully realized yogi. No doubt as you read these pages that will become most evident.

Once more, sincere gratitude and thanks go to Maha Lotsawa Erik Pema Kunsang, the translator of all of these texts and many of the oral teachings. These talks took place at Nagi Gompa, Kyabje Tulku Urgyen Rinpoche's hermitage in Nepal, above the Kathmandu Valley. The audiences consisted of anywhere from two to twenty-five people over the course of fourteen years.

Heartfelt thanks go to Tsoknyi Rinpoche, for sharing his impressions of his father's style. Special recognition and thanks are also due to the Tsadra Foundation and Eric Colombel, for sponsoring both the translation and compilation of this book as well as subsidizing its production. Additionally, I'd like to thank the editor, Anne Paniagua; my constant book designer, Joan Olson; the meticulous proofreaders, Lynn Schroeder and Michael Yockey; the cover designer, Mary Sweet; and the diligent transcriber, Tim Dufka, all of whose efforts have helped bring this publication to fruition.

The profundity of the Dzogchen teachings permeates every page of this book. The skillful presentation of Kyabje Tulku Urgyen Rinpoche brings them to life for each listener and reader. May we all realize the ultimate meaning of the Great Perfection and may these pith instructions remain for as long as there are beings to be influenced.

HISTORY AND OVERVIEW

The Buddhist tradition consists of nine vehicles, three taught by the nirmanakaya buddha, three taught by the sambhogakaya buddha, and three taught by the dharmakaya buddha. The three vehicles taught by the nirmanakaya are geared for the shravakas, pratyekabuddhas, and bodhisattvas. The three vehicles taught by the sambhogakaya buddha are called Kriya, Upa, and Yoga. The three vehicles taught by the dharmakaya buddha are called Maha, Anu, and Ati.

Within Atiyoga, there are subdivisions such as the outer mind section, the inner space section, and the secret instruction section. The fourth subdivision, called the *innermost unexcelled section,* or the *innermost heart essence,* consists of the special Dzogchen teachings themselves. It is said that the ultimate view of the teachings given by the nirmanakaya buddha is the view of the Middle Way, Madhyamika; the ultimate view given by the sambhogakaya buddha is Mahamudra; and the ultimate view given by the dharmakaya buddha is Dzogchen. In this way, although Buddha Sakyamuni had, of course, realized the nature of all nine vehicles, in his capacity as a nirmanakaya buddha, he publicly gave teachings appropriate for shravakas, pratyekabuddhas, and bodhisattvas.

In the name Dzogchen, Great Perfection, perfect or complete means that all the lower vehicles are perfected or completely contained within the Dzogchen teachings. The meaning of the word *dzog,* perfection or completion, is explained thus in the *Kunje Gyalpo* tantra:

> Complete as one—everything is complete within mind.
> Complete as two—everything of samsara and nirvana is complete
> within this.

'Dzog' means that the vehicle of Dzogchen contains all the teachings as well as all phenomena and the lower vehicles. Chen or great means that there is no method or means higher than this vehicle. Although we say that Dzogchen, sometimes called Atiyoga, is a dharma tradition, it is in actuality nothing other than the basic state of one's mind.

Turning to the practice itself, we can speak of Dzogchen as we can of all views, in terms of ground, path, and fruition. Traditionally we say, "The ground is Mahamudra; the path is the great Madhyamika, the great Middle Way; and the fruition is Dzogchen." Applied in practice, each of these three great views has its own view, meditation, action, and fruition.

In the system of Dzogchen, we can compare the ground to pure gold and the path to gold mixed with impurities that are slowly being purified. Fruition, the state of buddhahood, is once again pure gold, the attainment of stability in recognition of the primordially pure ground. The difference here between sentient beings and buddhas is merely the difference between gold mixed with impurities and pure, untainted gold.

Ground Dzogchen, defined as *essence, nature,* and *capacity,* which correspond to the three kayas, is the ground, or the basic state, for both buddhas and sentient beings. For a buddha, there is no straying onto the path. Sentient beings strayed into the confused state of what we call path when their essence, nature, and capacity were obscured by the three kinds of ignorance: the ignorance of single identity, co-emergent ignorance, and conceptual ignorance. Sentient beings are like gold mixed with impurities. In the case of the buddhas, on the other hand, their essence ripened into enlightened body, their nature ripened into enlightened speech, and their capacity ripened into enlightened mind. The ground itself being realized, fruition is like pure gold without defects and is called the union of ground and fruition. In this way, buddhas were matured into primordial enlightenment, and the three aspects of the ground became the three vajras: vajra body, vajra speech, and vajra mind.

When the essence, nature, and capacity of sentient beings are obscured by the three kinds of ignorance, the three vajras in their impure state become ordinary body, speech, and mind. The three kinds of ignorance are fleeting or incidental. The confusion that has arisen on the state of the path can be cleared away. When we remove the stains of the three kinds of ignorance, we can become re-enlightened instead of primordially enlightened. This is accomplished by following the oral instructions of a qualified teacher; through this we accomplish the three kayas.

> The ground is primordial purity,
> The path is spontaneous presence,
> The fruition is kayas and wisdoms.

In practice, recognizing our essence as primordial purity is the ground; recognizing our nature as spontaneous presence is the path; and recognizing spontaneous presence as our natural expression, devoid of a self-nature, is the fruition. Although we have strayed into confusion on the ground and path, by practicing in this way, ground and fruition can still be united in the final state of enlightenment.

The third Karmapa, Rangjung Dorje, taught thus about our basic nature in the following series of quotes: "It is not existent, as even the buddhas have not seen it." This means that the basic state of mind is not something that exists in a concrete way: even the buddhas of the three times have never perceived it. "It is not nonexistent, as it is the basis for both samsara and nirvana. This is not a contradiction; it is the middle path of unity." Contradiction, like the impossible instance of having fire and water on the same plate, does not apply here. The basic nature is neither existent nor nonexistent—these two are an indivisible unity. "May I perceive the mind essence free from extremes." Usually when we say *is,* we are contradicting *is not,* and when we say *nonexistent,* we are contradicting *existent.* But this middle path of unity is devoid of such contradiction. Recognizing and experiencing this is to attain the unified state of Vajradhara.

In Dzogchen terminology, nonexistence means primordial purity and existence means spontaneous presence; these are regarded as an indivisible unity. We can also say that primordial purity means *emptiness* and spontaneous presence means *luminosity* or *luminous cognizance.*

These two aspects of our basic nature, being empty and cognizant, are a unity. Why is this? Mind essence is empty while being cognizant, and it cognizes while still being empty. There is no obstruction between the two aspects. The empty aspect is called essence, the cognizant aspect is termed *nature,* and their unity is called *capacity.* The empty aspect is also called *dharmakaya,* the cognizant aspect is referred to as *sambhogakaya,* and their unity is called *nirmanakaya.*

This unity of being empty and cognizant is the state of mind of all sentient beings. As there is nothing special about that state, the practitioner should suffuse it with awareness. The path of practice is to become stable in recognizing this unity of empty cognizance suffused with awareness.

Malaysia

GROUND

The ground to be understood is the all-pervasive sugata essence.[8]
Uncompounded, luminous, and empty, it is the natural state of
   awareness.[8]
Beyond confusion and liberation, it is completely quiescent, like
   space.[8]
Although it abides without separation in samsara or joining in
   nirvana,[8]
Due to the great demon of co-emergent and conceptual ignorance,[80]
From the solidified habitual patterns of grasping and fixation,[8]
And the different perceptions of worlds and inhabitants,[8]
The six classes of beings appeared as a dream.[8]
Although this is so, you have never moved, and will never move,[8]
From the original condition of the essence.[8]
Endeavor therefore in purifying the temporary stains.[84]

First of all, the primordial ground in this context is the primordially free
yeshe, *(ye shes),* or rigpa, which is devoid of any fault, utterly flawless.
But it is also lomaten, *(blo ma bstan),* which in this context means undetermined, in the sense that a tulku is born but has not been given a name
or been recognized as so and so; it is not determined yet who that tulku
is. We can also say that it means *undecided.* In this case, undetermined
doesn't mean impure. It is primordially free yeshe. At this point, that
ground has not been recognized as either a buddha or a sentient being.

   It is an undecided or undetermined state, but it is not real ignorance, *ma rigpa,* because it is awareness wisdom. There is another type of
lomaten that is a vacant state of ignorance, where one doesn't know anything that hasn't happened yet. The primordial, original ground is called
lomaten in the sense of being undecided—not because it is an obscured,
ignorant state. It simply hasn't been named yet. This refers to the ground
of primordial purity, but then when the spontaneously present manifestation of the ground appears, there are other choices. It is in the sponta-

neously present manifestation of the ground that either Samantabhadra awakens to complete buddhahood by means of the six special qualities, and is therefore called *buddha,* or one falls into delusion through the three types of ignorance and is called a *sentient being.*

When the declaration is made, "I am the primordial buddha, the first of all buddhas," alluding to Samantabhadra, who has awakened through the six special qualities, this does not refer to a person, or man, who attained enlightenment. All the emanations and all the different manifestations appear from Samantabhadra. Regardless of whether they are sambhogakaya or dharmakaya, these are emanations, re-emanations, and so forth. They are all the expression of awareness wisdom, the original Samantabhadra, which is simply unmistaken wakefulness. That is the meaning of the original buddha, Samantabhadra. All appearances unfold from the expression of awareness, like the sun and its rays.

At the same time, what we call *sentient being* is the mistaken or deluded mind and all its expressions, which are the 84,000 different types of disturbing emotions. Nevertheless—corresponding to all the various manifestations of deluded mind—there is an equal number of manifestations of the sugatas, which are meant to influence or subdue through any necessary means. In other words, there are manifestations of the enlightened state that correspond in equal number with the manifestations of the deluded states.

There is a statement that says, "Dharmadhatu pervades all of samsara and nirvana." That is rigpa, the buddha-nature present in all sentient beings, which is none other than Samantabhadra. It is also called *space and awareness* or *unobstructed, empty cognizance.* It is not something we find only in nirvana; it is also present in samsara, because all sentient beings have consciousness. The essence of this consciousness is the buddha-nature. The main reason why sentient beings can awaken to buddhahood is because no one is without buddha-nature.

Vajrayana teachings are always structured as the three aspects of symbol, meaning, and sign. Samantabhadra as *meaning* is the unobstructed, empty cognizance present as the nature of mind of everyone. Samantabhadra as *symbol* refers to the paintings or statues in all different colors and shapes. Samantabhadra as *sign* is the vision of the deity that you will experience when you engage in the development stage for some time; the deity that appears is Samantabhadra as sign. Also, when engaging in the practice of Tögal, *(thod rgal),* the buddha forms that appear are Samant-abhadra as sign. In this way, there are three.

Some people wonder, "Why is Samantabhadra mentioned in these different ways? Sometimes they say Samantabhadra is your own mind. Sometimes he is this figure on the wall. Sometimes it is said that when you do Tögal practice Samantabhadra appears. When people practice development stage and chant mantras, a vision of a deity appears. Why are there so many different kinds of Samantabhadra?" Actually, uncer-tainty comes from not understanding the three types: meaning, symbol, and sign. The real meaning of Samantabhadra is the unmistaken wake-fulness, the nature of your own mind. When you recognize the real essence of your mind, it is naturally apparent.

During the development stage, try to visualize that there is a Samant-abhadra present in the celestial palace. That is Samantabhadra as sign. In one way, Samantabhadra is here in the sense of being the nature of our own wakefulness, but on the other hand, he is over there at the place where we are supposed to give the offerings to the celestial palace. Why is that? The one over there is a product of skillful means. When making an offering, there needs to be someone who makes an offering to some-thing. Those to whom the offerings are made should be in front of you. Without that, there is no real making of offerings. But at the end, there is always the ultimate way of offering, resting in the state free from holding onto the concepts of giver, offering, and recipient.

It is the same in the Seven Branch practice: we take refuge, pay hom-age, make confession, make offerings, make requests to turn the wheel of Dharma, supplicate to not pass into nirvana, dedicate the merit, and so forth. The real meaning is our unborn nature, sherab, *(shes rab)*. The other way is the means, to purify our habitual attitudes of concepts, which we have harbored for so long. At the end, there is always resting in the nonarising nature or essence of mind, which is totally free from con-cepts. In this way, there is first the skillful means aspect, and afterward the knowledge aspect—means and knowledge go hand in hand. The ultimate offering, the ultimate Samantabhadra, is our own unborn mind.

It is a fact that no matter what kind of universe, or world, sentient beings appear—regardless of their different shapes and configurations, whether created or formed—they always do so within space, not any-where else. When they abide and move around, it is always within space.

When everything falls apart, disintegrates, and disappears—when all beings die and vanish—this always takes place within space. They never come from some other place, exist in some other place, and disappear to some other place. There is nowhere else outside of space.

In the same way, all kinds of mental states, such as joy and sadness, as well as all spiritual practices—such as making offerings, visualizing, thinking this, feeling that—take place within the expanse of rigpa. Everything begins and ends within that. These states cannot vanish into any place other than the state of rigpa, which is, by itself, devoid of the three concepts of doer, deed, and object. That's why the expanse of rigpa is so precious, so basic. No matter how our state of mind flaps around, no matter what it chases after, the flapping and chasing take place nowhere other than in the state of rigpa. That's why it is so important to recognize rigpa.

All the galaxies throughout the universe that have formed, persisted, disintegrated, and vanished are just a play or drama displayed within space. There is no other place this could occur. The dramas of sentient beings could not be played out anywhere but within space. In the same way, any kind of mental play of happiness or sorrow that we can possibly drum up cannot take place anywhere else, other than in the expanse of rigpa.

In short, according to Dzogchen, the identity of all beings within the three realms can be expressed as essence, nature, and capacity—also called *dharmakaya, sambhogakaya,* and *nirmanakaya* or *body, speech,* and *mind.* All are in the expanse of rigpa, unmoved from basic space. When (rigpa) is recognized, no matter how it all dances about, appearing in all different ways, it is nothing other than children's play forming within space. The basic space of rigpa doesn't change in any way whatsoever. Only the different manifestations change, and they cannot harm space in any way. Once we recognize and attain stability in the space of rigpa, itself, nothing else really matters. Then everything is seen as children's play. That is the experience of a yogi who is stable in rigpa. Nothing can harm, disturb, or cause fixation no matter what arises, just as Samantabhadra exemplifies. Think about the analogy of space; it is extremely beneficial. That is the way it really is. The way it appears is how it seems to be. We think, "This person was born and now they move around. Now they have died. Now they are reborn again." That's only how it seems to be, the way it appears.

Only when we are deluded does it seem that there are myriad different worlds, experiences, and apparitions, but actually in the nondeluded space of rigpa, there is no increase or decrease, no change whatsoever. It is out of that realization that the vajra jokes and the amazing declarations are made. It is all talking about the unchanging space of rigpa. Rigpa is primordially endowed with the perfect qualities, just like the sun or a wish-fulfilling jewel. It is primordially free from all faults. This is our basic capital, the essence of mind, the buddha-nature, which we want to invest in through practice. We already have it and it is like a wish-fulfilling jewel or tree, like the sun itself, which can fulfill all wishes. It doesn't require any effort whatsoever or any striving. Simply leaving it in its natural state is sufficient. Progress comes through effortlessness, nonstriving. Honestly, since we already have it, how could we produce it through effort? If we didn't have it and had to search for it elsewhere, then we could strive and achieve, but it's not like that. This is the most precious, and it requires no effort. Don't modify; don't fabricate.

Space is never altered or changed; it never increases or decreases. Conditions like mist, fog, haze, or clouds can make it seem that space is changing. In the same way, our essence is fundamentally unchanging; the nature of rigpa cannot change. Only our dualistic thinking makes it seem to change. If you try to cultivate buddha-nature, that's just a concept. If you forget it, you are deluded. Once you recognize rigpa, the way to progress or put it into practical experience is through neither meditating upon it nor forgetting it. If you meditate, it is conceptualized; if you forget it, it is delusion. Practice uncultivated nondistraction.

It is unformed, like space, but its qualities are spontaneously present. Its unformed quality is like space. Its spontaneously present qualities are like a wish-fulfilling jewel. Not cultivating or meditating means that you don't have to cultivate space by meditating upon it. Try to think of space. Can you think of space without it being anything except a concept—without meditating, yet without parting from it? It is an empty, awake state; that's it.

Götsangpo, Gonpo Dorje once said, "Sometimes Samantabhadra is the wakefulness of empty cognizance, which is wide open and more immense than space. But sometimes it is the manifest emptiness, which is a form with a face, arms, and brilliant blue color. The meaning is rigpa. Right now, the falsity of all the words of the 84,000 Dharma sections is exposed. Leave it like that; that's it." Try to slowly understand these words; they are actually mind blowing.

The primordial, original ground is your present rigpa; it's not back there in the past. It's not up ahead and it's not behind you somewhere. Your unfabricated, present wakefulness is the original ground. No matter how much you check and investigate, this empty, awake moment is the primordial ground. But we forget and become distracted and then even what cannot be lost seems lost. We undergo all the different troubles, the suffering of the eighteen hells, while still having it. We never lose it, unless we become a piece of wood.

We are like a trader who has done really bad business and gone broke. Some traders begin with a big capital and lose more and more until finally they do not even have a single cup. That's the same as continually wasting buddha-nature. We must slowly reinvest the right way; do clever business deals. When we do really good business and get the state of Samantabhadra back in our own hands, this is called achieving true profit.

Otherwise, while already having Samantabhadra, we still have one loss after another until the basic capital shrinks down to only one rupee. If we keep that one rupee and reinvest it in our business, it can increase more and more until we finally regain ownership of Samantabhadra. Just joking, but actually, I'm not joking; among jokes, it is the truth. Right now, we are Samantabhadra, who is down to his last rupee. Slowly we have to increase that one rupee. If we get more and more money out of that, we can take ownership of the most valuable thing in the world. We win; the eighteen hells lose. We need to gain such profits.

When most people make a bad business deal, they sit with their nose down on the ground with a dark face and breath with deep sighs, saying, "Oh, I really lost money here. These are dark times." They beat their chest and say, "I really blew it this time. I made a big mistake, a bad investment." We have thrown away Samantabhadra by not knowing. Think about this well. If we can now do proper business, we can transcend the realms of samsara and step beyond the three realms.

TREKCHÖ PRELIMINARIES

There are preliminary practices for Trekchö, cutting through, which are called the khordey rushan, *('khor 'das rushan),* or the three doors khordey rushan, *(sgo gsum 'khor das rushan).* Rushan means making the difference or separating samsara and nirvana in terms of body, speech, and mind. Right now, even though our nature is the body, speech, and mind of all the victorious ones, the Buddha, because we do not recognize our buddha-nature, our physical body of flesh and blood obscures the indestructible vajra body. Our voice is intermittent—words and sounds that come and go, which obscure the unceasing vajra speech. Our discursive thinking obscures the vajra mind. Even though our being is really the body, speech, and mind of the awakened state, we appear to be the ordinary body, speech, and mind of a sentient being that wanders in samsara. In order to make the difference, in order to separate the two, we go through what is called the rushan, the separation practice.

To reiterate, the idea of the separation practice is that our ordinary body, speech, and mind—the material body, our voice, and our thinking—have their source in the body, speech, and mind of the awakened state. If we track down where this whole thing actually comes from, we find that it comes out of the enlightened body, speech, and mind. But at present, in our deluded state, we need to make the distinction; we need to separate, as if water and milk were mixed together. We need to separate the milk from the water. That is the idea of the separation practices.

The rushan, or the separation practice, is distinguished in the view itself. Even though by nature we are the three vajras of body, speech, and mind, at the same time, all sentient beings have ordinary body, speech, and mind. By going through these practices, we are able to make the distinction, in order to separate what is called *innate ignorance* from *innate wakefulness,* and that distinction is made in the view itself.

This is an incredibly profound practice, much more profound than any ordinary virtuous action. It is said that compared to doing a hundred thousand circumambulations and offering a hundred thousand butter lamps, it is more profound to engage in a practice like this for even

a short while. In general, compared to all the practices, such as the preliminary practices, the ngöndro, the normal development stage, and so
forth—the normal types of meditation—it is much more profound to
engage in the training of the nadis, pranas, and bindus, *(rtas, rlung, thig
le)*. But compared to the trainings and mastery in nadis, pranas, and bindus, it is much more profound to practice the Dzogchen teachings of the
rushan, Trekchö, and Tögal. In this way, we should understand that each
level of vehicle is much more profound and effective than the ones below.

In the different Dzogchen cycles of teaching, there are different
ways of practicing the rushan and sometimes there are different levels of
rushan. These are preliminaries for Dzogchen, the special preliminaries.
First, there are the three parts for body, speech, and mind. Body is the
vajra posture. Speech is the speech yogas of HUNG. Mind is the inquiry
into the arising, remaining, and disappearance of thoughts, which are
normally called the arising, dwelling, and ceasing. Through these practices, we discover that what we call mind does not arise from anywhere.
It doesn't remain anywhere. It doesn't go anywhere. It is in fact emptiness itself. We come to understand this, not just as an idea or theory, but
as an actual experience. By looking into whether thoughts actually arise
from somewhere, remain anywhere, or go anywhere, we discovered they
don't; it is just emptiness. This is seeing emptiness in actuality. We have
already been introduced to the nature of mind; we've had it pointed out.
The state of rigpa, proper, gets pointed out really clearly afterward anyway, though recognition of the natural state of mind is already occurring.

In addition, the Dzogchen preliminaries include the extraordinary version of shamatha and vipashyana, here called nalbab, *(rnal dbab)*, remaining in naturalness, and sorshug, *(sor bzug)*, sustaining the freshness of the
original state. Nalbab means arriving at the natural state. Sorshug means
sustaining the freshness of that natural state through daily activities. Without losing the continuity of recognizing mind essence, we bring it into
movement or daily activities. Nalbab involves just resting evenly in what
was recognized through the mind inquiries, and sorshug indicates that we
then bring that into activity, without losing its continuity.

Up to this point, we've been dealing with the extraordinary preliminary practices for Trekchö. After this comes the pointing-out instruction
according to Garab Dorje: *Three Words Striking the Vital Point, (Tshig
Gsum Gnad Brdeg)*. The first is to recognize our own nature. The second

is to decide on one point. And the third is to gain confidence in liberation. These teachings are categorized under the main practice.

However, it is possible to have already recognized your own nature during the preliminaries, rather than having to wait for the pointing-out instruction. There is the story from the previous lives of Ngaktrin Rinpoche, the former incarnation of my guru Samten Gyatso. At the time of the third incarnation of Ngaktrin, as a small boy, he stayed at Lhachab Gompa. He was playing around like a boy does, and an old gonla, the lama who does all the protector practices, said, "Don't play around like that; look into your mind." Then the boy stopped and asked, "Yeah, but how do I look into my mind?" He responded, "Just let your mind look into itself." Then he reflected and looked into his own mind, which he saw to be empty and clear, wide awake without thoughts. He recognized mind nature right then.

Later when he grew up, he enlisted in the retreat center at Palpung Monastery in Eastern Tibet. He became the retreat master and finally became a great siddha, who had clairvoyance and could perform miracles. He became a really great master. During all this time, he received teachings on the pointing-out instruction from many great masters. Nonetheless, he realized that what they pointed out and what he recognized were not different from what the old gonla had already shown him. So, he always said his real root guru was this old gonla when he was a kid. He was just eight years old when he recognized rigpa.

It is not that the state of rigpa somehow shifts into a higher gear, becoming improved or more refined. The empty cognizance that is recognized from the beginning is nothing other than what is realized later. It is not like the case of visualization, where for example, in the fourfold intent of approach and accomplishment, you first visualize the seed syllable and the garland of mantra. Then, the next day, the lama says, "Now you step up to a higher level." Then you visualize that it spins and radiates light and that it sends out a lot of different things. Finally, the whole world becomes deities and mantras and so forth. The state of rigpa is not like that. What is recognized in the beginning is the same as what is recognized later. What Ngaktrin Tulku realized during his life was the same as what the old gonla pointed out when he was a kid. In the same sense, it is possible to have already recognized the nature of mind during the preliminaries of the extraordinary shamatha and vipashyana. Ngaktrin Tulku is the same as Samten Gyatso, who was my root guru, but I was telling about his former lifetime, the third incarnation.

Please understand that these two preliminaries, the nalbab and sorshug, the extraordinary shamatha and vipashyana, are incredibly profound. They can be summarized in just one sentence that Longchenpa often mentioned in his trilogy *Resting in the Nature of Mind:* "Rest your tired mind." Our mind has been so exhausted going through life after life of trials and tribulations; finally, we are told by Longchenpa, now simply take a break. That is exactly what the teaching here is all about. Instead of making thoughts over and over, churning out one thought after the other, let everything settle. Just recognize the natural state as it is and remain in that. Since the state of rigpa itself is totally free of thoughts of the three times, when we recognize rigpa, we have no impetus to create or fabricate any further thought of chasing after some memory of the past or planning some event in the future, because rigpa itself is free of the thoughts of the three times. So, it is impossible for any thought to take place and remain while recognizing the state of rigpa. That is the true rest that Longchenpa admonishes us to apply. Once we let our weary, tired, and exhausted mind rest, then it is like a person who has completed his task. There's a very simple way for us to understand this: We are trying so hard to get our long-term visa for Nepal, going through all kinds of painstaking efforts—bribing and filling out forms, whatever. Finally, we get the visa and we can take a rest, like the person who has completed his task. That's the idea here. It is quite likely that even through the preliminaries we can recognize the natural state of rigpa itself, even though they are the preliminaries.

QUESTION: How do we actually structure these practices with sessions in a practical way?

RINPOCHE: Let me make this suggestion: It is better to practice these things in a retreat situation, because we are less distracted. There are fewer diversions and, therefore, there is more merit, and practice is more effective. So, it's best to do these practices while in a retreat situation. That goes from the very beginning of preliminaries all the way up.

Practice each session within the framework of the three excellences. That is extremely important. Start out with refuge and bodhichitta;

practice whatever it is in the main part of the session, like the *Lejang* of *Kunzang Tuktig;* then finish by making dedication and pure aspirations. When doing the rushan, do the sadhana practice once at the beginning of the session. Work down to the mantra and do at least 108 recitations of the mantra at a minimum. It doesn't take very long, just at the head of the session.

Once you have finished with that, as the body of the session, do whichever of the separation practices you are engaged in: for body, the three-pronged vajra; for speech, the four speech yogas; and for mind, the investigation into the arising, dwelling, and ceasing—or nalbab or sor-shug. Practice this till it is time to eat and once you have eaten, relax a bit. Then do an afternoon session later in the day. When doing the rushan, practice it as two sessions in one day.

In the general framework, there are four sessions a day: pre-dawn, morning, afternoon, and night sessions. But for the focus on this practice, do it in two sessions: one in the morning till noon and the other in the afternoon, beginning after you eat lunch and take a rest. At this time, do the dissolution and re-emergence for the *Kunzang Tuktig* and dedicate the merit and make aspirations. In this way each session is within the framework of the three excellences.

The number of days you spend on each part depends on how long your retreat is. If you do a month, divide it up within a month. If you do just ten days, divide it up within the ten days. That's totally a personal matter, how long a stretch of retreat you decide to do.

In the afternoon session at the end, there is an option to add what is called the *fulfillment,* confession practice, and also the petition offering to the dharma protectors. That's optional.

For the other sessions, I think it's more convenient instead to practice the *Kunzang Tuktig* sadhana just in the pre-dawn session, and, in the night session, do the very short daily practice of Vajrasattva, as was arranged by Kyabje Dilgo Khyentse Rinpoche. That is more convenient. That is how I suggest structuring one day for retreat practice of the rushan. For the main part, every session is nothing other than recognizing mind essence.

SHAMATHA AND VIPASHYANA IN DZOGCHEN

In all three vehicles—as a matter of fact in all nine vehicles—the words shamatha and vipashyana are used. The same words are used but with different meanings, and these meanings become more profound with each successive vehicle. You accomplish the state of realization of a buddha through the unity of shamatha and vipashyana. So, you always use the words *shamatha* and *vipashyana,* but as you go through the vehicles, the meaning of each becomes increasingly more profound. In the case of Dzogchen, we are taught the extraordinary shamatha and vipashyana.

There are two types of shamatha: conceptual shamatha, which involves concepts, and nonconceptual shamatha, which is the practice of naturally resting in awareness. Without departing from the state of non-conceptual shamatha, the natural resting in awareness, you engage in sor-shug, the practice of sustaining freshness, in order to develop the power of vipashyana.

According to the general dharma system, one should cultivate sha-matha and then pursue vipashyana. Pursue here means to track down, seek out. The first practice is to cultivate something and the next is to look for the one who cultivated it. Vipashyana is the practice of look-ing into who the meditator is. First you meditate in a conceptual way and finally you inquire, "Who is this meditator?" That is called pursu-ing vipashyana, seeking insight. That was in short about shamatha and vipashyana according to the conventional vehicles.

Both shamatha and vipashyana are included or contained within these practices of nalbab and sorshug. In fact, there is no attainment of buddhahood disconnected from shamatha and vipashyana. When we slightly put down shamatha and vipashyana, we are only talking about their ordinary, conceptual aspects—since a conceptual act cannot be the cause of enlightenment. On the other hand, the extraordinary shamatha is resting in the stillness free from conceptual thinking. This should be combined with the recognition of that, which is vipashyana. In that way, shamatha and vipashyana are unified. This is also called the unity of awareness and emptiness. When awareness is inseparable from emptiness, then shamatha and vipashyana are automatically unified; that is the extraordinary approach.

From the shravaka vehicle all the way to complete buddhahood, there is no way around using the words *shamatha* and *vipashyana*. However, as I keep reminding, their meaning is not the same. As is said, "Same term but superior meaning." How is that? For example, a small child is the same one who later becomes a fully grown person; it is the same child with the same mind but there is a huge difference in ability and strength. Similarly, the words shamatha and vipashyana are used on different levels but there is quite a huge difference in the extent to which qualities are manifest. A small child doesn't have the learning, experience, courage, or physical strength of a twenty-five-year old. In the same way, it is said that the realization of buddhahood cannot be attained unless we depend upon the union of shamatha and vipashyana.

Shamatha, nalbab—and vipashyana, sorshug—are categorized as the Dzogchen preliminaries for Trekchö. A most vital part of the preliminaries is the examination of the coming, staying, and going of mind. Once you resolve that, you understand rigpa unmistakably. In short, you know rigpa to be empty. This understanding of it being empty is not just an assumption. The outcome of examining for yourself is that you can decide definitively that it really is empty. This is unlike in the past, where any understanding that mind is empty is nothing but a mental fabrication; there is no real definitive certainty.

On the other hand, by means of looking into the coming, staying, and going, you can one hundred percent resolve that everything, from the aggregate of form to omniscience, is empty and devoid of a self-entity, exactly as the Buddha taught. This understanding takes place through your own experience without any need for intellectual knowledge. What the panditas say—that all phenomena are empty and devoid of a self-entity—is based on intellectual understanding. A yogi simply stays in the mountains, and after reflecting on this, she or he directly experiences rigpa.

In this regard, there are three steps: intellectual understanding, experience, and realization. As for experience here, you resolve that rigpa is empty, that it is beyond arising, dwelling, and ceasing. The actual practice, however, is what we repeat again and again, saying, "Don't wander; don't be distracted!" Unless you apply it (the recognition) in practice, your state remains indifferent.

The testament known as *Deyje, ('das rjes),* says:

Then be skilled in bringing
Body, speech, and mind to the natural state.

The *Deyje* is a testament of the four buddhas, from which this quote has been taken. You should become skilled in remaining in naturalness.

What is the importance of resting in naturalness, nalbab? It is talk of unfabricated naturalness. The previous practices of body, the three-pointed vajra; speech, the four speech yogas; and mind, looking into the arrival, remaining, and disappearance of mind, are tiring. So, you come to unfabricated naturalness, letting mind rest in naturalness.

The meaning of *rnal* is the same as in yoga. Yogi in Tibetan is nal-jorpa, *(rnal 'byor pa),* one who brings into mind, which is *('byor),* or takes to heart the nature of rnal, which means the unfabricated, natural state, uncontrived naturalness. That is what comes after the three previous separation practices, through which you have become very tired and exhausted. In order to take a rest, to refresh or restore yourself, after being totally exhausted through the previous practices, you do what is called remaining in or resting in naturalness.

There is no past thought; it's gone, so there is no need to follow any past thought. The future thought has not arrived, so what is the point of inviting it? Mind is free of arising, dwelling, and ceasing. You have established the fact of emptiness through experience, and you have ascertained that the past thought is gone and that you are the one creating thoughts. The same is true for the thought of the future. Do not follow after the past or the future thought. For the moment of the present thought, when you look into what thinks, you do not find that it has any visible form, color, or shape. It is without anything to be seen, in any way whatsoever. Rest evenly in that state. Remaining in naturalness, there are no thoughts.

Just to backtrack a little, when looking into the present moment of thought and seeing that it has no form, color, or shape—that there is nothing whatsoever to see—rest evenly in that. There is a thought-free state of remaining, which, in relation to the two types of dualistic mind, stillness and thought-occurrence, is more the stillness, the quietness aspect, in which the body remains at ease and the voice flows freely— actually uncontrolled, like a sitar where all the strings have been cut. As for the mind, thinking remains without projecting or dissolving thoughts. Here comes a two-line quote to support that:

Not seeing is the supreme sight,
Not finding is the supreme find.[5]

This means not seeing in the sense that you are not seeing mind as having any form, color, or shape; thus, you are not seeing it as a concrete thing. That itself is seeing the nature of mind, which is the supreme sight. Not finding, not being able to find the mind as being any concrete substance whatsoever, is itself the supreme, the most eminent discovery.

Thus, on a comfortable seat, place your body however it feels at ease, such as in the bodhisattva posture, and remain still. Silent and without controlling your breath, let your speech rest.[6]

Uncontrived means that to make exclamations, such as calling some- body's name, is to converse, asking, "How are you?" and so forth. It also indicates you are not controlling or contriving the flow of breath, which is what produces speech. *Uncontriving* means you don't try to place the breath in any specific way.

Let go of all your mind's thoughts—good, evil, or indifferent—and rest in naturalness.[7]

Good thoughts refer to dharmic thoughts, dharma practice; evil ones relate to the three poisons; and indifferent thoughts occur when your mind stays without noticing or knowing anything. Give up all thoughts of conceptualizing any of the five sense objects.

Naturalness, *(rang babs),* is a very important point. It means rest- ing without placing the mind. If the mind is placed, it is not in a state of naturalness. In ordinary shamatha, there is no naturalness, because in shamatha the mind is placed in a peaceful state. How can there be naturalness? To rest without placing anything is naturalness, which is just like a water mill, where the water has been disconnected or diverted. In this way, let your three doors of body, speech, and mind rest or remain as they naturally are in the ground itself. Here, in speaking of the ground, we should understand ground within these three: ground, path, and fruition. Ground means the state of primordial purity itself. This is the practice of abandoning body, speech, and mind within the state of primordial purity.

Like water clears when left unstirred, by freely leaving your three doors unaltered in their basic nature, your mind will remain still.[8]

If you mix mud with water and leave it for a few hours, all the soil will sink to the bottom and the water will remain completely clear on top, but if the water is disturbed then it will become muddy again. If you engage the three doors in activity and do not know how to let them rest in naturalness, it is like stirring up muddy water. Here, again, basic nature refers to the primordially pure state and the mind that remains in stillness, which is the unfabricated stillness. When we say basic nature, *(gzhi thog),* it is the original or basic state, which also means awareness.

To reiterate, this section here, Resting in Naturalness, and the subsequent one, Sustaining Freshness, are the extraordinary types of shamatha and vipashyana. Freshness here means the original or virgin state of naturalness itself, as cultivated in the previous practice. Sustaining it means that you maintain it through activities. It corresponds to the vipashyana part of Dzogchen. In order to develop the strength of the vipashyana, which means clear seeing, you need to engage in activity. Otherwise you don't develop the strength.

If you only remain in the sitting posture, with the stillness of shamatha, then you don't fully develop the vipashyana aspect in Dzogchen. In order to develop the vipashyana aspect, do not depart from the state of naturalness, which as I explained before means not following past, present, and future thoughts. In this way, you do not depart from, lose, or move away from the state of naturalness. While keeping the state of resting in naturalness, move the eyes around in various gazes and move the body in different ways. Here different doesn't refer to the body movements of Anu Yoga but just in diverse ways. Instead of sitting still, start to move the arms and legs, get up, walk, and so forth. Also, with the voice say different things, make different utterances, and speak different words. In this way mingle movements of body, speech, and mind with the practice.

You train like this because it is the extraordinary form of shamatha and vipashyana. In ordinary shamatha, the moment you move the gaze, the moment you move the body, immediately your attention has a tendency to be distracted. The stillness is lost. Here in order to train in daily life activities, first, you move the eyes, the body, and the voice.

As I keep mentioning, the Dzogchen shamatha is Resting in Naturalness, and Sustaining Freshness is vipashyana, the clear seeing, the introduction to awareness. But here the words *shamatha* and *vipashyana* are not used; instead, we refer to them as sustaining a state of awareness and remaining without moving away from the state of awareness. The first is shamatha and the second, mingling this with the path of action, is sustaining freshness—the vipashyana.

In the practice of sustaining freshness, you need to do different actions. An ordinary meditator's meditation is disturbed or destroyed by ordinary activities like walking, eating, talking, sleeping, and so forth; meditators have this fear. Therefore, you do this practice in order to clear away this fear. Actually, while resting in naturalness, awareness is already being introduced, pointed out. In order to mingle it with daily life, you do the sustaining freshness practice. In this practice, you need to use bodily activities to remain without moving away from the natural state.

There are different kinds of gazes applied in this practice: the peaceful gaze, the wrathful gaze, looking downward and upward, and so forth. Apply them and let the brightness, the sharpness, of awareness increase. Don't let fixation take over! It is fixation, in any case, that ruins it for us. So, without giving in to fixation, rest in awareness.

You also move the body and limbs in different ways just like the tai chi exercises I'm doing these days, except here they should not be learned exercises. You should just move spontaneously, acting out whatever comes into your mind. Also, say all different things, without any restriction as to what should and should not be said. *Practice* refers to resting in naturalness, which is awareness and sustained freshness; thus, you never move away from awareness.

When you are feeling delighted, depressed, attached, or angry, you should just rest in naturalness, which is the state of empty awareness.

Naturalness, again, means the unfabricated, the real. At this time, both the object that is grasped outwardly and the mind that inwardly fixates are spontaneously freed without any place or object.

Gazing in different ways, while performing various physical activities, and while uttering different words and sounds, try to mingle these with training in mind-essence. The term *zangthal* is used in relation to awareness. Zangthal means clarity, *(gdangs cha)*. Without leaving this state, engage in the daily activities. Do not get carried away during the activities! In this way, the sorshug practice is the method of training in vipashyana.

When stable in this, while conversing in crowds, no matter which disturbing emotion of the five poisonous thoughts arises—such as desire, anger, praise, blame, joy, or sorrow—simply rest in the natural state of emptiness. Like firewood added to a fire, these thoughts will become fuel, and they will disappear, placeless and spontaneously freed. When a fire is ablaze and you add more firewood, it will flare up and there will be no harm caused toward the view. In fact, the clarity will be even greater. The different emotions of aggression, passion, and delusion will cause no harm at all; they will be aids. Although there is a seeming thought activity, once awareness has been recognized, aggression and passion have no object or place.

Rigpa is cognizant yet not obscured or blocked. An example of obscured is when you forget or become distracted. If you start to follow one thought after the other, the brightness of awareness becomes obstructed. It doesn't become completely obstructed or lost, but it becomes kind of covered, veiled. Distraction is the worst enemy; if you wander away, then the essence is kind of lost.

When you are in rigpa, whatever appears is like a reflection in a mirror; it is appearing, yet empty. The mirror and the reflection are not apart or different. The reflection is visible, but there is nothing tangible, nothing to hold; although there is nothing tangible, it still appears. While appearing, there is nothing to hold; this is an example for the state of awareness being unobstructed. There is cognizance yet no fixation; there is nothing to fixate on or hold. The unity of appearing and being empty, just like the reflection in a mirror, is called being empty while appearing. Like the reflection in a mirror, it has shape, it has color, but no concrete substances to grasp. Yet while being empty, it is still visible. This is called the unity of being empty and apparent like the reflection in a mirror.

QUESTION: Can you explain again how nalbab is different from ordinary shamatha?

RINPOCHE: The nalbab practice is shamatha without support. Prior to this, you have practiced with body, speech, and mind and tried to seek the mind here and there, examining and examining and becoming really tired. Nalbab is for the purpose of reviving from this tiredness. In other words, taking rest. This taking rest is the extraordinary shamatha practice. Once again, by examining very minutely the coming, staying, and going of the mind, you resolve in actuality that it is emptiness; you decide one hundred percent that the mind within is empty.

Also, outer appearances that you perceive are emptiness. This is because appearances, nangwa, *(snang ba),* are nangtong, *(nang stong)*— empty appearances, or appearing while being empty. First examine any place from which an appearance could arise, any place it could dwell, and any place for it to disappear. Then you decide that all of this—whatever appears, whatever dwells, and whatever goes anywhere—is totally empty. You do not find any of these places at all. There is no place outside where anything could come from because all appearances are appearing and empty. Anything that is real should not be able to be burned by fire. Everything, the world and beings, can be consumed by fire. Something not empty should not be able to be burned by fire, because when burned it means it disappears.

In this way, you resolve that all outer things are empty and also the mind within is really and truly empty. In this case, you don't need to repeat the statement that mind is empty or think it is probably empty. You can directly and actually understand that this is so, that mind is empty by means of examining the arising, staying, and going. You examine both the object and subject, determining that there is no place outside, inside, or in between; there is nothing that comes and goes either. Both of these have been resolved. Then you have truly ascertained emptiness, decisively, without even an iota of doubt.

Once you have resolved this, the nalbab practice means that you rest in exactly that resolution, at which point, you don't need to think, "This is how it is." Simply resting naturally in that understanding of emptiness is nalbab—resting naturally in emptiness. Once everything has been resolved to be empty, you don't need to create emptiness. Any made up emptiness is fake; but here, there is no need to make up anything. This is true emptiness. Without having to keep an intellectual idea, remain naturally in the experience of it. This is the true or real understanding of emptiness.

Shamatha and vipashyana cannot be disregarded or eliminated, as awareness wisdom is resolved through shamatha and vipashyana. In this case, the extraordinary shamatha is to resolve and rest in the true emptiness itself—not just as an idea but in actuality: Nalbab means that through direct experience, you resolve emptiness and rest naturally in that. Nalbab is the true, real shamatha practice of not creating anything artificial whatsoever, simply resting in the experience of emptiness. Sorshug means that you do not deviate or depart from that state. Try and reflect on this.

QUESTION: In the Dzogchen teachings, the practices of nalbab and sorshug are placed before the actual Trekchö practice. Has one been introduced to the essence at the time of nalbab or sorshug or not?

RINPOCHE: Yes, one has, of course; why not? If one really practices the correct nalbab and sorshug, then the nalbab is resting in awareness and the sorshug is not losing the continuity of it, mingling it with the path of action. This is when it is practiced correctly. In the Mahamudra system of shamatha and vipashyana, the first steps are called *one-pointedness* and then *simplicity*. In the first, one-pointedness, one practices mainly shamatha and in the second, simplicity, mainly vipashyana. In these two stages, there is still some involvement in conceptual mind. The practice of Dzogchen is a bit different. Therefore, it is said that the nalbab refers to shamatha and the sorshug to vipashyana. They are not called *shamatha* and *vipashyana* here, as they are in the Mahamudra system. If they were, there would be some concepts involved. But from the very beginning, the Dzogchen practice is without concepts, without conceptual mind. Why shouldn't the essence be introduced from the very first?

QUESTION: Then how come the three points are placed afterward?

RINPOCHE: There is nothing wrong there. They are placed under the view; whereas the two other parts are placed as preliminaries. In the

Dzogchen system, shamatha and vipashyana are designated as preliminaries. Actually, nalbab means nonfabrication *(ma bcos pa)* and sorshug
means not losing the continuity of naturalness. If one has been introduced to the essence in Dzogchen without nalbab, one won't be able to
accomplish anything. There is a saying for this in Kham: "The bottom
is showing from outside." If the door is open, even if one is standing outside, one can still see the innermost part of the room with all the images
from outside. Although the nalbab is placed as a preliminary, according
to the sequence of chapters, it does not mean that one should abandon it
and try to get to something that is higher or more profound. The essence
is being introduced, since there is a use for it in the very beginning. If one
hasn't been introduced, it is still possible to get the teachings on *The Three
Vital Points, (Tshig Gsum Gnad Brdeg),* and still not recognize, isn't it?

In short, it is merely placed as a preliminary practice and if one has
recognized at this point, then one might feel that *Tshig Gsum Gnad Brdeg*
is not very important. *(Rinpoche laughs.)* It looks afterward like these
three points are very important, so one thinks, "Oh maybe they are not
that important." In short, one has been introduced to the nonfabrication
and to the naturalness, which in general refer to the shamatha and then
vipashyana.

As it is said, "Sometimes the preliminaries are more profound than
the main practice." If there is somebody who is going to be introduced, he
will have recognized already at this point. If one is somebody who is supposed to recognize, the view is quite remarkable. There is the tradition
of pointing it out right away. This is exemplified by the story about the
previous incarnation of Tsangsar Samten Gyatso that I just told.

The story was about how he recognized when he was young without any master. Simply an old monk said, "Oh you little naughty tulku.
Don't play around like that. Don't wander. What is the use of being distracted?" The small boy asked, "What is *not wandering*?" "Look at your
mind itself; that's it," the old lama said. That is where he recognized the
essence. He said that after that there was nothing extra that he had to be
introduced to or have pointed out. He recognized right there and then
and he became a great, accomplished master.

Here is an example of his extraodinariness. It happened sometimes in
the wintertime in Eastern Tibet, where this great master lived, that the
water melting from the snow would freeze and make barriers of solid ice

as high as three-storied buildings. These would block the paths and make it impossible to travel. On the rooftop of Ngaktrin Lama, there would never remain any snow, no matter how much would fall in the wintertime. It would melt due to his tummo practice.

On the other side of the mountain pass, one of his major sponsors had passed away. On the way was a river that overflowed and had made huge ice curtains. These rose to a height of two or three stories and there was no way to go through. A message was sent for Ngaktrin Lama to come and do phowa, the ejection of consciousness. He replied, "I'm coming!" All his attendants tried to dissuade him and said, "How can you go? Do you want to die in the ice water? If you have to travel around, it will take you two or three days. There is no way. How can you, an old lama, go there? Forget about it." But he said, "No, it is improper if I don't go. He has been a very kind patron of mine. If I fail to reach there, it will be a breach of samaya. Tomorrow morning, I am going myself!" The servants had nothing to do but obey and thought that now they had to walk around the long way. But the lama said, "No, no, that will not be necessary at all." The next morning, he said, "Last night I cleared the way." It meant that in his tummo practice that night, he had melted the ice curtains. All the ice on the whole mountain pass had turned into water. The next morning there was not even a flake of snow anywhere. All had melted due to his miraculous power and that morning they could travel freely. When asked, "How can this be possible?" the lama responded, "Last night I practiced some tummo; I melted it into water."

This was the kind of master he was. He had a very great practice. The foundation for his practice, the one who introduced him to mind nature, was the old monk who would do the pujas for the dharma protectors. He introduced him when he said, "Don't wander." When being introduced, there are sometimes these strange stories, if one has the karmic potential. It doesn't always fit the traditional sequence. There are some people who are introduced during the preliminaries. Actually, nalbab and sorshug belong to the preliminaries in Dzogchen, whereas the main part is *Three Words Striking the Vital Point.*

WORDS ARE LIKE RICE HUSKS

QUESTION: I sometimes wonder whether shamatha practice involves wakefulness, and if so, whether it is contrived.

RINPOCHE: The word shamatha means abiding peacefully. There is essentially some bliss in that peace or calm, and the abiding aspect means there is fixation. Ordinary shamatha is the same as delight or bliss, and abiding means grasping or fixating on bliss. When there is no fixation, no clinging to the wakefulness, it is not ordinary shamatha; it is the naked vipashyana, clear seeing. Thus, the ordinary shamatha state arises with a slight attachment, with a slight fascination in it; that is the definition of shamatha. On the other hand, vipashyana, clear seeing, is wide open, awake.

Paltrül Rinpoche has described this state of vipashyana as being bare but wide open; this wide-openness is inexpressible, indescribable. With such wide-openness, you cannot merely abide in peace in the shamatha state, because there is no abider and nothing to abide in. If you say 'abide', it means abiding in the empty state, that the empty abides in something. Of course, the mind is empty, but if you say that this emptiness abides, then the emptiness refers to a fixation on the peace, the calm, the bliss. The abiding means that there is fixation on that sense of peace. So just remaining, holding onto this bliss, thinking, "What a fantastic meditation I have!" you almost dare not move your body at all for fear that "If I move the body, the state will collapse."

When you have bliss and attachment to the feeling of bliss, there is duality, and the seed or the cause for rebirth in the three realms of samsara is thereby still sown in your being. This is why mere shamatha practice does not bring liberation and enlightenment. If there is peace or calm, there is some delight or bliss, and then there is abiding in or clinging to it. Fixation accompanies this bliss, this ease in feeling, "So comfortable, so relaxed!" It is like feeling your body is not there at all; and if you move the body you feel, "Now, my meditation will disappear." You fear, "My meditation will vanish; it will disappear."

In other words, ordinary shamatha means holding on to peace, whereas vipashyana is nakedness: wide open and indescribable. This is the true meaning of vipashyana, the vipashyana of dharmakaya, the dharmakaya awareness, rigpa. This is what is meant by the naked state of dharmakaya. As it is said, "By the great lightning gaze"—nowness is like a flash of lightning descending from the sky—"by the great lightning gaze, both buddhas and beings are freed." 'Buddhas' here means good thoughts, and sentient beings means bad thoughts. In such awareness, both good and bad thoughts are freed. Otherwise, good thoughts such as devotion, respect, and shamatha would remain. The nakedness of vipashyana is merely free, fresh—no buddhas and no beings. This does not mean actual buddhas and actual beings. The statement refers to good thoughts and bad thoughts, indicating that you should be freed from both so-called positive and negative thought states. Good thoughts are devotion, relative devotion, and relative compassion. Relative here means that a concept is involved. These must all be destroyed, freed. 'No buddhas' means that the good thoughts are freed; 'no sentient beings' means that our deluded experience and ego-clinging are equally liberated. Again, by the great lightning gaze, both buddhas and beings are freed. Listen to that. Recognize how it is in that first instant. There are no good thoughts, no bad thoughts. That is the meaning of freeing both buddhas and beings.

Don't cling, don't become fascinated by your particular degree of wakefulness. Thought-free wakefulness is completely clear, as the mind does not apply or arrange any concepts. It is the first instant in which nothing is made, constructed, cultivated, or manufactured; it is your present, uncreated freshness.

If you have the feeling, "I must make my meditation state a little more wakeful," you should realize that this feeling is born of intellectual understanding. You should be free of that. If you are too detailed in your approach, too concerned about this, then the meditation will not be successful because it is just conceptual mind, which wants to be very correct. This must also be abandoned. Otherwise, there is some concept involved. If you think, "Now I know. I know I am aware of this," there is a conceptual aspect to the experience. That which is aware is actually awareness wisdom. We needn't try to know; by itself it is wakeful, nonconceptual. Awareness wisdom is not something that we have created conceptually, by or from our intellect. If you think that, you are wrong, you err. Or you may think, "There is some knowing. This is not right." Without any knowing, without cognizance, we would be unconscious. This knowingness or knowledge, however, is self-existing. It is not something we have manufactured.

This is the crucial point. Most people think that when they really examine this wakefulness of self-existing wisdom, it is just conceptual mind. They think they should attain something superior to that. But nothing whatsoever is superior; one has reached naked awareness itself.

You can be too particular. Some people think, "Self-existing wisdom is without a knower." They think there shouldn't be any knowing at all. Particularizing too much like this, you become trapped by fixation. But rigpa, awareness, has self-cognizant presence of mind, self-cognizant mindfulness. By thinking, "Isn't this sense of awareness just conceptual mind? It is probably just a mental fabrication. I need something totally unfabricated. This is not enough," you develop a kind of suspicion or fear. Better to remain totally loose in that very instant, as it is, not making it worse and not trying to uplift or improve it. This is what you should decide on. There is nothing other than that. You need not think, "There must be something better," because in this very moment, awareness is nakedly manifest.

Believing there is something better than this, some people think, "This state is not correct. It is not self-existing wisdom. There is some conceptual involvement here!" But you have not created your awareness; it is self-existing, self-occurring. Were it fabricated even the tiniest bit, it would be dependent on conceptual mind. But it need not be manufactured. That's the genuine awareness with no error whatsoever.

What is the natural state, the actual state of awareness? It is the first instant. Don't defame or praise it; don't exaggerate or denigrate it. Yet we are not to blame if we slip into fabricating a little. Since beginningless time, we have been fabricating the unfabricated. When we say, "Let go into nonfabrication," isn't that itself also unnatural? Isn't letting go also a fabrication? We use words because we have no other way to proceed, but saying, "Let go, rest loosely!" doesn't mean that there is something that is being let go of and somebody who lets go. True letting go is without these two, beyond duality.

When you have finally attained stability in your practice, relying on such words as, "Let go, rest loosely!" can be quite damaging. How can words compare to the naked, self-existing awareness itself? Words are just like rice husks. You will gradually cast words away as your view deepens, as it becomes more profound. When the view reaches fullness, you will really know how much damage words cause. The practitioner should then recognize how submerged or entangled in words he or she has become. But you cannot notice that right now. The view is free from viewer and viewed. When you have grown accustomed to rigpa through a correct view then you will understand that, realizing, "I have just been clinging to words. The words and what they mean are so different."

In the true state of Dzogchen, it is said you should: "Herd primordially free rigpa with innate mindfulness." Nurture it as you would a herd of grazing cattle. Innate means uninterrupted. Then, after that, rest freely. Dzogchen teachings use the words rest freely a lot. When nurturing the primordially free rigpa with innate mindfulness, without being distracted or carried away, rest freely just as it is. In this context, self-abiding nondistraction is called mindfulness. But such mindfulness is without duality. When the primordially free rigpa is nurtured by innate mindfulness, the rigpa is nurturing or sustaining itself. Mahamudra uses the word watchfulness or keeping guard, indicating a sense of watching. For some people, without some watchfulness or keeping guard, without some mindfulness, there is no abiding and the meditation is lost. Without this support they have no meditation. It is said, "By fabricated mind, one is led to the natural state."

Fabrication leads you to the natural state, to the genuine truth. Were a beginner to proceed without the duality of a watcher and something watched, just resting freely, with no previous practice in this, his or her mind would be left without any support. Mahamudra definitely emphasizes mindfulness as the main part of meditation. In the first stage of the path of Mahamudra, in one-pointedness, mindfulness is mixed with shamatha. When you reach the stage of simplicity, mindfulness is discarded. In general, you can say that the Mahamudra system treats beginners very kindly. Depending on your karma, your interest will be in Dzogchen or Mahamudra.

When Tsewang Drakpa, Chokgyur Lingpa's son, was asked to explain the general teachings of Dzogchen, he said, "Don't ask me for mind-teaching. I am a person who made it to the roof of the house without using the stairs. Through my explanations you won't understand anything. You won't be helped at all. Don't ask me for mind-teachings; ask some other teacher." He was one of those who took the sudden approach and, therefore, said, "You can't ask me for mind-teaching. Somebody who explains should know the path, should tell you which step to take first so that you should go slowly up the staircase in such and such way. I have no practical knowledge at all. Were I to explain my view to you, it would not help." Mahamudra, on the other hand, leads one to the effortless by means of deliberate mindfulness.

In the Dzogchen system, in the very moment of recognizing your distraction, you have arrived at rigpa. For example, when striking a match, the flame appears the instant the match is struck, simultaneously. Likewise, at the moment of noticing the distraction, you arrive at rigpa. If you fail to notice the distraction, there is of course nothing at all. While being distracted, while wandering, you are unaware of that. When you cease wandering and notice "This is ignorance!" without rejecting it, that itself is sufficient. But as I have already mentioned, you must understand when there is distraction and when there is not. This is very important. Not knowing the difference between wandering and not wandering, you can easily think, "I am completely without distraction." Many people stray from the view in that way, and such an artificial attitude cannot destroy delusion. When thoughts are not freed or destroyed, how can you be free from samsara? The root of samsara is conceptual thought. Without being overpowered by thoughts, just rest, self-contained and self-sufficient, in nonconceptual wisdom. That is the view. The view is not something to be achieved from elsewhere.

You must recognize that awareness is not something to be artificially prolonged. Nor should you try to shorten the duration of nondual awareness. Allow the moment of naturalness to exist as long as it lasts by itself. Neither try to prolong nor to shorten it because that would be just a conceptually based undertaking. If it's long, it's long; if it's short, it's short. If the nondistraction lasts for a long time, let it be; a thought of nondistraction is useless. Do not have nondistraction where you think, "I am without distraction." Rather, have a freely self-abiding naturalness that is neither foreshortened nor lengthened by your intentions.

In that moment of naturalness, none of the three poisons of aggression, passion, or delusion arises. The natural state contains none of the three poisons and no thoughts of the three times. If thoughts of the three times exist, then as they have a place to adhere to and something to follow, the basis for passion, aggression, and delusion to arise is there. When past, present, and future do not exist, the three poisons have nothing to adhere to or follow after. When the three poisons are not present, nothing will grow, as they are the roots of the three realms of samsara, the seeds of the desire realm and of the form and formless realms. No crop grows if no seeds are planted. There will also not be any cause to stray into the three realms of samsara.

The thoughts that do arise while resting in naturalness are self-occurring and self-liberated, the expression of rigpa. When recognized, these thoughts, which arise from you, are liberated and freed. They dissolve back into the space of rigpa. This is uninterrupted, self-occurring self-liberation. Without gaining confidence in this freeing of thoughts, even though you have recognized your essence, you are unable to destroy delusion. Delusion accompanies the thoughts that arise as an expression of rigpa, unless you have attained the state of exhaustion of phenomena beyond concepts. But right now, thinking of ground, path, and fruition, we are at the stage of the path and have not yet realized the view of fruition.

Thoughts occur from you; they don't come from elsewhere. They are the expression of rigpa. Again, a thought arises from the expression of rigpa, and again it dissolves into the space of rigpa. With training in this again and again as path, you become used to it; the force of the thoughts decreases and rigpa becomes uninterrupted. Finally, phenomena and concepts become exhausted; they finish. Upon reaching this level, you have no distraction. While undistracted, the thoughts that used to occur from you do not arise. When the strength of the thoughts is released into the primordially pure space, rigpa is said to be self-sufficient, to have seized its own seat of power. Seizing its own seat of power means that thoughts have dissolved into rigpa.

COMPARING MAHAMUDRA
AND DZOGCHEN

In Mahamudra, you are introduced to mind and then you train with awareness. The practice is mixed with mind until reaching nonmeditation. Then the practice is only rigpa, the ultimate view. In one-pointedness and simplicity, you exert lots of mental effort, through which fixation greatly reduces and obscurations are cast away. It is like peeling off different layers of corn; first one is peeled, then the next and the next. In Dzogchen, from the very beginning you are introduced to nonmeditation, nondistraction. Dzogchen has the three sections of mind, space, and instruction. The mind and space sections are introduced before the Mahamudra introduction. The intent of the *Kunje Gyalpo* tantra is the same as the intent in Mahamudra.

According to the words of Künkhyen Tsele Rinpoche, also called Tsele Natsok Rangdröl:

Mahamudra and Dzogchen
Differ in words but not in meaning.
The only difference is that Mahamudra stresses mindfulness
While Dzogchen relaxes within awareness.[9]

Mahamudra stresses mainly mindfulness. 'Mindfulness' or 'presence of mind' means to apply mindfulness or watchfulness. While Dzogchen relaxes into awareness; this is the mere difference. As it is said, "In Dzogchen the ultimate view is to relax into awareness," which refers to nonfixation, nongrasping—(to remain) in the continuity of nongrasping. As it is said in Mahamudra, "It is necessary to apply mindfulness."

(In Mahamudra), *you then train with appearances by utilizing whichever of the six sense perceptions that occurs, without keeping or discarding.*[10]

In Dzogchen you 'train with awareness' *(rig thog tu rtsal sbyang)* and in Mahamudra you 'train with appearances' *(snang thog tu rtsal sbyang).* The meaning of *training with appearances* is not inhibiting any experience *(snang ba).* It is certain that forms will appear to your eyes and that sounds will appear to your ears; experience is unobstructed, intrinsic. To train means that whatever forms appear in your field of vision, however varied, just recognize the watcher; that is the training. According to Dzogchen, awareness does not need to depend on external appearances. Simply remain in rigpa. Whatever appearance may occur—without trying to prohibit, inhibit, or encourage it—train in awareness itself. Here, 'training', *(rtsal sbyang),* means developing a skill, becoming practiced, such as doing physical exercise. Similarly, students in school train by developing some skill, learning something.

According to the Mahamudra system, it is a little bit uncomfortable to train with appearances. There is a lot of talk about appearances in the beginning. However, without recognizing awareness, there is no way to train with appearances. After recognizing rigpa, you can train on appearances or experiences, in that the experiencer is rigpa.

In the other case, when training with awareness in Dzogchen, whatever occurs as an experience is beyond benefit and harm. You abandon all appearances and only rest in rigpa. Train in that. In Mahamudra, you train on appearances of the five sense objects. We have the five sense organs and the five external sense objects. Whichever of these may appear or be experienced, you look into the essence of that.

You train in this way so that experience does not cause any harm. In the beginning, experiences may be harmful or unpleasant, meaning that uncomfortable sights, unpleasant sounds, and so forth will happen to a meditator. But the experiencer or perceiver of these experiences is the mind, without which there would be no experience, just as a stone or a piece of wood does not perceive anything. Without mind there is no experiencer, because all experience is personal experience, *(rang snang).* Once you acknowledge that experience is personal experience, you can train in that. In Mahamudra, you train on experience without any delusion. In short, in Mahamudra you train with outer appearances, and in Dzogchen you train with inner rigpa.

We can say it like this, but as a matter of fact, appearances and rigpa are a unity. You don't need to inhibit anything, because perceptions are beyond benefit and harm. You do not have to block anything out; all appearances are beyond benefit and harm. In this way rigpa and appearances are a unity. In Mahamudra, when you remain in rigpa, without having any fixation or clinging toward any appearances that may occur, this is the first of the perceptions of the six collections (of sensations). They occur but you do not cling to this occurrence; instead, you train in this nonclinging. The six sense perceptions refer to form, sound, smell, taste, touch, and mental joys and sorrows. When we say the six collections, we have to take into account the various mental joys and sorrows, the five senses, and mental objects. We do not need to cast them away or abandon them. We don't need to adopt or keep them either. We experience them without rejecting or accepting.

Ordinary sentient beings, on the other hand, cling to perceptions; first they cling, and then they become attached. First there is the cognition or appearance that is called 'holding something to be there.' One fixates on a perception. After that there is attachment to whether it is good or bad. All sentient beings have clinging and attachment. For instance, if you have eyes, then a visual image is sure to appear, right? You perceive it. For example, you perceive this and think, "Oh, this is a tape recorder." First you think—that aspect is called 'holding it to be there.' After that you discriminate, thinking, "Oh, it's a good one." Then, in addition to fixation, you have attachment. Thinking it is not good is anger, and thinking "I don't care" is stupidity. These three tie us to samsara.

A yogi practitioner has eyes and perceives things. If you have eyes, you will have visual perception, unless your eyes are closed. Whoever has eyes will have visual perception, but whatever is perceived becomes empty perception, *(snang stong)*. If you recognize the essence, when forms appear, they become the unity of appearance and emptiness. While appearing, they are empty. While being empty, these six collections do occur or manifest. Appearing and being empty occur as a unity. The word unity has great significance. Don't divide appearances as being there and awareness as being here. Let appearance and awareness be indivisible; this is what the Kagyüpas teach. To divide appearances as being there and mind as being here is what sentient beings do. Practitioners, however, do not divide these two, thinking appearances are there and mind is here. They practice the unity of appearance and mind, which is the meaning of one taste. That is the reason why things become smooth, easy for the practitioner; without that there would be no way to attain ease.

Here you train without keeping or discarding. This means that the training you develop is not in the realm of conceptual mind—it is beyond conceptual mind. To bring onto the path means that you mingle the practice with the path of action, the daily activities, without losing the continuity. If the continuity is lost, then you have not brought the practice onto the path.

Finally, you train in appearance and emptiness as a unity. Thus, though there is a difference in terminology, the essential meaning is identical (in both Mahamudra and Dzogchen).[11]

To develop training on appearances comes after being introduced to emptiness. This is according to the Mahamudra system. You should recognize the four parts without three. Then, in all the paths of action, daily activities, no matter which of the six sense perceptions you experience—since they are self-occurring and self-liberated—you will be able to develop the training, the power of training.

A mother bird will train her babies to fly. Although they do not have the power to fly when they are very small, their father and mother will fly with them and show the chicks how to do it. Then the baby birds will train in the skill. When they are able to fly properly by themselves, they will separate from their parents. When we say training the skill, if you have not first been introduced to what you should train in, then there is no skill to develop. Once you have been introduced to and have recognized mind nature, as primordially empty and rootless—that which is empty since the beginning and is free from any basis—then you can train in that recognition.

This is different from the Hindu system, where you just imagine things to be empty and meditate, cultivating that. If you train in that way, it becomes like the mountain stream frozen by the ice-cold wind. Water is uninterruptedly flowing and naturally free. But, when the freezing wind comes in the wintertime, the water becomes stiff and solid. Likewise, if you have not recognized mind nature, there is no skill to develop. You should train in the expression, in the manifestation.

In the Mahamudra system, they talk about essence, manifestation, and expression. The essence is unborn, the manifestation is unobstructed, and the expression is manifold appearances. In our tradition, we talk about the essence, nature, and capacity. The essence is empty, the nature is cognizant, and the capacity is all-pervasive. These are the dharmakaya, sambhogakaya, and nirmanakaya. On the other hand, Mahamudra terminology refers to unborn essence, unobstructed manifestation, and manifold expression. First, you are introduced to the unborn essence as being the empty essence. Afterward, you train in order to develop skill during perceptions, the unobstructed experience.

Appearance and emptiness have to be a unity, since the very beginning of primordial time. The Dzogchen teachings refer to this as the unity of primordial purity and spontaneous presence. This is how it is from the very beginning. It is not something that we have to put together. It is impossible to make a temporary unity of these two. Since primordial time, primordial purity and spontaneous presence have been inseparably united.

Through Trekchö, you understand the view of primordial purity. Through Tögal, you realize that spontaneous presence is self-display, *(rang snang)*. Neither of these has any self-nature, *(rang bzhin)*. The spontaneous presence does not have any self-nature; you cannot take hold of the deities. No matter how much you beat them with a stick, they would never feel any pain. *(Rinpoche laughs.)* Just joking! Appearances do manifest as deities and you can see them, but you cannot take hold of them with your hand in any way whatsoever, nor can the four elements harm them. They are like forms of rainbow light. That is the meaning of spontaneous presence. When this understanding takes place in the yogi's mind, then he or she becomes at ease without any troubles. Practitioners never become more and more depressed, more and more narrow-minded, because they understand things as they are.

Since the very beginning, appearance and existence are of the same nature as the three kayas. This reference to the three kayas means that the essence is free from constructs. As I repeatedly remind you, the essence is empty, the nature is cognizant, and the capacity is unity. This is how awareness is. Sentient beings' essence is also empty, their nature is luminous or cognizant, and their capacity is unity. Guru Rinpoche explains what is called the 'unity of emptiness and cognizance suffused with awareness[8]'.

Luminosity and emptiness have been a unity since primordial time. In the case of sentient beings, this unity is suffused with ignorance. All sentient beings have empty cognizance, because they are pervaded by sugatagarbha. Yet they are suffused with ignorance; they are the unity of empty cognizance suffused with ignorance. That is how a sentient being is, whereas the yogi or practitioner experiences empty luminosity with the core of awareness. Think carefully about this line, as everything is contained in this quote, "Empty cognizance suffused with awareness[8]."

If a person asks you, "How is mind? What is mind? Tell me briefly." Then you can say, "It is the unity of emptiness and cognizance suffused with awareness." Mind is complete within that sentence. Its essence is empty; its nature is cognizant. Its capacity is that these two cannot be taken apart. That is the meaning of unity, impossible to separate. The emptiness and luminosity cannot be divided, right? That is the state of affairs in all beings, yet they do not experience it.

As is stated in the *Mahaprajnaparamita:*

Transcendental knowledge, (*prajnaparamita*) is inexpressible, inconceivable, indescribable, nonarising, and unceasing—the essence of space itself. It is the experience of individual cognizance, self-cognizant wakefulness or wisdom.

In the case of sentient beings, it is the experience of an individual ignorance, but for yogis it is the unity of emptiness and luminosity suffused with awareness. The wisdom, yeshe *(ye shes),* refers to the cognizant aspect, namely rigpa. Sentient beings are of the ignorant aspect. Therefore, sentient beings are described as emptiness and luminosity suffused with ignorance.

In Kham there is a saying: "Tell all, like a sack turned inside out." You have a sack in which you keep things. You then pour them out and turn the sack completely inside out, so nothing is left behind; everything is emptied out. Likewise, in this statement, Guru Rinpoche has turned his sack inside out; he has completely disclosed everything. It is the unity of cognizance and emptiness. Since the very beginning, it is cognizant and empty; these two are a unity. The yogi is suffused with awareness, cognizance. Rigpa means 'knowing.' All sentient beings are suffused with ignorance. In this statement, the essential meaning of one hundred lines is contained. It is complete; Guru Rinpoche has turned his sack inside out. (*Rinpoche laughs.*) Hasn't he? Didn't he completely lay it bare?

THREE WORDS STRIKING
THE VITAL POINT

Garab Dorje emphasized Atiyoga, especially the Dzogchen view of the outer, inner, and secret sections of mind, space, and instruction. He especially concentrated on the fourth section of the 6,400,000 Dzogchen tantras, which he condensed into the three statements mentioned below.

What are the three words striking the vital point? As the first of the three statements instructs: 'recognize your own nature,' which is buddha-nature itself—empty cognizance with a core of compassionate energy. This nature is empty in essence yet naturally cognizant. These two are indivisible, and that is the compassionate capacity. The first of the three 'words' of Garab Dorje is called recognizing your own nature for what it is. That is the exact pointing-out instruction itself.

Buddha-nature is the very basis or source from which all worlds and living beings, whatever appears and exists, originate. How is the buddha-nature? It is empty in essence and cognizant by nature, and its capacity is endowed with a core of self-existing awareness. This is the universal ground from which everything arises.

We should understand that it does not fall into any categories, such as being an entity that exists or does not exist. If we assert that buddha-nature is or exists, that is incorrect because it does not: it is not a concrete thing with distinguishing characteristics. It is wide open, like space. However, we cannot assert that it is nonexistent, that it isn't, because this nature is the very basis or source of everything that appears and exists, everything that comes into being. Buddha-nature does not fall into any category, such as being or not being. Similarly, it surpasses the category of beyond being and not being as well.

It is like space. Can we say that space is? Can we say that space isn't? We can't. Space itself does not comply with any such concepts. Concepts made about space are merely concepts. Space itself is beyond any ideas we can hold about it. Buddha-nature is like this. If you say that space exists, can you define space as a concrete entity? But if you say space does not exist, that's incorrect because space is what accommodates everything, the world and all beings. If we think space is that which is beyond being and not being, that is not really space; it is merely our concept about it. Garab Dorje's first statement is to recognize our own nature. We need to acknowledge how this nature actually is.

I asked you to recognize your own mind and give a reply as to what you could see. You said, "I don't see a thing." Right? That's because the mind is free from the limitation of something that is, so, of course, there is nothing to see. But your mind is also not non-existent because, if I clap my hands, you agree that you have heard the sound, right? If the mind were non-existent, there would be no knowing of the present sound.

This Buddha-nature of yours, which is primordially free from the two extremes of being and not being, is said to be a unity. What does unity mean in this context? Unity means that, right now, visual forms, sounds, smells, and so forth are all present in your experience. If buddha-nature were nonexistent, there could be no such experiences. But if you say buddha-nature does exist, then what is it that experiences buddha-nature? Can you pinpoint it? It's empty, right? There is nothing to confine these two, the perceiving aspect and the empty aspect. While being empty, there is still experience. Yet, if you look into the perceiver, there is no thing. There's no limitation between the two. If it were confined to just one or the other aspect, there should either be an appearance that remains or else there should be an absolute void. However, at the same time that a vivid perception is occurring, that which perceives is totally empty. This is called the unity of appearance and emptiness, the unity of awareness and emptiness. The perceiving aspect eliminates the extreme of nothingness, while the empty aspect eliminates the extreme of existence.

In this way, you can say that existence and nonexistence are a unity. This unity is not something we can make up intellectually. That is why it is called the 'view beyond intellect or concepts.' It is also called thatness, 'just that'. Knowing 'that' is what we refer to as recognizing your own nature. The moment you recognize your own mind and you don't see a thing, this is called 'seeing the empty essence'. Buddha-nature is unlike space, which doesn't know anything, because we already agreed that there is knowing, which refers to the cognizant nature. Can these two aspects, the empty essence and the cognizant nature, be separated? If not, that means they are a unity. This is what we should recognize when recognizing our buddha-nature. It is called recognizing our nature.

Now we come to the second statement, which is called 'to decide on one point.' The empty essence is called dharmakaya, while its cognizant nature is called sambhogakaya. The unity of these is called 'the unified capacity,' which is all-pervasive; this is called nirmanakaya. Once we recognize our own nature, our buddha-nature, then we should decide on one point: that the three kayas of all the buddhas are present in just that.

The third statement is 'to gain confidence in liberation.' It is said that meditation is not the most important, liberation is. Mere meditation, such as the state of stillness, like shamatha meditation, does not liberate you. Here 'liberation' can be described as four or five different types.

The great master, Vimilamitra, described three ways of liberation that have three degrees. These can be applied either to the progress of a particular individual or to the three types of capacity that individuals have. The first is similar to meeting someone with whom you are already familiar. The second is like a knot tied in a snake, which is untied when left to itself. The third is like a thief entering an empty house. These are the three examples used to describe (the levels) of liberation. The most exalted is the third, a thief entering an empty house, which has neither harm nor benefit.

First of all, we should understand that awareness or rigpa is primordially free or 'pre-liberated' and is within all sentient beings. It doesn't have to be re-liberated. The state of rigpa, our nature of awareness itself, is primordially liberated. However, because we have not acknowledged this, we have strayed into confusion, and the way we think, while in the state of confusion, is not liberated.

When tied down by ignorance, which method of liberation is needed? Thoughts are not obstructed; there is no way to stop thoughts. You need to know that thought is self-liberated. Thoughts cannot be suppressed. Knowing the essence of the thought makes it possible to liberate it. This is like meeting a man you already know. Once you perfect the training, it is like a thief in an empty house. Rigpa has a natural strength.

Thinking is what needs to be liberated. The way to liberate thinking is to practice in accordance with this quote that I previously mentioned: "Sustain the primordially free awareness with unfabricated mindfulness." `Unfabricated' or `innate mindfulness' means `without a technique' such as thinking, "Oh, I should do such and such to this thought." In the beginning, if you have already recognized your nature once, you have caught the scent of it. Once you get a whiff of the nature, it is as familiar as something you already know. The arising of the thought and its liberation are simultaneous. On the path, this is gaining confidence in liberation.

There is a saying that goes like this: "If you know how to meditate but not how to liberate, then aren't you just like the meditation gods?" The main practice of the meditation gods is shamatha. Shamatha does not bring liberation, and the path to perfect buddhahood is blocked by shamatha. No liberation goes as high as the realm known as the peak of existence. Liberation is the key point.

When you start to think once again, getting involved in a new thought, since you have already recognized the nature previously, when you recognize the thinker, that is the point at which you are meeting someone with whom you are familiar. You should recognize the thought as it arises, so that it is liberated simultaneously with its arising. This is unlike the thinking that takes place in the mind of an ordinary person, which is called `black continuity' or `black diffusion' whereby there is no knowledge whatsoever about such things as who is thinking, where the thought comes from, and where the thought disappears. Rather, an ordinary person is totally and mindlessly carried away by one thought after another. That is definitely not the path of liberation. Once you have caught the scent of it, then the thought is liberated upon arising. This is like meeting someone you already know; you do not doubt who he is. As soon as you see him, you know who he is. It is the same with a thought; when you recognize it, it is liberated. This is like the example of drawing on water. Recognition and liberation are simultaneous.

As you grow more and more accustomed to this, when a thought moves, you have an immediate recognition of the nature, so there is no need to apply any technique at all. The thought is liberated by itself, just as a knot tied in a snake does not have to be untied by anyone, because it unravels by itself. This exemplifies becoming more stable in the training. Finally, the ultimate [level] of liberation is like a thief entering an empty house; there is nothing to liberate and there is no liberator. This is called stability or perfection in training. A thief entering an empty house does not gain anything and the house does not lose anything. All thought activity is naturally liberated without any risk or gain whatsoever. That is the ultimate achievement and is, therefore, the third of the three levels. This is confidence in liberation.

Now I will make it easier to understand. To be introduced to your nature, the four parts without three: the past thought has ceased; the future thought hasn't arisen yet; and if the essence of present thought is recognized, and the thought is not followed after, this present thought will collapse. If it is not recognized, it will not collapse. These are called `the changing thoughts of the three times.' There is a fourth time, once the essence is recognized, which is called the `fourth time of the unchanging innate nature.' This occurs when you are not thinking about the past, the past thought has ceased; you are not thinking about the future, the next thought hasn't arisen yet; and you are not accepting, rejecting, or tampering with the present thought. When you do not get involved in the present thought, it simply vanishes. There is a short gap, which is beyond description. It is free from the thoughts of the three times, so it is timeless. It is called the `fourth time of timelessness.' Recognizing that is called `recognizing your own nature.'

You see it the very moment that you let your mind recognize itself. It is seen the moment you look; you see there is nothing to see. Isn't that right? What you need to see is that there is nothing to see. There is a famous statement: "That fact that there is nothing to see is clearly and vividly seen." Because it is empty, it is certain that there is nothing to see. It is empty; it is not a concrete substance, but the empty has a knowing quality, emptiness, because of the `ness' the cognizant quality that is consciousness. The empty quality defies the extreme of existence, while the cognizant quality defies the extreme of nothingness. When recognizing that, most people say, "I don't see a thing." What is it that sees that no thing is seen? If there were no cognizant quality, how could there be the claim of not seeing a thing? Would space see no thing? The cognizant quality is what sees that there is nothing to see. This is called seeing emptiness—seeing that there is no thing to see. It is not something hidden from us; it is totally direct.

When I give mind teachings, almost everyone says, "I don't see a thing." The fact that there is nothing to see proves that our nature is empty, but the fact that we `see' that there is nothing to see proves that there is also a cognizant quality. This is called `seeing in the very moment of looking.' Directly. It is not that we get to the nature of mind slowly, and it is not that we missed it by searching too high or too low for it. It is not that we only see half of it, while the other half remains hidden. It is seen the very moment of looking. In the moment of seeing, it is free, free of thought. There is no thought, right? Afterward, when you say, "Oh, now I see that there is nothing to see," that thought arises subsequently. It is not liberated. The first moment is enough. It is sufficient. It's right on! Because it is so close, it is very easy. We expect something special to happen, but at that moment all thoughts have been cut through. That moment is what is meant by, `recognizing one's own nature.'

The second statement, `deciding on one point,' means to resolve on being free from thought. In particular, this moment of awareness is called the `sovereign nature of the three kayas.' We recognize directly the fact that there is nothing to pinpoint, this essence, knowing that is the cognizant quality. We cannot separate these two aspects. They can never be separated because they are a unity. In this way, they are 'the sovereign nature of the three kayas.' There is nothing higher or superior to this to decide upon.

Our essence, nature, and capacity are the dharmakaya, sambhogakaya, and nirmanakaya. Additionally, they are the three vajras—vajra body, speech, and mind—of all the buddhas, which we are supposed to achieve. They are also the basis for the body, speech, and mind of all sentient beings. There are no sentient beings that are without body, speech, and mind—and these are the basis for enlightenment.

It is our thinking that causes us to continue in samsara. The moment, the sovereign nature of the three kayas, is free from thought and we remain free from thought, there is no continuation in samsara. We should gain confidence in this. Right now, it is only a short moment, but it is, indeed, free from thought. When this becomes unceasing, will there be any of the three poisons? Is there any greater quality than that? To be free from thought and yet know everything, that is wakefulness. It is said, "Free from thought, yet everything is vividly known." If there were no wakefulness or wisdom quality, it would be pointless to be free from thought. The wisdom, compassion, powers, and capacity—as well as the buddha activity to benefit others—all arise from this wakefulness. The word buddha in Tibetan is sangye, *(sangs rgyas),* purified perfection, which means that the dualistic consciousness with the five poisons is purified, while the wakefulness or abundance of wisdom qualities is perfected. That is called 'awakening' or 'enlightenment.'

This is, in short, the essence or very heart of the *Three Words Striking the Vital Point.* If you want more details, there is the whole Tripitaka, the commentaries of the masters, the one hundred thousand Nyingma tantras, and so forth. One great master once said, "All the thousands of books and scriptures are taught for the sole purpose of realizing these three words". The Buddha's sole purpose for giving teachings is for us to recognize the empty nature, to train in that, and to attain stability.

The blacksmith can swing his hammer around in the air, but he must always land it directly on the anvil. In the same way, the Buddha taught all different kinds of teachings, scriptures, and so forth, but they actually all boil down to a single point. Although the blacksmith swings his hammer around in the air, he has to strike a single point on the anvil. The hammer striking that spot on the anvil is analogous to the *Three Words Striking the Vital Point.*

What do we mean by vital point? If you want to kill someone, you go for the vital points in the physical body—a knife wound in the heart strikes at the vital point. If you want to 'kill' or 'cut the life force' of deluded thinking, there is no method other than recognizing buddha-nature. Do you understand how to kill someone? Cutting off the nose or the ears will not readily kill the person, will it? Stabbing him in the foot won't kill him either. But if you stab him directly in the heart, by the time you pull the knife out, the victim is already dead. If you want to 'kill' delusion, you have these three words.

Now, I have spoken like a simpleton, but, in short, recognize your natural face. Is something seen or not? Not seeing a thing proves it is empty. You see that, right? Seeing that proves there is cognizance. This emptiness is able to cognize. Empty space doesn't cognize. That is called empty cognizance. 'With a core of awareness' means that we experience this personally, but ordinary beings do not. They are always in a state of 'black dissipation.' Actually, the rigpa or awareness is never really lost or dissipated. It's not that we totally lose it and it then returns like a divine personage descending upon us. It's not like that at all. No one has ever been without it for even an instant. But we are carried away in `black dissipation' or darkness.

There is another proverb from Kham. There is a mountain in Kham called Ngomo Lang Tang, which is at the end of a very vast plain. When people walk toward it, it seems to be constantly just in front of them, so there is a proverb about it that says, "When walking for one day, there is Ngomo Lang Tang; when walking for two days, there is Ngomo Lang Tang. The distance is so vast it seems as though you aren't getting any closer. In the same way, when I give a teaching, I speak about this point and when I give another teaching, I also speak about just this. It is like the squeak of a small sparrow. A sparrow squeaks in the same manner every day. My teaching is always the same. I squeak one evening, and on the following evening I make the very same squeak.

There was a master named Gendun Chopel, who died just a few decades ago. Some people came to him claiming that they had had this and that vision or experience, while some people returned from a place called Uddiyana, which is renowned to be the terrestrial realm of Vajrayogini, where there are terrifying charnel grounds and frightening eternal fires and so forth. They came back and told him, "We didn't see anything. It's just a normal place." In reply, he told them, "If you don't see the unchanging nature of mind, from which you have never been apart for a single moment, then how will you ever have visions of deities through sadhana practice?" He meant if you are unable to see what you already possess continuously, how can you expect to see fantastic appearances through sadhana practice?

In India, in the past, there were other masters like Kyungpo Naljor or Tilopa and Naropa, who visited Uddiyana and described the visions they had of Vajrayogini's pure realm. When normal people went there, they returned saying there were just some big boulders and a little pond of water. To this Gendun Chopel replied, "If you can't even see your unchanging nature, which you have never been separated from, how can you expect to perceive Vajrayogini's pure land?"

All sentient beings are never apart from this unchanging, innate nature of mind for even an instant, yet they don't see it. Just as the nature of fire is heat and the nature of water is wetness, in the same way, the nature of our mind is rigpa, awareness. We cannot be separated from this, but we don't notice it. How can we expect to have any special visions?

We must first be well-established in dharmata, then it is possible to see the city of Vajrayogini. That means we should have attained accomplishment, but we do not even see our unchanging nature, from which we have never been separated. If we didn't have the buddha-nature, who could be blamed? Just as water is always wet and fire is always hot, in the same way, the nature of our mind is always awareness wisdom. We cannot be separated from this; it is innate or intrinsic.

Understand that there are three steps: recognizing, training, and attaining stability. The first of these steps, recognizing, is like acquiring the seed of a flower. Once you acknowledge it as the seed of a flower, it can be planted, watered, and grown. When it is fully grown, different colored flowers will bloom perfectly. Similarly, you first need to recognize the nature of mind. Thoughts are not the nature; it is the essence that needs to be known. That is like the flower seed. You must first acknowledge that it is, indeed, a flower seed. In the same way, you should acknowledge that the naked awareness of the four parts without three, which has been pointed out, should be acknowledged as your nature. It must then meet with the right conditions. To cultivate a seed, it must have warmth, moisture, and so forth; then it will certainly grow.

In the same way, you must first know the dharmata nature of mind; next, you train. Training is repeating this short moment of recognition many times, again and again. As a support, you should have devotion to enlightened beings and compassion for unenlightened beings. Devotion and compassion are said to be a universal panacea, like a single efficient technique. A famous quote says, "In the moment of love, the nature of emptiness dawns nakedly." Both compassion and devotion are included in the love mentioned here. Short moments of recognition, repeated many times and supported by devotion and compassion, are called 'training.'

In short, this means nondistraction. In the beginning, it takes effort to not be distracted. Then slowly it becomes effortless, and you become used to it by training. You give water, warmth, and protection to a seed once it has sprouted, so that it will continue to grow. Likewise, you progress by training in nondistraction again, again, and again.

Finally, there is stability. When this moment of nondistraction lasts day and night, unceasingly, what will that be like? All movement will have been destroyed. When the three poisons never arise again and the qualities of wakefulness become fully manifested, will we be ordinary human beings or divine? A small candle flame or the ember from a hearth is the same fire that can set the whole mountainside ablaze. When the moment free from thought and endowed with wakefulness—which we can experience right now—becomes unceasing day and night, what will we be like, ordinary or divine? Is there anything more divine than possessing all the wisdom qualities utterly free from the three poisons? Isn't that what we call `divine?'

We can deduce from this that we need training. We must grow up, just as a new-born baby must grow up. The way for us to do this is through training. The child born this morning is the same person who grows up to be a twenty-five year old, right? He is not someone else. Right now, our nature is the buddha-nature. When fully enlightened, it will also be the buddha-nature. Right now, our nature is unfabricated naturalness, just like space, unmade. The essence of mind is like space, which does not need to be altered. It is just this way by itself. Do we need to imagine or fabricate the space in this room? It does not need to be manufactured. That is how the nature of all beings is. But we need to sustain this through unfabricated naturalness—nothing to meditate, nothing to fabricate.

Our nature, which is unfabricated naturalness, is like the sun shining. In ordinary beings, its expression—the rays of the sun—turns into conceptual thinking, which obscures the sun. If we just let it be as it naturally is, without trying to modify or fabricate, there is no way to err or stray from the view. It becomes unnatural and fabricated when we try to manufacture something or modify or try to do something. Check yourself: is the moment that you call `your nature' something you need to make and then maintain in an unnatural way or is it something you simply leave unfabricated, as it naturally is? This you can check for yourself. If you start to say, "Well, it's not exactly right. It needs to be a little different." or "Well, I guess this is it. Maybe it's not it!" or "Oh, now I've got it. Well, I had it!"—all these thoughts are not what we mean by `unfabricated naturalness.'

QUESTION: What is the defect of the meditation gods, the dhyana devas?

RINPOCHE: There are four meditation god realms, and one is born there due to practicing those meditations. By accomplishing these concentrations here, we will be born in those places. They have meditation but their meditation is with concepts, and, therefore, they are unable to attain enlightenment. In the realms called the summit of existence, one dwells on this idea: "It is endless like space. Consciousness is infinite. There is nothing whatsoever. It is beyond being and not being." But all of this is just thinking. As long as there is thinking, there are concepts, and one wanders through samsara because of conceptual thoughts. If thoughts are not transformed into the wisdom of nonthought, there is no enlightenment, so there is no way that the meditation gods can attain enlightenment.

One is first deluded down from the summit of existence, from 'neither being nor not being.' One is deluded down to nothing whatsoever, then to infinite consciousness, next to infinite space. One is deluded further down to the seventeen realms of form, then further down to the six realms of the gods of desire. When confused or deluded, one has fallen from the summit of existence. We say that at the summit of existence there are the four meditations or four concentrations according to the general vehicles. When it says that one should go beyond the four concentrations at the summit of existence, it means that thinking there is neither being nor not being is just a thought. When we go beyond thinking, we are beyond the summit of existence and samsara is abolished.

It is a subtle thought that is able to produce the coarse ones. It is said that the first concentration is the samadhi with conceptualization and discrimination. It is like a blazing fire. The second concentration has both joy and bliss. The third concentration has no delight but bliss. The fourth concentration is the samadhi of equanimity. Here, this equanimity is conceptual equanimity. It is not the equanimity of the buddhas, because the samadhi of equanimity, or resting in evenness, is free from resting and not resting. A samadhi where something is placed in meditation is of no use. It must be free from the thoughts of placing and not placing in evenness. Freedom from both placing and not placing in meditation is the samadhi of the buddhas. It is like space; a smart person does not argue whether it exists or not. One cannot say that space exists or that it doesn't. But a foolish person disputes whether space exists or not. It is said that foolish people argue the existence of space, while the learned ones are free from arguing about it. The concentrations or meditations of the devas have something upon which they meditate.

With Dilgo Khyentse Rinpoche

POINT DIRECTLY TO
NAKED AWARENESS

Although the Dzogchen tradition has a gradual system of preliminaries, the special characteristic of Dzogchen is that it directly points out naked awareness, self-existing wakefulness. This is for suitable students with sharp mental faculties. Instead of going through many preliminaries, the master introduces them directly to their mind essence, to their self-existing awareness, comprised of three aspects: essence, nature, and capacity.

To ascertain the essence of the mind, we ask whether it is compounded or uncompounded. That which is compounded must have material substance and that which is uncompounded must be substanceless. Substanceless means that there is nothing for the eyes to see, for the ears to hear, and for the hands to hold. This substancelessness is said to be the empty essence of mind, the dharmakaya. Thus, we say, "In the empty essence, dharmakaya."

If this emptiness were a total void, there would be no talk of the buddhas attaining enlightenment and of sentient beings wandering in samsara and the hells. Space is not like that. Without being void, the emptiness is naturally cognizant. Thus, we say, "In the cognizant nature, sambhogakaya." This refers to the hosts of sambhogakaya deities; the nature of sambhogakaya is cognizance. Sambhogakaya means "something with perfect abundance." If something is totally void, it cannot possess perfect abundance. The emptiness itself has perfect abundance; that is called sambhogakaya.

As it is also said, "In the manifold capacity, nirmanakaya." Capacity here means union; the unity of emptiness and cognizance is called capacity. The term *manifold capacity* means that the capacity is all-embracing and unobstructed, not just in one or two ways but as the inconceivable dharmata. 'Manifold' means that the unobstructed original wakefulness of self-display manifests a compassionate variety. It does not refer to external coarse substance but to the unobstructed self-display; capacity here is the unobstructed aspect of emptiness and cognizance. Manifold means 'all-embracing.'

Dzogchen is said to possess great advantages but also great dangers. This is because all teachings are ultimately and finally resolved within the Dzogchen system. This act of resolving can be of two types: resolving through intellectual understanding and resolving through personal experience.

To resolve the teachings through personal experience has a great advantage. Having had naked awareness pointed out and having recognized it directly, one simply makes that the main part of practice. At this juncture, the path to enlightenment is very swift and direct, and the benefits are inconceivably great.

On the other hand, there is great danger when one appropriates the teachings intellectually, assuming that "In Dzogchen, there is nothing to meditate upon. There is nothing to view. There is nothing to carry out as action." This conceptual nihilism is completely detrimental to progress, because the final point of the teaching is nonconceptual; it is beyond intellectual thinking.

The major mistake occurs when one intellectually conceives of what Dzogchen is and holds on to that concept tightly. It is very important to incorporate the teachings into personal experience through the teacher's oral instructions. Otherwise, to have the idea that "I am meditating on Dzogchen" is to completely miss the point. Self-existing wakefulness has been present within the mind-stream of all sentient beings since primordial time. This presence is something that should not be left as theory but should be acknowledged through experience. First recognize it, then train, and attain stability in it. That is when Dzogchen has great benefit. There is actually no greater benefit than this.

When words convey mere intellectual understanding, then concepts preclude experience, and these concepts lack the nonconceptual quality. To rely on conceptual mind is merely to rely on the intellect, whereas to remain in the continuity of naked awareness and to grow used to it is what is truly called 'experiencing.'

The principle is the same whether one talks of Madhyamika, Mahamudra, or Dzogchen. As Shantideva said in the *Bodhicharyavatara,* "When one's intellect holds neither the concept of concreteness nor that of inconcreteness, that is the state of not conceptualizing." As long as one's mind is not free from concepts, one has merely understood the view intellectually and it is nothing more than theory. One might then think,

"Dzogchen is primordially empty; having no basis, there is nothing to meditate upon, no need to do anything. If I meditate in the morning, I am a buddha in the morning. When I recognize at night, I am a buddha at night. The destined one need not even meditate."

Incredible as it may seem, the Dzogchen view can purify the subtlest cognitive obscuration. Merely assuming this is so, however, as many people have done in the past, assuring themselves that they need not either meditate or practice, is to completely miss the point.

To guard against that, practicing according to Madhyamika or Mahamudra, where one goes along step by step, alternating theory and experience within the structure of theory, experience, and realization, is much more beneficial. Proceeding gradually, one becomes clearer and clearer about what is to be resolved and one finally captures the dharmakaya throne of nonmeditation. This graduated system provides some reference points along the various paths and levels.

In Dzogchen, however, the master will, from the very beginning, point out the nonconceptual state, instructing the student to remain free from concepts. If a student thinks, "I am free from concepts; I am never distracted!" while walking around with vacantly gazing eyes, he or she has strayed into intellectual understanding.

Such understanding will not help us when we have to die. Tilopa told Naropa, "Theory is like a patch; it will wear out and fall off." After dying, we will undergo various pleasant and unpleasant experiences, intense panic, fear, and terror. Intellectual understanding will not be able to destroy those fears; it cannot make confusion subside. It is useless to ascertain that one's essence is devoid of confusion. Such patchwork thought is ineffective in dealing with one's confusion at the moment of death.

One needs to recognize and thoroughly acknowledge the view of one's essence. Constructing it from concepts is useless. Simply hearing that there is a delicious meal to be eaten but not eating it, you cannot know what the food tastes like. One must, moreover, be totally free from the slightest flicker of doubt about the state of naked awareness. Concerning stability in awareness, Jigme Lingpa said, "At this point there is no need for one hundred panditas and their thousands of explanations. One will know what is sufficient. Even when questioned by these scholars, doubt will not arise."

The main point is to become stable in awareness through experience, not through intellectual understanding. When a qualified master encounters a worthy student, iron strikes flint, creating fire immediately. When two such persons meet, it is possible to be free from doubt. The proof of having recognized the mind essence is that one feels no doubt, no matter how much one may try. If it is possible to start doubting, thinking, "I wonder how it is; what shall I do?" that understanding is intellectual. This difference between theory and experience is what I was referring to by saying that Dzogchen has both great benefit and great danger.

When a practitioner is introduced to naked awareness, he or she will be able to attain enlightenment in that very body and lifetime. This is because in the moment of recognizing the essence of awareness, the cognitive obscuration is absent. This is called touching the fruition. In this there are three aspects: taking ground as path, taking path as path, and taking fruition as path. Receiving the pointing-out instruction means that one takes fruition as path. That is why it is so precious. Do not let recognition stray into mere theory.

Experience is considered the adornment of awareness. Awareness exists within all beings; whoever has mind has awareness, since awareness is the mind's essence. Mind is like the shadow of one's hand, and awareness is like the hand itself. In this way, there is not one single sentient being who lacks awareness. We might hear about awareness and think, "I understand, awareness is such and such." This mental construct is totally useless—from the very first, the absence of mental fabrication is crucial. As is said, "Within the naked dharmadhatu of nonfabrication, wakefulness dawns—spontaneously present." To introduce awareness is to point out the absence of mental fabrication. Otherwise, it becomes an introduction to mere discursive thought. (*Rinpoche laughs.*)

POINTING OUT

To recognize your nature, that is the first vital point.

If you have not recognized the view, there will be nothing to sustain through the meditation, so it is essential to first recognize the view. That is to say, you are introduced to the self-existing wakefulness present in yourself, which is not something to be searched for elsewhere. It is not something arising within your being that wasn't already there.

Let me go into a bit more detail about the first point in the teaching of the *Tsik Sum Nedik (Tshig Gsum Gnad Brdeg), Three Words Striking the Vital Point*. Tsik sum means three words and ne is the vital point, just like the vital point in our body is our heart. Striking the vital point is analogous to striking the heart with a weapon if we want to sever the life force and kill someone. Likewise, to cut through the life force of confusion, which makes sentient beings continue in a confused state, we need the weapon of awareness wisdom. By means of that, we can kill the life force of confusion. That is the meaning of hitting the vital point. Therefore, the teachings are called the *Three Words Striking the Vital Point*. To repeat, these three words or statements are as follows: recognize your own essence, decide on one thing or on one point, and gain confidence in liberation.

In order to kill the life force of confusion, we should understand what is meant by the state of confusion. Here we use the analogy of gold. In its original state, gold is simply pure. Then it can get covered with dirt or defilement, so that one doesn't know it is gold. The original state is the same as the state of the primordial buddha, Samantabhadra, where no confusion took place. It was simply the original state of pure gold itself. Samantabhadra didn't have the cause of confusion and, therefore, didn't need to clear anything away. That is called the state of primordial enlightenment.

We, on the other hand, did not recognize our own nature, and, therefore, did not know that gold was gold. Thus, our nature became as if covered by defilement. That is the confusion of not realizing our own nature. What happened, at that point, is that we did not recognize the three aspects of our nature, which are called essence, nature, and capacity. They were obscured by three kinds of ignorance. It is said that the empty essence was obscured by the single-identity ignorance. The cognizance, or luminous nature, was obscured by the co-emergent ignorance. Finally, our unobstructed capacity was obscured by the conceptual ignorance. We did not recognize what our nature actually was and fell into temporary confusion. This is the state that is like gold being mistaken or confused with something else. The defilements, like the dirt on gold, are the three ignorances. However, the actual basis is essence, nature, and capacity—awareness wisdom, self-existing rigpa. This is what destroys the three ignorances. Once the temporary ignorance is cleared away, it is the fruition. For us it is impossible to be primordially enlightened; that has been lost. What is necessary now is to become re-enlightened, recognizing the primordially pure essence of wisdom, which we already have. By doing that, it is the same as having the gold that is covered with dirt, purifying it, and ending up with pure gold itself. That is called the re-enlightenment.

The end result, the fruition we can attain, is not something that comes from another place. It comes from us, from what we already have to begin with, just as in removing the defilement of the gold, we end up with the pure gold, as it was originally. The confusion, or the state of being obscured, is not something eternal. It is a passing or temporary thing, and because it is temporary or passing, it can be cleared away. This is just like the sky being obscured by clouds: the clouds are temporary or momentary, and because of that, it is possible to end up with a clear, cloudless sky once again. The buddha-nature that all sentient beings have is not temporary or passing. We have had this enlightened essence since primordial time. It is present in all beings, just as oil is present in sesame seeds—if you squeeze them, there will always be some oil.

The buddha-nature essence is primordially pure; its nature is utterly or perfectly pure, and it is also free from temporary defilements. There is another analogy used for our enlightened essence. In previous aeons, like the golden aeon, there was something called the wish-fulfilling jewel. One could make special wishes to this jewel, and they would all be fulfilled. Our enlightened essence right now is like a wish-fulfilling jewel that got dropped in a mud hole and was not noticed. Nobody knew what it was. Similarly, the enlightened essence of all beings is something we already have but it is not evident; we are not aware of that. If we knew that there was a wish-fulfilling jewel in some mud hole, we could take it up, rinse it, and put it on the top of a pole. In the past ages, people would put it on top of a pole with banners and make wishes that would all be fulfilled. Likewise, if sentient beings can have their enlightened essence pointed out, and if they recognize it, it is the same as purifying the wish-fulfilling jewel.

There was one story of a lama, a kind of unconventional, accomplished lama in Kham. He would do prostrations to anybody and also join his palms even to dogs and pigs. Other people would say, "Why are you doing that? It is just a dog." He would respond, "They also have the enlightened essence. What about the pig, the dirtiest animal? Yeah, they do too. The enlightened essence is still inconceivably precious, even though it is in such a form." Somebody said, "Hey lama, haven't you gone a little crazy to go and prostrate to dogs and pigs?" He said, "Actually not. You are the ones who are crazy, not knowing what the enlightened essence is. I am not prostrating or paying homage to the dogs and the pigs, but to the enlightened essence that is within them."

Right now, we find ourselves in what is called the path, and that is the same as the wish-fulfilling jewel that has fallen in the mud and is being mistaken or confused with an ordinary stone. Still we have our enlightened essence, which is no different in quality or size from that of the primordial buddha, Samantabhadra, or a dog or a pig.

The first sentence in the *Three Words Teachings,* is to recognize your own nature, the enlightened essence that you already have but haven't been aware of or acknowledged—that is what you recognize now. When it says, "Recognize your own nature," it doesn't mean recognize somebody else's essence. It means recognizing or acknowledging what you already have since the beginning. The key instruction is how to recognize your own essence and how to cut through or kill the life force of confusion—this is called four parts without three.

Our enlightened essence is not some conditioned thing. It is unconditioned. In the conditioned three times, we have the thoughts of past, present, and future. They are changing, whereas the unconditioned and unchanging nature is like space. The conditioned thoughts are like clouds, and they move away. The unconditioned nature is like space, unchanging. Space means the openness right here. We need to be free from the three conditioned, changing times and to recognize the unconditioned fourth time, which is simply called the timeless time.

The three times are merely concepts. There is no other conceptual thinking that is beyond or apart from the three times. When you are free from conceptual thinking, you experience timelessness. This timeless time is also called the fourth time of equality. We talk about four parts without three, which simply means the three times with conceptual thinking. When free from that, automatically there is only the unconditioned nature left. That is what is called awareness wisdom.

To identify the timeless time, you need to get to the immediate present. The present is when you hear the sound, like when I clap my hand. In the present moment, when hearing the sound, the past thought has ceased and the future thought hasn't come yet, but there is still an involvement in what is known as the present. This is called the present thought. Sentient beings are incapable of stepping out of present thought; instead, they attach a new thought activity to the previous one, and it becomes a continuous chain, which is called samsara.

Instead, in the present moment when the past has ceased and the future hasn't arrived, don't follow or continue the present thinking. How do you do that? Don't accept or reject; then the present vanishes as well. There is no concept—the moment there is no thought involvement in the three times that is the naked state, rigpa. At that moment, there is no covering of the thoughts of the three times. There is only our essence itself, nothing else. What obscures the essence is the thoughts of the three times. When there is no thinking of the past, no anticipating the future, and no conceptualizing the present, in this absence—the vanishing of thinking—there is the essence itself, nothing else. That is called recognizing the nature.

When you recognize your nature, the thoughts vanish; there is simply the essence itself. Then it lasts for a few seconds, not longer than that, because since beginningless time until now we have had the opposite habit. But this short moment is flawless. It is flawless because it has not been overtaken or corrupted by conceptual thinking yet. It is thought free.

Some people think that because there is no thinking, we become incapacitated. It is not like that at all, because there is a natural luminosity present. Luminosity means that luminous cognizance is still present. We are not oblivious. Some people think they become mindless because there is no thinking, but mindlessness or oblivion means that somebody knocks you out. When you are knocked out, then it is all right to say that the thoughts ceased without knowing anything either. What I am pointing out here is called thought-free knowing. There is no thinking taking place, but still the capacity to know is unblocked. The mindless thought-free state is different. When knocked out, the present vivid experience is brought to a halt. However, in the thought-free moment of knowing rigpa, the present sense experience is not blocked at all.

Right now, try to remain without involvement in past, present, and future. All sense impressions are not blocked. You see whatever is present, right? You can still hear whatever sound there is. Even though thoughts have ceased, awareness doesn't cease. You are free of conceptualizing but the quality of knowing is still present. Everything is perceived through the senses yet there is no conceptualizing. This is called the vividness of appearance. In that short moment, there is no thought involvement concerning past, present, or future. That is called cutting the thinking in itself.

When the three times are absent, there is the fourth time of the great equality, which is actually timeless. This is how the nature of mind is pointed out according to the tradition called the four parts without three. As long as there is concept or thinking, there is time, but the absence of thought or concepts is the timelessness, the time of the timeless time.

When you talk about the four parts, you need to be free from three— free from past and future, and also not conceptualizing the present moment. By conceptualizing the present, the present exists. If we are not involved in conceptualizing what is perceived in the present moment, there is no thought left at all. The four parts without three style is the tradition of Dzogchen.

According to Dzogchen, you first investigate whether you can find a thought that arises, remains, or ceases. Failing to find any such thing in the thinking, you can establish with certainty that the mind is utterly empty, just like space. Can you say that space comes into being, that it remains anywhere, or that it ceases to be? When we look closely and scrutinize how the mind really is, we cannot fail to discover that it is beyond arising, dwelling, and ceasing. Just as the space here has no arising, dwelling, or ceasing, in the same way, empty mind doesn't arise, dwell, or cease either.

Mind is still cognizant. Mind perceives. The mind being empty and able to cognize is a unity that doesn't arise, dwell, or cease. As long as we fail to clearly see this unity being empty and cognizant, we get involved in unaware thinking that arises, dwells, and ceases. Once we recognize the indivisible, empty cognizance, we realize what is beyond arising, dwelling, and ceasing. Being unaware of that and merely involved in normal thinking, the thinking will still arise, dwell, and cease. As sentient beings, we are controlled by this expression of normal thinking, which arises and ceases, arises and ceases. However, once it becomes the empty cognizance with the core of awareness, this knowing aspect sees what is beyond arising and ceasing. In the absence of thought, how can there be something that arises or ceases?

The ultimate or final thing to discover about the nature of mind is that it is empty and thought-free yet cognizant. We do not know that. We get so busy, always forging, forming, and creating everything that we make; this is called samsara. Yet these two, essence and expression, the nature of mind and the thinking, coexist. They are co-emergent, like flame and its heat, the sun and its sunlight, the ocean and its waves, the body and its arms and legs, the sky and its clouds. If we try to look, where do the clouds exist? They do not exist anywhere outside space. To what are the arms and legs attached? They are directed by the brain. The heat of the flame or the smoke from the fire comes from the flame or the fire itself. The wave in the ocean is dependent upon the ocean itself; it does not exist independent of the ocean.

In the same way, the pleasure and pain we feel are based on the empty mind. They don't exist anywhere else. The moment we recognize what it is that feels happy or sad, we cannot help but connect with the empty mind. At that moment, pleasure and pain vanish, collapse, disappear. Conceptual thinking can be disbanded, discarded; it disappears. The outcome of this disappearance is called awareness wisdom.

How do we recognize the fourth without the three? We recognize it through a pointing-out instruction or introduction. The method is to abandon conceptual work and recognize that moment, free from conceptual thinking; it is also called cutting through. Let's say we have a string here that is blocking free space. If we cut that in one second, the whole thing falls apart, and there is a moment without anything joined together, just like clear space. When free from the past and future, and also from the thought of the present, there are no thoughts. When we cut the string, everything becomes one space. Right now, the conditioned thinking is blocking or interrupting the unconditioned. Usually we talk about the present, but the present refers to the present thought. If we can recognize the nature of the present thought, we discover the fourth time of timelessness. There is no kind of thinking that is not about the past, the present, or the future. When free from these kinds of conditioned thoughts, we experience a timeless moment free from any concepts. It is called the unchanging wakefulness.

There are various means to recognize this awareness wisdom. In a strong moment of emotion, like faith, if you suddenly acknowledge your own mind, because of the strong emotion, there is no thought left behind in the mind. At that moment, the enlightened essence is not obscured by anything whatsoever. Similarly, in a moment of strong compassion for other beings—one that is so overwhelming that tears come to your eyes—there is a moment when no thought is left in your mind. If you recognize your mind essence at that moment, there is nothing to obscure this unchanging wakefulness.

Likewise, you have that kind of feeling in a moment of shock, great fear, or panic, when, for example, a tiger or lion suddenly jumps out from somewhere and is about to eat you. If you have some stability in practicing, at that moment the mind is totally divested of concepts. It is very easy to recognize the essence. Most people, because of the panic, become kind of oblivious. Before becoming oblivious and losing your senses, there is a moment where you can recognize the naked wakefulness directly, the fourth without the three. Also, if you have run up a mountain without taking rest anywhere and you are totally exhausted, there comes a point where you can't run any longer. You simply sit down, out of exhaustion, and then your mind stops totally. The awareness, however, doesn't stop. Most people, though, become oblivious or mindless at that point.

It is said that the moment conceptual mind ceases, the dharmakaya is nakedly manifest. At the moment our conceptual thinking is brought to an end, there is nothing other than naked wakefulness present. There are many different words for mind—like mind, thinking mind, and consciousness—which is what sentient beings have. Those words always refer to a state of mind where the essence is not realized or recognized—but you can recognize the essence within thinking.

Any being with a mind will have a thought happening. When a thought occurs in your mind, instead of looking at what is being thought of, recognize what is it that thinks the thought; look into its source. At that moment of looking into the source of the thought, you cannot find any specific place or pinpoint it in any way that this is exactly where it came from. It has totally vanished, nothing. It is not because one is not very bright or unlucky or kind of missed it. Actually, it is because it is the unconditioned nature, which is like space. There is not a thing as such to find. It is not that there was a thing to find and one missed it. One actually found that there was not a thing.

There is also a way of recognizing the essence after the thought has vanished. For example, a master will shout very forcefully and suddenly, the sound PHAT, which is the unity of means and knowledge. It should be abrupt and forceful, just like a flash of lightning or a thunder crack. Because one's mind doesn't have a chance or time to have any concept yet, there is kind of a gap or moment where there is nonconceptual wakefulness. Since there is no time for a thought to arise yet, there are a few seconds, not very long, where one can and should realize one's essence. What should be recognized is without fabrication, the naked, present wakefulness, which is unconstructed.

There is one song that says the mind is free from concepts, the fresh nature. When, for example, the sound PHAT has been exclaimed suddenly and forcefully, it is said that our wakefulness, the basic state of mind, is totally naked. Naked means that it is stripped of all the different kinds of emotions or concepts that we usually have—the five, six, or different numbers, such as twenty-one or eighty different kinds of thoughts. At that time, none of these has a chance to arise. This is the authentic four parts without the three, the fourth time. The mind is totally naked, like a stainless crystal. That is the introduction by means of shouting PHAT.

There are two basic ways of pointing out the mind essence, from within thought and when the thought has ceased. In either case, pointing out is not enough. The master can point out mind nature, but the student has to recognize it. The two ways of pointing out are either when the mind is still or when the mind is moving. Before I talked about the mind when there is thinking, recognizing what is it that thinks. Now I am explaining about mind when it is still.

According to the root verses of the *Tsik Sum Nedik,* you should first rest naturally without deliberately trying to think of something and without trying to either concentrate or not think. At that time, there is no strong thought; it has disappeared. You are remaining in the alaya, in indifference. When simply resting like that, without any deliberate thought activity, that is shamatha, and of the two, ordinary and special, it is the special shamatha. This needs to be destroyed. This is the introduction within stillness. When remaining in that smooth state of equanimity, suddenly and forcefully shout the mind shattering PHAT, which is sharp and not premeditated. As Paltrül exclaims, "How wonderful! Emaho!"

> Nothing whatsoever—totally disengaged.
> Disengaged but utterly open.
> A total openness, which is indescribable.

Not fixating outwardly or holding inwardly is the shamatha without support, an indifferent state that needs to be blown apart. After shouting PHAT, the abiding is destroyed. Here, when you simply rest, there is no thought going on, but there is still some subtle fixation on that stillness and that has to collapse. After you shout a sudden, very strong, and sharp PHAT, the abiding and not abiding are destroyed. It shatters that fixation so there is only the dharmakaya awareness left. Then there is a blank and free state, which is indescribable. Recognize this as the dharmakaya awareness. This is the introduction to naked dharmakaya through stillness.

There are two different ways of recognizing the essence of mind: when it is still and when it is thinking. The introduction through movement is when a thought arises; here you recognize the one who has thoughts. By recognizing the knower, you are introduced through movement. At that time, simply remain naturally free. In recognizing your own rigpa, the movement disappears. Recognize the dharmakaya awareness.

All sentient beings have arising and ceasing (of thought); mind will not only stay or only move. A thought doesn't arise by itself. It needs the circumstances of a mental or external object, our senses, and our conscious mind directed toward that—these three are the basis of movement. There have to be some factors coming together for a thought to arise. Movement comes when there is the external grasped object and the inner fixating mind. When thoughts of happiness and sadness arise, if you simply look directly, as it is said in the very well-known Mahamudra teachings, then the essence of thought is the dharmakaya. When a thought arises, if you immediately recognize who is it that thinks, the thought self-vanishes, self-evaporates. Once the thought vanishes, there is nothing but unimpeded awareness.

Thoughts do arise and there are different ways of recognizing essence, as I previously mentioned—through a strong emotion like devotion or compassion, or with the strong exclamation of PHAT, or simply recognizing who it is that thinks. Through any of these ways, the thought will disappear. Recognize (the essence of) the thought and the thought will vanish. It will be traceless, as in the example of writing in space. It does not stay; this is the example.

Since beginningless time, we have been so accustomed to conceptual thinking. We need the moment where a thought has vanished, just like a cloud-free sky, which is only pure sky. Pure sky means without anything to obscure. Likewise, when a thought has vanished, there is nothing to obscure our enlightened essence. However, if we deliberately try to throw the thoughts away or prevent them from arising, that is simply another thought, and it will cause more obscuration. The thoughts are like the natural expression of our empty essence. They are not something we can block or suppress. If you try to suppress thinking, it increases; you cannot throw it away. You cannot suppress it. What has to happen is that it should spontaneously dissolve. The moment a thought has vanished, the wakefulness left behind is nonconceptual or thought free. I have now spoken about the method of being introduced (in various ways).

The first thing that is important is, if one hasn't recognized, one should recognize. The second point after that is, *to decide on one point.* It is not that somebody decides on one point because you should decide on one point. But by recognizing one's essence, then naturally, the doubt will fall away, and one decides on what the essence is. One's mind cannot be resolved by somebody else; it has to be resolved from one's self. At the moment of being free from doubt, you have resolved. If you cannot tell me, "This is how it is, I decided on that," I will still feel, "Yeah, he says so, but is it really true or not?" Since the essence is a moment totally stripped of conceptual thinking, and one experiences that, it is very easy to decide 'that's it.'

The essence of dharmakaya is simultaneously free from thoughts and naked. That is how it should be. There is also another way of being free from thought while being kind of dull and stupid. That is not called nakedness. It should be a moment free from any concepts but at the same moment wide awake, cognizant. That is the naked dharmakaya. There is one quote that says, "Free from concepts, the original, fresh essence." Original means it is our primordial, pure essence, and fresh means it is not adulterated, covered, or spoiled in any way by the different disturbing emotions and so forth. The very instant a thought vanishes, there is a moment that is fresh and wide awake. It is not an oblivious state, where we are dull or murky or half-fainted, as if somebody knocked us out from behind. This is something that we understand in the post-meditation; it is not something we ponder in the meditation.

In the very instant of this immediate awareness or wakefulness, the three mental poisons—attachment, anger, and stupidity—are not present. What can be more special than that? When we have a flame, a hair will not be able to remain in it. Likewise, in this moment of nonconceptual wakefulness, thoughts such as the three poisons will not be able to stay.

In the *Tsik Sum Nedik* teachings, the first point is how to recognize if you haven't recognized. That is the moment free from thoughts of the three times, the immediate kind of wakefulness free from concepts. That's it. As it is said, "It is free from all defects," which means that the three poisons are not present at that time. You should first recognize what has not been recognized. This was about what should be recognized. After having recognized, you should enhance that.

This is the pointing-out instruction, according to the Dzogchen tradition. In Mahamudra, there are three other words used. In Tibetan, they are called *(gshi, gdang,* and *rtsal)*, which mean essence, manifestation, and expression. The essence is nonarising; you need to establish that in order to realize Mahamudra. The unobstructed manifestation is exactly the same as the cognizant nature. In the expression, there are myriad displays; it is the same as the capacity, which is the indivisibility of being empty and cognizant. According to Madhyamika, you need to transcend extremes. Extremes here means conceptual formulations, such as it is like this or that. In other words, totally free from extremes means that you remain without formulating any construct or concept whatsoever, until it is only wide open and bare like space.

Our nature, or basic state, is defined or described as empty, cognizant, self-existing wakefulness. When you start to try to alter, improve, forge, or form that, it gets spoiled. You capture your natural seat, which is the original state as it is, before starting to create or form anything. This is an extremely subtle, but very simple, noncomplex state, the unity of being empty and cognizant. But when we start to talk about it, we also have to eliminate the ideas about how it is not. All the different ways of establishing exactly how this basic state is and how it isn't become very, very complex. According to how subtle that explanation is, you have all the different levels of vehicles and so on. But on the other hand, what about letting it be as it is, without having to formulate it? Then it is like that at the outset, simply leaving it like that is the path, and realizing fully just as it is, is the fruition—not three different things.

In Mahamudra, there is a famous statement that says: "Basic wakefulness is utterly subtle, extremely subtle. It is indestructible like the center of space. It is more subtle than subtle." In other words, it is not something that can be held as an object of thought; it is indestructible like the center of space. The indestructible vajra here means the changeless quality, unchanging. You need to recognize that which is unchanging—like space itself, it doesn't begin, doesn't have a middle, and doesn't end.

The third statement in the pointing-out instructions of Mahamudra is this: you are your own father. Relax or rest in the experience that is beginningless and endless. These are the vajra words used in the pointing-out instructions in Mahamudra.

The *Prajnaparamita* is the precious teaching of Lord Buddha himself. This also contains the pointing-out instruction, which is the transcendent knowledge or prajna. It is inexpressible, inconceivable, and indescribable. In other words, it is not something that can be made an object to be spoken of, thought of, or illustrated through example. It is called transcendent knowledge because it transcends the prajna intelligence, which in the normal sense is discrimination, discriminating knowledge, which means to discern, and to conceive. The state of transcendent knowledge is not something that is either discerned or discriminated.

First of all, the main thing to understand when recognizing your nature is that the present moment is being pointed out. It is right now. It's obvious that there is present mind. No matter how much you look into it, you never find a thing about which you can say, "That is what it is," even if you look for a million years. Like Machig Labdron said when she was talking to some demon, "You demon, besides the empty movement of an empty mind, I don't see you as having any existence. Even the enlightened buddha does not see you anywhere." She was pointing out to the demon that it is actually empty as well.

No matter how much we analyze and try to track down the mind, we don't find anything other than it being just empty. This should be completely settled. You agree? The example is that it is like space, but we cannot settle that it is space, because then it becomes a void, noncognizant state, so we can't say that either. It is not space; it is empty, but space doesn't know anything. This empty whatever we call it can also cognize. That is called in Tibetan salwa cognizance, *(gsal ba)*. This is the 'ta' in shunyata in Sanskrit.

These two are indivisible. You cannot separate being empty and being cognizant. Even though we may be completely uneducated or stupid, we can acknowledge as a fact that we don't find something called *mind;* it is empty, and also this empty *whatever* can still cognize. It is not like space that cannot. We can know that our mind is empty because it is cognizant; it is the knower of all things. Without this knowing, this capacity to perceive, this world would be completely empty. Even forms and sounds and so on are empty forms, empty sounds; they don't know anything. The knower is the cognizant quality. The elements that make up the world— earth, water, fire, wind, and space—are all lacking cognizance.

Aren't you completely sure now that there is nothing more important or precious than mind itself? Mind is the one that experiences everything, all pleasure and pain. It is also this mind that makes all the trouble and creates samsara, when it is empty and cognizant yet unaware or ignorant of its own nature. In this moment, when it is empty and cognizant and knowing its nature, the thinking has been cut in itself. In the very moment of knowing the indivisible, empty cognizance, it is impossible for thinking to remain. Within knowing, ignorant thinking has no place.

However, when being in the state of indivisible empty cognizance that is unaware or ignorant of its own nature, it is very possible to be involved in thinking, the deluded thinking. That is how sentient beings function. Indivisible empty cognizance that knows its own nature is called the immaculate dharmakaya, which is in itself not something to be created through meditation or forgotten through distraction. This is the first point.

How do we connect with this? It is the present moment of wakeful-ness. Don't try to form or tamper with it. Leave it as it is. When know-ing itself, it is called the awareness wisdom, rigpa yeshe. Do not try to accept or reject. Do not think there is a promise or some threat through hope and fear. It is the immediacy of nowness. It lasts for a few moments unmixed with discursive thinking, then it slips away. We start to forget. Once we forget and become absentminded, thinking reoccurs. But before we forget, the state of rigpa itself is not something we need to meditate upon. It is there by itself. It is once we forget that thinking starts.

In the first stretch of a few seconds, it is empty and yet it is awake. No need to do anything to that. The outer objects are not blocked. Mind within is not nailed down. There is nothing to do to mind or appearances. This is what is called 'the great equality.' When there is great equality, it is oneness. Do not reach out to what is perceived; do not focus in or con-centrate on the perceiver.

In the first few seconds, is there any thought activity? That is called rigpa, which is stable in itself. You have reassumed your natural seat, which is not an act of meditating. There is no need to meditate. There is no doing, no reference point as to an action.

This is what has slipped away through ignorance since beginningless time. Of the two types of ignorance, co-emergent or innate ignorance and conceptual ignorance, conceptual ignorance is the thinking, the thought movement. The co-emergent ignorance is the forgetting. Once we for-get, then we think. But when we remain unforgetting, there is no way to start thinking. That is called purifying ignorance in the ground, in that short moment, because during that moment there is neither forgetting nor thinking. Once we forget, thinking reoccurs. Thus, you train in short moments, many times. This is a very important phrase: short moments, many times. It is not that rigpa will come down from the sky and take possession of you. It will never happen. Nor is it like being hit by a flash of lightning, where all of a sudden all discursive thinking vanishes and there is only rigpa. That doesn't happen either. You don't have to think of that as being something other than what is right now.

It is not that we visualize the state of rigpa and the real rigpa comes in and dissolves into that. It is not like that either, as in the development stage. In short, leave present wakefulness without trying to improve it, without trying to alter it. That is sufficient.

In the beginning, we do need to have the observer and observed. But as we become more and more accustomed, we can transcend the observer and observed. There has to be the idea to recognize our nature. Otherwise, we will never notice. Once we get more stable, we experience arriving in the natural state, but not through any deliberate effort whatsoever. But to get to that, you need to train, meaning get used to it, like learning something by heart. You can do this, just as I know the Seven-Line supplication by heart. When I was young, I had to learn it, and now I can chant it without any second thought at all. It means I got accustomed to it, I learned it. In the same way, you need to grow used to and train in the natural, unfabricated state of rigpa. By training in that, you will get used to it, and it will become like second nature.

When arriving in rigpa, within basic space, conceptual meditation is naturally dissolved. You can take a rest within the indivisible state of awareness and space, like a person who has completed his task. Being at ease is the outcome of training. Besides this, there is no other nature of mind to be pointed out. It is not anything other than what is in you. But still, at this point, you need to get the smell of it. Besides that, there is nothing to do; there's only naturalness. The essence is not an act of meditating because it is not made up. It is not within our power to make the essence of mind. If we could, we should, but it is not something that we can create, because it is the flawless dharmakaya itself.

The teaching that I have given is the pointing-out instruction on recognizing your nature, the first of the three vital points.

ENHANCE THE RECOGNITION

What you are recognizing is the instant free from any conceptual thinking. For example, when you were an infant, your father left for another country and came back when you were twenty-five-years old. You will not be able to recognize who he is unless somebody points out and says, "Here is your father." That is the meaning of being pointed out and recognizing. Another example is about a fool who lost himself in the marketplace and was running around asking where he was. The people said, "Don't be stupid; you are right here." He replied, "Oh yeah, here I am" and found himself. You recognize your own essence in the same way, just as a fool who lost himself then recognized where he was. After recognizing, you should enhance that—by repeating short moments, many times.

It should be short, because when the moment is short, there is no time for new thoughts to come in and obscure it. If you try to make it last longer, it becomes merely a conceptual idea. But you need mindfulness or re-mindfulness; otherwise, you will never even think of recognizing your essence. To begin with, you need a deliberate mindfulness to recognize—just simply rest free from the concepts. After you get more accustomed and grow used to that, the mindfulness becomes effortless.

You do not prolong the state by deliberately trying to rest in it for a long time or by cutting it short either. Let it be as it naturally is, according to its own stability, which is called unfabricated naturalness. Leaving it short helps for nonmeditation. Repeating it many times helps for nondistraction.

First, it is important to recognize your essence. Next, you need to decide "that's it," without doubt. Finally, the third vital point, or the third sentence, is called *gaining confidence in liberation*. What does liberation refer to here? It is the liberating or the freeing of your thinking as it arises. We always have thoughts and emotions coming up, but these thoughts are a projection or an expression of our own essence. Simply recognize the essence of the thought as it arises. It arises from you and it dissolves into you. It arises and dissolves, just as when you draw with a finger on the surface of water. You make the drawing and it disappears,

73

vanishes. You make another one and it also vanishes. The thoughts or conceptual thinking we have do not come from some other place. The thoughts arise from within us. They come from the awareness, our nature. Therefore, when we recognize that which thinks, the thought itself dissolves back into our nature. That is the meaning of *arising from itself, being freed into itself.* It is never said that thoughts come from somewhere else but have to be freed in us. It is called *self-occurrence and self-liberation.* The thoughts are coming from our own nature, and when we recognize them, they simple vanish, dissolve into our nature again. That is the meaning according to the *Tsik Sum Nedik,* which says, *Self-occurring self-liberation, without interruption.*

Ordinary shamatha practice, where you try not to think, doesn't mean that the thoughts have been liberated; they simply become kind of frozen. That is the same as squeezing a fart inside, not letting it come out. There is nothing to smell outside but the cause is retained within. You do not become enlightened simply through shamatha. The reason why shamatha is not enough for enlightenment is that our basic nature, the awareness wisdom, is primordially and originally beyond arising, dwelling, and ceasing. It is totally free from these attributes, whereas the state of shamatha is simply trying to rest in a state where the thoughts have ceased, deliberately. It is not the natural freeing. Shamatha is like putting the awareness in prison and trying to catch it. The teachings in the *Three Words Striking the Vital Point* instruct us to recognize the dharmakaya in the liberation, not to recognize the nonliberated dharmakaya as in shamatha.

Shamatha doesn't mean free from thoughts, it means that the thought has somewhat subsided. Whereas vipashyana, wakefulness, is the thought having been liberated. The difference between being blocked versus liberated is the same as the difference between being constipated versus going to the toilet.

The key point of self-liberation is like a bubble: It arises within water. It dissolves within water again. The thought arising from your own nature dissolves into that nature again. In the same way, you recognize the dharmakaya of what is liberated. Since the thought is a manifestation of dharmakaya, it arises from within you, and again by being recognized, since the essence of the thought is dharmakaya, it dissolves into one's essence, dharmakaya.

This is how to practice while we are still ordinary people. Thoughts will arise until we become what is called an arya, a noble one, and even then, there are some thoughts. Thinking is only exhausted in the state of buddhahood. It is like arriving on an island of pure gold; we can't find any ordinary stones. If the state free from thoughts were merely a blank, dull, oblivious state, there would be no point whatsoever. Actually, awareness at that point has the potential of having incredible qualities—inconceivable.

The difference between ignorance and awareness is the difference between night and day. In the night, we can't see anything if it is really dark. Awareness is like the sunlight in the day. Likewise, now we only really perceive what is just in front of our nose. Another thing, when we see, usually we think that our eyes see; actually, it is the mind that sees, because a corpse also has eyes, but it doesn't see anything. Our different sense organs are made of dead matter. What actually perceives is done through the senses, but not by the senses—it is the mind. Actually, that which experiences is mind or consciousness. It is not the eyes or the other senses. Of course, they are used for example; without the eyes, we don't see visible form, but the perceiver is really the mind.

When we think about what the mind is, intellectually, we should never think of it as being a concrete or material thing, a substantial entity. It is insubstantial or nonmaterial, but at the same time, it is not a blank physical space. It has the ability to cognize.

The *Song of Karmapa*[12] says this about the nature of mind:

> It is not existent since even the victorious ones do not see it.
> It is not nonexistent since it is the basis of samsara and nirvana.
> This is not a contradiction, but the Middle Way of unity.
> May we realize the nature of mind, free from extremes.

These two seeming contradictions, one excluding the other, are not like that. They are an inseparable unity. That is the Middle Way. All other viewpoints and philosophies hold up to being either nonexistent or existent. There is always some extreme. But the true view—how it really is—expresses that there is a simultaneous unity of being and not being. We cannot say it is, because there is nothing to find. But we also cannot say it is not, because it is the basis of everything cognized and experienced. This unity is like the unity of water being wet and of fire being hot. You can't take those apart. That is the unity we are talking about here. It is like the unified state of Vajradhara, the complete enlightenment of unity.

It is said that to hold on to the mind as being something concrete is to be as stupid as a beast or a cow; but to hold on to the opposite, thinking there is nothing, would be even more foolish. If you think the mind is a thing, that is one kind of concept. If you think it is nonexistent, that is also another kind of concept. If you think, "Oh these two are a unity," that is a third kind of concept. The moment free from any concepts is the natural unity, as it is. The first moment is naked wakefulness, free from any idea that the mind is this or it is not this, or it is both, a unity. When free from thoughts, it is a unity by itself. You cannot combine or make a unity; it is self-existing. It hasn't been made up and is not a construct or a thought. Rest in the present naked wakefulness. If you simply rest without thinking it is this or it is that or it is unity, that is the same as using a single bridge to cross a hundred rivers after they have flowed together.

For enhancement, in short, have devotion to enlightened beings, the Three Jewels, and compassion for unenlightened ones, or all sentient beings. Be diligent and do not stray from this unfabricated natural state, which doesn't need to be maintained or sustained. It also doesn't need somebody to sustain it. Recognize yourself, and, at the same, time let the mind face itself. Give up everything, all other concerns. Then you will have arrived back to square one, the primordial state.

CHARACTERISTICS OF
MIND AND RIGPA

There is the all-ground, the all-ground consciousness, the mental cognition, and the defiled mental consciousness, according to the classifications. The first one, the all-ground is just delusion. It is a blank state, vacant. When we stay in that state, there is no thought, but there is also no awareness. There is no freedom, which is why it is the basis for samsara.

After that is the all-ground consciousness, which is cognizant and still without thoughts, but there is fixation. It is not free like rigpa or all-ground wisdom. Then there is the mental cognition, subtle thought activity. The defiled mental consciousness is gross thought activity, like passion, aggression, and so on. There are the five sense consciousnesses, and they are also cognizant but nonconceptual. In the sense cognitions, like visual cognition, there is cognizance but no thought about it at first.

If we move our head and look, then in that first instant we have no thoughts, just visual cognition. We haven't gotten to the stage where we say, "Oh this is a wall," or "This is such and such." Those are called concepts or ideas, and with these concepts, we get into the mental consciousness or the defiled mental consciousness.

The yogi way of practice is through the five sense openings, which are wide open; the mind is unfocused, without reference point; and awareness is totally free or uninhibited. When you are like that, you are what is called all-ground wisdom. Through shamatha practice, you only get back to the all-ground. It is the friend of the all-ground, the helper. It is attending the all-ground.

The all-ground is a limited state; rigpa is unlimited. That is the difference. Rigpa is open, unimpeded; you can know that. The all-ground state is more vacant or blank. The difference between these two states is the difference between being wide awake versus blank and oblivious. There is a big difference. You can check it out actually, by yourself. If a beginner stays for too long in rigpa, it can become blank and vacant. That is why it is best to train in rigpa for short moments repeated many times.

My own root guru, Samten Gyatso, said, "What is the use of sitting for a long time in the state of stupor, the stupid meditation state? We have been there like that since beginningless time anyway, sleeping in the nest of the all-ground, the alaya. Better to practice for a short moment, but completely wide awake." He says that the main point of practice is to do short sessions but many times—short periods repeated many times. When Samten Gyatso came into a room, people could not bear to look at his eyes. He was overwhelming to look at; his eyes were very special. You can see in the eyes whether the yogi has good practice or not, because when the eyes are very bright and clear, it is due to remaining in rigpa. If the eyes are kind of dumb and dull, then not. They say that in Kham.

QUESTION: Since the characteristics of consciousness are to be conscious and cognizant, can you explain further how that is different from rigpa?

RINPOCHE: The cognizance of consciousness is with fixation, whereas that of self-existing awareness is without fixation. The difference lies in whether or not there is fixation. They are the same words but with different meanings. Self-existing wakefulness is conscious and cognizant, while consciousness is also conscious and cognizant. In the words they are the same; there is no consciousness that is not cognizant or aware. Otherwise, how would anything be perceived? It is the characteristic of consciousness. Still, one is with fixation, and the other is without it. Awareness is without fixation. It is the essence, and dualistic mind is its expression. The essence is without fixation; it is conscious and cognizant.

Consciousness, which is also cognizant and aware, is with fixation. In the beginning, we don't know how to make this difference. But if dualistic mind were to be without cognizance and consciousness, how would we know anything? Dualistic mind does have cognizance and the ability to cognize.

QUESTION: The five sense consciousnesses are cognizant yet nonconceptual. How are they different from the nonconceptual wisdom?

RINPOCHE: All eight consciousnesses belong to dualistic mind; they are different divisions of it. What does cognizant yet nonconceptual mean? When we see something, the eyes perceive it, if we have eyes. There is a form; there is cognizance of it. Nonconceptual means that the eye consciousness itself is not able to create any concepts about what that form is. That is the meaning of cognizant yet nonconceptual.

Nonconceptual *(rtog med)* means that there are no concepts about whether a thing is this or that. Upon meeting objects, consciousnesses are cognizant yet without concepts. That is what nonconceptual means. The mental consciousness is what thinks, "This is a statue; this is an offering bowl," and so forth. It is not the same as the nonconceptual awareness wisdom. In the first moment, when the sense consciousnesses meet with their objects, there is no concept of perceiving something. The sense organ itself, like visual perception, does not know that. That which perceives, the mental consciousness, will think, "This is a hand."

The five senses do not perceive. The all-ground is said to be that which is completely blind, deluded, and the defiled mental consciousness is that which is dualistic. The five sense consciousnesses are cognizant yet nonconceptual. The mental consciousness is subtle thought activity; the defiled consciousness is gross mental activity registering likes and dislikes. This is something we should understand.

The five sense consciousnesses are cognizant yet nonconceptual. Cognizant means that we understand, we cognize. *(Rinpoche claps his hands.)* Do you hear this? When we think whether this is nice or not, that is the defiled mental consciousness. The five senses do not have this cognition.

QUESTION: Previously you mentioned that there are two kinds of thought occurrences, conceptual and nonconceptual.

RINPOCHE: In the nonconceptual state, there cannot be any thought occurrence. Nonconceptual cannot be called thought occurrence. It should be called thought expression. Thinking and thought occurrence are the same. What I mentioned before was nonthought. Concerning nonthought, there is the nonthought of thought and the nonthought of awareness. The nonthought of thinking is delimited, whereas the nonthought of awareness is unobstructed, unlimited. In the nonthought of thinking, thoughts are unbridled, with one thought following the other. Wakefulness is the nonthought of awareness. In the nonthought of awareness, both fixation and attachment have collapsed. Cognizance, however, has not collapsed; if it does, then the state of mind is obstructed.

QUESTION: The occurrence of thoughts is obstructed. What does that mean?

RINPOCHE: Yes, because only one thought can occur at a time. When the second thought comes, the first one has finished. It doesn't stay right?

QUESTION: Yet there is still occurrence.

RINPOCHE: Yes, of course. The characteristics of consciousness are to be conscious and cognizant. It has cognizance; it does know. It can know but it cannot know the three times simultaneously. Consciousness is like a dog: it only notices what is exactly in front of it. Likewise, the cognizance of grasping mind cannot know what is in front, in the middle, and in the back—or the three times— simultaneously. It only notices what is directly in front of it, whereas, the wakefulness of rigpa can know the three times simultaneously. This is the knowledge of all the buddhas. Without rigpa possessing these qualities, Guru Rinpoche wouldn't have been said to possess "The five higher perceptions of the future, the five higher perceptions of the past, and the five higher perceptions of the present." These are mentioned in the life story of Guru Rinpoche. He wouldn't be able to possess these unless they were the qualities of awareness wisdom, (*rigpa ye shes*).

All enlightened qualities are qualities of rigpa. If rigpa couldn't know the three times simultaneously, the enlightened knowledge would not be there. The reason why it is so important to recognize rigpa is that it is not enough to recognize grasping mind, (*sems*). That would just be noticing, "Oh, now this is a statue, this is a torma, this is a mandala plate, and this is a Chenrezig statue." Just noticing the thoughts is what we mean by being conscious and cognizant, which are the characteristics of consciousness or mind. It does know, but only what is immediately present. It cannot notice the three times simultaneously.

Again, the nonthought of mind is total blankness, like being knocked out with a stick. The nonthought of awareness is free from thought occurrence. Thought-free means that there is no need to have one thought coming after the other. It is like a mirror, where many things can present themselves. Both cases are called nonthought.

Yes, as it is said, "Similar words with different meanings." The word is the same, but the meaning is different. In the case of stillness, occurrence, and noticing (*gnas 'gyu rigs gsum*), we use the word *rigpa*. Also, self-existing wakefulness is called rigpa. When we practice these two, the difference is as big as the difference between the sky and the earth. In the case of stillness, occurrence, and noticing, rigpa means that you just notice whether the mind is still or whether there is thought occurrence. Yet the word rigpa is used. On the other hand, self-existing awareness is free from being still and free from thought occurrence. It hasn't been hampered or obstructed into being nonthought. That is why it is called awareness wisdom.

QUESTION: You mention a seeming thought in the state of rigpa. How does this differ from ordinary thought?

RINPOCHE: The difference between the seeming thought and an ordinary thought is the difference between whether or not there is dualistic grasping or fixation. The expression of rigpa is a knowing that does not fixate in a dualistic way. It is like the quote from *Chöying Dzöd*, "Is vividly awake or cognizant, but without holding on to subject and object." It is the expression of the expression of rigpa that fixates in a dualistic way. But the expression of rigpa itself does not fixate. It is cognizant without fixation.

The expression of the expression of awareness is the deluded mind, which apprehends objects where no real objects exist, and apprehends an 'I' where no real 'I' exists, and so forth. However, the expression of rigpa, itself, is clear cognizance, which does not fixate in a dualistic way. There is a knowing of whatever there is but no holding on to it; it is a natural cognizance.

The expression of the essence is rigpa. It is like the circle of the sun. The expression of the expression involves grasping and fixation. From that expression comes deluded mind, the expression of the expression. The initial expression is like the rays of light from the sun, the cognizance of rigpa. The expression is this knowing quality. Then this (secondary) expression produces deluded mind. The natural cognizance of rigpa does not hold in a dualistic way. If there wasn't any knowing, it wouldn't have the name rigpa, which means knowing. It is the expression of the cognizant that gives rise to the deluded.

It is a seeming movement. There is a knowing taking place, but it is not real thought, deluded thinking. With a real movement, there is grasping and fixation. A real movement always takes place because there is an object. The other one is just a seeming movement. There is no moving of the mind toward anything that is apprehended as an object. A seeming movement is an act of cognizing without dualistic fixation.

QUESTION: Can I say in a rough way that while resting in rigpa, I can see the cup there, but I don't sit there and think that is a cup? I know it is a cup anyway without having to think or label it.

RINPOCHE: Rigpa is unobstructed. Without straying from the essence, it says, there is the visual cognition of the cup taking place. Definitely you know it is a cup, but you have not fallen into dualistic fixation.

QUESTION: Do you label it as cup; do you call it cup?

RINPOCHE: If you learned the word cup, automatically that word cup will come about. But you don't go further than that. There is no straying into the defiled mental cognition and, thereafter, the subsidiary disturbing emotions, such as, "I like it; I don't like it; where does it come from; I want to get one." It doesn't get that far. Merely the arising of the word cup doesn't harm anything at all, because there is no following up on that. There is no accumulation of karma.

The five senses are wide open, and the mind is unfocused, not pinned down. The reason is that all the sense objects in this case appear within the expanse of rigpa, just like images being reflected and appearing within a mirror. The mind does not have to pursue or reach out toward an object as being out there. It is the object that appears like an image in a mirror. If that weren't the case, as I said earlier, the buddha-knowledge would be absent. The difference between sems and rigpa is that sems strays onto the object but rigpa doesn't. Sense objects manifest in rigpa. Rigpa doesn't have to reach out for the object. That is the main difference. Once you start to say, "Oh, there it is" and "That is what it is" then it is called straying, wherein the sems strays out to the object.

This means that rigpa has no conceptualizing and discerning, whereas sems always involves first conceptualizing and then discerning. Vividly awake or clear, the five senses are not blocked and are without thought—meaning they are wide open without conceptualizing and discerning. When there is no straying into these two, conceptualizing and discerning, the root of samsara is cut. Rigpa is free from conceptualizing and discriminating. Only sems conceptualizes and discriminates. To know without conceptualizing and discriminating is what we mean by a seeming thought movement, which is not a thought; it is not thinking, because all thinking involves conceptualizing and discriminating.

DIFFERENTIATING SEMS AND RIGPA

In the present moment, we, ourselves, can know whether or not there is fixation. Any fixation, or attempt to hold something with a thought, is either past, future, or present. But if we narrow it down, past thought has finished, it's gone, and the future has not really come yet. There is only present thought. The question is, "Am I entertaining the present thought or am I letting it go?" If it is let go, there is nothing other than the essence at that moment. There is no way to miss it; there is no way to screw it up. There is only present consciousness, and when present consciousness is in the act of pursuing, aimed at something, it's not natural mind; it's ordinary mind. The attempt to correct or improve is called *fixation*. When not involved in that, and it just disengages, there is nothing other than the essence at that moment, no fixation.

In both Dzogchen and Mahamudra, what's being pointed out is the four parts without three. The four parts without three is also what's being put into practice. Four parts signifies the thought of past, present, and future. When consciousness is free from these three, there is only one left, which is timeless time, the great equality. The past and future thoughts need to be abandoned. The present thought is judging and evaluating, and that's what we call present thinking. When we just let go of that, there is nothing left other than the fourth time, timeless equality.

When doubting this, questioning if this is the real thing, your doubting is another present thought, just like anything else. Who is thinking the thought? Who is doubting? What is doubting? Recognize in a flash, then the doubt vanishes; it doesn't remain. It is possible to doubt, definitely, and you don't have to blame yourself for that. Recognize what it is that doubts, and the doubter vanishes like a knot on a snake, which naturally unravels. In one way, it is not bad to have doubt. It's better than being vacant and sitting there being absent-minded, not really noticing what is occurring and calling that the practice. When you notice that you have doubt, you are cleaning up in a detailed way, so notice the doubt. That is not really such a big problem. Just look into who feels the doubt and then it vanishes.

When you start to judge, there are different ways to misapprehend the view and different ways to go astray, thinking, "I am probably making this and that mistake. I wonder what I am doing wrong now?" All these thoughts are merely thoughts. You can call them doubt, but they are only thoughts. When you examine who is thinking this doubt—in a flash, naturally—and let go of doubt, and it vanishes like any other thought.

Doubting thoughts naturally vanish at that moment, just as when the sun shines, the darkness cannot remain. In the presence of the light turning on, no darkness stays behind. You can put a hair in a flame but it will not remain. In the same way, in the moment of recognizing the thinker—no matter whether you're doubting or thinking anything else—that thought cannot remain.

Thoughts can take many shapes; for example, you could say, "The lama taught very nicely and correctly, but I am not so sure I really understand or, even if I did understand, if I can really apply it. Or when I apply it, I'm not sure whether I am doing that right." These are different forms of thoughts. In the moment of recognizing the thinker, the concept or thought does not remain; nothing is left except rigpa.

One of the most important words in the Dzogchen teachings means both direct and immediate; the moment of remembering and recognizing is simultaneous. For example, when I tap the tabletop, you immediately hear the sound it makes, cognize the sound. There is no hesitation. You hear the sound right away. In the same way, the recognizing—the intention to recognize and the act of recognizing—is immediate, right away, direct. There is no chance for any doubt; there is no time to doubt. Instead of investigating, "Should I or should I not feel doubt?", completely ignore that question and go directly to looking into who thinks this, immediately.

It is said that 'the great flashing gaze' means that the moment of recognizing is immediate and abrupt, just like a flash of lightening. The great flashing gaze liberates both buddhas and sentient beings. Buddhas means good thoughts; sentient beings means bad thoughts. Both good and bad thoughts are destroyed, because it's like a flash of lightening that suddenly appears within the sky; it's instantaneous, immediate. Trekchö is a direct cut, not a sloppy, slow one. At that moment, there is no time to start speculating about whether it's this or that, whether it's recognizing or not recognizing—meaning whether it's a good thought or a bad thought. Both are totally cleared away.

In one of his Dzogchen teachings, the fifth Dalai Lama said that recognizing rigpa requires the oral instructions of the vidyadharas. He said that recognizing rigpa should be as immediate as raising your gaze momentarily. It shouldn't be slow, where you get to it in a roundabout way. It should be right then. If you look down in the direction of your nose, that is shamatha. If you raise your gaze, at that moment, there is nothing but rigpa. Let go in naturalness and look up: at that very instant, there is nothing but naked rigpa. That's an important key point. To recognize mind essence, the quicker and sooner, the better.

The first and the second moments are clean, genuine; afterward, we start to think different things. For sure we have all different kinds of thoughts. We have not broken out of the hive of conceptual thinking. We are still encased in the physical body, and the circulation of the different things in the body creates all different kinds of thoughts. We are not totally free from that. We are not beyond feeling doubt. However, whether we feel doubt or not, the important thing is to apply the gaze of the great flash of lightning at that moment. It immediately cuts through.

It's best to be an easygoing imbecile. That is how you should be, an easygoing idiot. Recognize once and don't worry too much about it. Merely carry on and don't speculate a lot, like an unintelligent person, who doesn't question too much about things and also is easygoing, kind of relaxed, not upset about this and that. That's much better than being too clever, too smart, and too critical about fine details, because then you get carried away and start to think things. So what? Just recognize; it's a new opportunity to look at mind essence and carry on from that point. It's not that you have to have a sense of loss and say, "Oh I used to have the view but now it's gone." This is not really the correct view. "If I could just change this in some way." All of these thoughts are judging the experience to see whether it's correct and they're trying to improve it. That attempt, itself, is the obstacle.

During the moment of rigpa, thought cannot arise, even if you try to think in the moment of rigpa. The thought has no real power, no real potency. It is said that when you are really in the continuity of rigpa, even the attempt to make a thought is unsuccessful. Once the continuity of rigpa fades, for sure you can start thinking.

The main difference between sems and rigpa is that during rigpa, thought cannot take root. Even if you try to think, there is not real substantial thought. It's like pouring mercury onto dust; it doesn't mix. But the state of sems, normal thinking, is like pouring water on dust; it completely becomes mingled immediately. Rigpa does not fixate on objects or fall under the power of thoughts, whereas sems does.

Try and remain in rigpa and make a thought. It should be stable rigpa, the naturally stable rigpa. That's the difference between sems and rigpa. In the state of rigpa now, try and think, "I want to go to the kitchen and eat. I need to do such and such." The moment rigpa is lost, you get caught up in that thought, and it's like pouring the water on soil. Check yourself to see whether it gets lost or not.

Rigpa is unobstructed, unimpeded, so you notice and feel everything. It is knowing without holding. Try right now: "I will drink some tea. I will go over there." You can act without being distracted. Sems is not like that; it has no inherent stability. It immediately gets caught up. The state of sems immediately gets caught in thought. The state of rigpa does not lose the continuity; it remains undistracted.

Let awareness break out from the subconscious gossip. Invigorate or elevate rigpa out of that undercurrent of thought. On the other hand, it says, "Don't care about anything. Be completely carefree. Don't judge, don't evaluate. Be like a small child. If you are happy, you laugh; if you are sad, you cry." Too much judging, too much evaluating, "Is it right? Is it not?," will make it murky.

Recognize a little bit once in a while and forget in between; that's how it is. It's not that you recognize rigpa and it stays like that continuously; that doesn't happen. Within the state of rigpa, appearances can take place. Different things arise because rigpa is unimpeded. It is not stuck in a frozen state. Otherwise, it would be impossible to have the unity of development stage and completion stage. If, as soon as completion stage begins, you get stuck in that, development stage would be impossible, so how could there be any unity? It is said that the perfect practice is the unity of development and completion stages— all the deities can be manifested while never leaving the state of the essence, rigpa.

That is not the same as normal thinking. Normal thinking is either gross or subtle. Subtle thought is called subconscious gossip or undercurrent of thought, which is analogous to a small flow of water going underneath a heap of straw. The straw cannot stop the water, but the water doesn't make all the straw wet; it is still dry on top. In the same way, you can sit and imagine that you are undistracted, but you still have some background commentary going on, or you are criticizing, thinking, "This is not really right. Maybe this should be so and so." That is subtle thinking. At that point, it helps to pull rigpa out in the open—where you relax inwardly but concentrate a little outwardly. Also, it helps sometimes to shout PHAT.

It's also important to be totally free from any attempt to meditate—even a hair-tip of trying to meditate. When you shout PHAT, there should also be no watcher. Nothing to meditate, not even an atom of something to cultivate. When you shout PHAT, there's not even a hair-tip of an observer or something to be seen. However, at the same time, at that very moment, there's not even an instant of distraction or forgetting. It says, "Keep mindful in the state of undistracted nonmeditation." What kind of mindfulness is this? It is unfabricated mindfulness, which is none other than rigpa. There is no act of cultivating or meditating, and there is no forgetting it. There is no deliberate, artificial mindfulness either.

The moment there is no distraction or attempt to cultivate, how can there be any doubt? While attempting to meditate or cultivate something, you can have the choice of thinking, "I am successful or not successful in trying to do this." Since there is nothing, not even an atom of something, to be cultivated, how can there be any doubt about that? Furthermore, there's not even a flicker of forgetting it: Undistracted with unfabricated mindfulness. No cultivation with unfabricated mindfulness. Try that right now. How can there be any doubt? Nothing to make; nothing to forget. Natural mindfulness or unfabricated mindfulness simply means 'not forgetting.' The moment you forget, of course, you have no mindfulness, no presence of mind.

Don't expect or believe that rigpa is something special or something amazing; it's not. But sems and rigpa don't coexist. When one is present, the other subsides. When rigpa is forgotten and thinking occurs, then rigpa subsides. It's just like darkness and light, which are not together at the same time. In undistracted rigpa, sems is latent. The thoughts of sems lead us into distraction, whereas rigpa knows sems but does not get carried away by it. The difference between them is that in the state of rigpa, the different expressions of thought take place, but rigpa doesn't get caught up in them. It does not get caught up in the power of that thinking, whereas sems does, and that is the difference.

Losing rigpa is called sems taking control, sems taking over. But in the state of rigpa, nothing is blocked off: sights are seen, sounds are heard; anything takes place. It is said that the essence of rigpa is like space or sky and that thoughts are like clouds. Have you ever heard that the sky is controlled by the clouds? It is said that the essence is like the sun itself. It is primordially uncompounded, naturally cognizant.

Just practice what I taught here and slowly, slowly it will get more and more simple to recognize and easier to maintain. That does not happen from one day to the next or in one or two weeks or months. Don't keep drilling it; leave it wide open. An example I often use is this: When traveling to Bodhgaya from here, you'll find that it's not a straight, easy road the whole way. There are ups and downs. Sometimes it's really smooth but sometimes it's really hard. That's how it is when we have a physical body, with the aggregates, elements, sense factors, and so forth. They make all different kinds of situations, and that affects our state of mind. Nonetheless, you will arrive if you continue on the journey and do not stop off on the way. Buddha-nature is present all the time. However, you need to recognize it. It's like the sun itself in the sky. It is naturally radiant, naturally clear, and primordially uncompounded, like the sky. Within this, maintain the continuity. Remain undistracted, looking again and again.

Most importantly, don't hammer the point. Don't get too caught up in this; be carefree. If you keep hitting a sensitive area, it makes it difficult. The state of rigpa is free and easy, and you should not try to confine it and make it more uptight. Be free and easy, carefree. Rigpa is like a good friend you already know. It's not someone you are going to lose. In the first and second moments, there is a recognition of rigpa, and then it's forgotten. As long as you are not stable in rigpa, this will happen.

When we are not trying to tamper with or improve the present consciousness, we are in a state of rigpa, itself. What muddies it up is when we try to improve it, to alter it. The present mind is empty and cognizant. Any attempt to improve or make it something else is called sems. The moment we let go, that's rigpa. Rigpa and sems are not two different things that are like two hands touching. They are the essence and its expression, the sun and the sunlight. That is their relationship.

Your present mind, present consciousness, is the unity of being empty and cognizant. If it is consciousness, of course it is cognizant. This is easy to understand. Space is empty but not cognizant. When we look at the essence, we can of course say it's like space—it's primordially uncompounded but also cognizant.

Something like space, which is only empty, is not cognizant. We, on the other hand, are empty and at the same time cognizant. There is no question about that. That is primordially so, primordially empty, but with no basis. There is no source where it comes from. And this baseless empty state is also able to know; it's conscious by nature. That's the definition of yeshe. 'Ye' means primordially present and 'shes' means conscious of cognizing objects. But when this original consciousness is fettered by fixation, it's called ordinary consciousness, *(rnam shes)*. Very simply, it's like this: when this present mind is not involved in improving or trying to correct anything, through hope or fear, then it is rigpa by itself. It is original consciousness, unspoiled by fixation, which means trying to improve or alter. Leave your present mind without trying to make anything. One statement says, "Your present mind free from fabrication is the real Samantabhadra, which has never been apart from you. In the state of recognizing, rest naturally." Without recognizing, it's not going to help. The recognizing, or the knowing of this, is called rigpa. Just let be in the state that is empty and cognizant with a core of awareness. No need to hope or fear anything or accept or reject; that itself is sufficient.

QUESTION: I know that the physical body is indispensable, but sometimes it creates an obstacle to practice. How should we approach that?

RINPOCHE: We must understand that the body is just a guesthouse, a temporary dwelling. Some dwelling places are good, some bad—there are various kinds. When we travel a long distance, the different places we stay in cannot all be good. Since mind is the most important—if the mind is independent and can function by itself—why should the dwelling place matter? Don't worry about it. The body is just a guesthouse offering various pleasures and pains. You should not be governed by them.

During practice, this physical body is both a help and a hindrance. Without a body, we would be a bardo consciousness, lacking independent power or force. Through the blessing of having a body, we do have some power. This body is actually an immense advantage, and yet it brings hindrances.

As I just mentioned, if we travel to Bodhgaya, unless we fly, we pass through mountains and valleys, ups and downs, rivers and gorges. There are comfortable places, steep places, all different kinds of places. Likewise, our body, made of aggregates and elements, has within it the self-existing wisdom, which is tied down by it. Due to the function of the five elements, the channels, and winds, we sometimes feel at ease and sometimes disturbed. Sometimes, even without an external cause, the mind can become irritated. We can suffer, even without any external, painful object. Although the enlightened essence itself experiences no suffering or pain, as we are tied down to the momentary habitual patterns and elements, our experience within the body varies. But as long as we persevere, regardless of ups and downs, hills and valleys, if we don't stop anywhere, sooner or later we will arrive at our destination, Bodhgaya.

We should focus our minds on simplicity, the state of buddhahood, nonconceptual wakefulness. Aim your mind at that. Although you will not arrive immediately, if you aim toward it, as if intending to go to Bodhgaya, then, no matter what happens on the way, if you never give up you will arrive. Since harm occurs in the mind, whatever disturbances arise in this body from aggregates, elements, and sense factors, just let them go again and again into unfabricated naturalness. Then you will reach your destination.

Attach no importance to, and don't be concerned about, whatever happens, whatever you experience. Really, this body is a great advantage. Without it, you could not look into mind essence. In the hells, among the hungry ghosts, or in the animal realm no one ever recognizes mind essence. That is how it is.

As long as we have a body of aggregates, elements, and sense factors, various experiences can occur. But your aim should be self-existing wakefulness. 'Aim' literally means the way you point your nose, your home place. Turn your nose toward home, toward what is ahead of you, in front, and not behind. (*Rinpoche laughs.*) For example, whenever I go abroad, my home place is Nagi Gompa. Your home place should be what is self-existing—free from concepts—primordial wakefulness, yeshe. Yeshe means wakefulness, which is primordially free from distraction.

When distracted, you have no wakefulness. The undistracted aspect is wakefulness—unconfused and unmistaken. If you're confused, the wakefulness is gone.

QUESTION: When shouting PHAT, it seems like we are prepared for it, sometimes. Then it is not really abrupt.

RINPOCHE: Such a PHAT will not be able to cut thoughts.

QUESTION: Then how should we shout?

RINPOCHE: It should be shouted in the very moment of thinking it, that very moment. Well, actually we are not to blame. If we have caught the smell of it, then it is difficult not to be prepared. Now you should try in the very moment of feeling prepared; you should shout PHAT. It should be simultaneous; it will be beneficial if you try to shout very fast. If you just think and afterward shout, it will be, as they say in Kham, that one has caught the smell of it. That will not be able to disperse thoughts. Shouting PHAT is to scatter a thought, to disperse the thought, revealing non-conceptual wisdom.

The thought is impossible to throw away because it is inherent or co-emergent. It does not remain if pressed down. You cannot do anything. You can maybe suppress coarse thoughts, but the subtle ones are impossible, as shown by the previous example I gave of water flowing under dry straw. The straw underneath will be wet and water can flow. Subtle, fine kinds of thoughts can obscure the essence, even without being noticed. That's how they can move. PHAT can cut through both coarse and subtle thinking. PHAT is the syllable of prajna and upaya. The method for using it is to shout it abruptly, suddenly.

It is not only the shout of PHAT when being introduced to awareness. The student can sometimes sit with his back to the master. Suddenly, the teacher shouts and the student becomes really 'moon struck.' In that moment, he should recognize. Otherwise, one will fall oblivious, which would be useless. One should be clearly wakeful, without falling unconscious.

Malaysia 1981

THE WATCHER AND THE WATCHED

When it seems like there is a watcher, look into this watcher and it will disappear. Maybe this watcher is just a concept. On the other hand, maybe you have to say that there actually is one when you are a beginner. You can say that there is a kind of watcher, because you haven't really become acquainted with the nonduality of watcher and watched. It is said in both Mahamudra and Dzogchen teachings that it should be like space, free from both watcher and watched. But as long as the watcher and the watched have not become mingled, sometimes it feels like there is a watcher and something being watched. It is like that, and why not—unless you are like Garab Dorje, who immediately mingled watcher and watched and was beyond distraction, and who was a sentient being when he sat down and a buddha when he stood up again. Other than him, everybody else takes years to get to the same stage, where there is no watcher and watched. All the Kagyü lamas take this long.

You should check yourself to see whether there is a watcher and something being watched, whether there is duality or not. If you were to ask, "What is the thing that is watched?" or "What is the watched?" it is this thought: "The master said there is something called the *unity of cognizance and emptiness.* That's how the mind is. There must be such a thing!" To think in this way, you mentally form something to watch, which is the cognizant emptiness. The mind is the watcher, thinking, "I must look at this cognizant emptiness." You think, "Oh, there is this cognizant emptiness. I'm seeing it" or "I'm not seeing it." That is the duality of watcher and watched.

In this case, concerning the watcher, you do not have to consider that watchfulness is over there. Mindfulness should occur by itself. This is due to the kindness of having practiced. When it occurs, it remains freely. This resting freely is extremely important. In Dzogchen terminology, 'resting freely' is defined as 'resting freely without meditating outwardly.' Due to the power of having become acquainted with the free resting of not meditating on something actual being there, you will rest awake in awareness. At that point, watcher and watched are mingled. Until then you need to apply watchfulness. It is like a herdsman looking after the cattle, questioning, "Are the animals doing well; are they eating grass; are they drinking water?" The watchman has to look after that. As it is said, "As long as you look outwardly, like a herdsman watching cattle, the view will be theoretical." When the theoretical view has collapsed, you say, "I have arrived at experience." This refers to the absence of watcher and watched. There is no need for duality of watcher and watched, because mind rests freely, awake; it has arrived in awareness. There is no need to produce thoughts such as "It is right; it is not right." This comes slowly and gradually by being diligent.

For sentient beings, even though the essence is primordially pure, like the perfectly clear sky, and has been within us since the beginning, we do not recognize it. Instead we have fallen under the power of discursive thinking. We have been in samsara for an unfathomable amount of time—vast stretches of time, and the tendencies associated with that are strong and recurring. Based on the fact that we have failed to acknowledge mind's essence, the expression of buddha-nature takes coarse, subtle, and extremely subtle levels of experience, almost all the time. It is like the sun shining in the sky. When the light hits the surface of water, moisture gathers in the sky, forming clouds, and we cannot see the sky. That expression obscures it. It is exactly the same case with our buddha-nature. We have wandered in samsara due to discursive thoughts. Since we have not recognized the expression of the essence, different levels of manifestation occur. On the coarse levels, there are three poisons, but on a more subtle level, there are meditation experiences or the meditation states, which are blissful, clear, or thought free.

There is something even more subtle than that, which is called the cognitive obscuration. Even though the sky is stainless, it is obscured by the watcher and what is watched. When free of the watcher and what is watched, the cognitive obscuration vanishes. The watcher and the watched are subject and object. Another name for the cognitive obscuration is indecisiveness, indecision. It is not a gross fixation but a very subtle fixation, which is exactly the cognitive obscuration.

On the sutra path, the cognitive obscuration is only purified at the end of the tenth bhumi, through the vajra-like samadhi, the very grand empowerment of the rays of light. According to Vajrayana, it is purified by means of the four joys. The four precepts provoke the four increasingly deeper levels of emptiness.

When we are practicing, in the first two instants we are free of the watcher and watched. As time goes on, it slowly degenerates. That is why in Trekchö we shout PHAT. In the four empowerments, this is what is called the precious word empowerment. Word means "PHATA, PHAT"! Simultaneously with the shouting, the subtle experience dissolves. We have the vase empowerment, the secret empowerment, the wisdom knowledge empowerment, and the precious word empowerment. Each one is more subtle than the preceding one. The ultimate path is the precious word empowerment. The primordial, perfect emptiness is decided upon as being empty; there is no need for doubt. It is cognizant emptiness, free from falling into any fixating.

Dzogchen has the tradition of shouting PHAT, which disperses the watcher and what is watched. Thinking of and shouting PHAT should be simultaneous. If you first think slowly, "Okay, here it comes; let's see what happens," that kind of PHAT is not effective.

Of course, all of the different vehicles teach on emptiness. All of them talk about emptiness, but the vase empowerment doesn't really purify the subtle cognitive obscuration. Neither does the secret empowerment, which purifies the nadi, prana, and bindu. It is only right at the borderline between the third, the wisdom knowledge empowerment, and the fourth empowerment that we actually deal with the cognitive obscuration. The first empowerment is appearance and emptiness, the second is clarity and emptiness, the third is bliss and emptiness, and the fourth is awareness and emptiness. The emptiness becomes subtler, until ultimately the viewer and the viewed fall apart.

Empty cognizance, for some, is the idea of what has to be kept in mind, what has to be realized and practiced, as I mentioned earlier. The guru said, "Mind essence is not only empty, it is also cognizant. I need to realize that, and that is the whole point here." That subtle notion does not destroy the watcher and watched. When shouting PHAT, instantaneously, the ultimate is only svabhavikakaya. What has obscured dissolves into the expanse of space. It is beyond fabricating mind, thoughts, the conventional. The view is beyond that which is thought of by mind. The mind is the one watching. When there is no mind, and the watched and the watcher mingle, then what is there to sidetrack or obscure us?

Basically, totally give up this whole thing of watching mind essence as some thing that is empty cognizance, with you as the practitioner who is doing it. You should simply and totally cast this to the wind, so to speak. As long as there is some exercise in holding subject and object, there is no real transcendence of dualistic mind, the true state of rigpa. The watching is like putting a hook in a piece of meat and holding on to it, so that no bird can fly off with it. Without these two, the watched and the watcher, as it is said, "If duality does not become oneness, there is no enlightenment." The ultimate path of buddhahood is beyond any duality, dualistic grasping. The duality is that subtle holding on to watcher and watched. This is not nonduality.

Attain stability in freely resting. Once you have established the natural state, the watcher and the watched are mingled into one. You are completely free, easy, and open. But subtle doubt can happen. Sometimes you are free of the watcher and the watched; sometimes it seems totally easy. There is no problem whatsoever recognizing mind essence; it's totally effortless. But sometimes it seems incredibly difficult, when it is agitated or drowsy. Sometimes it seems like there is some kind of murkiness, as you say, a subtle haze. It is not totally clear. This occurs because you have not established the natural state yet.

First of all, you need to be free of the three poisons. Based on that, you need to be free of the experiences of bliss, clarity, and nonthought. Based on that, you need to be free of the watcher and the watched, the very subtle obscuration. The fruition of being free of these is self-arisen rigpa. Thus, it is said.

When you become accustomed to the natural state, then whatever arises does not harm. There are no difficulties. Until that happens, there will be pleasant and unpleasant experiences. The example I often use is going to Bodhgaya. On the way, there are mountains and plains, all kinds of roads and landscapes. If we approach this journey by simply letting whatever arises appear, without getting sidetracked, applying only rigpa, ultimately the cognitive obscuration will be cleared. It is like that.

We definitely have not become established in the natural state, where the recognition occurs uninterruptedly for one or two hours straight. When the recognition only lasts for a few minutes at most, that is not called establishing the natural state. What lasts is shamatha practice, which is mind. One merely thinks that one is undistracted, and this type of meditation can last for one or two hours.

You need to understand no watcher and nothing watched. This is the essence, free of any concrete thing, which means no watcher or watched. If there is a thing, it is the watcher and the watched. The true natural state is free of any concrete thing. It is free of any intellectual positioning. The other views of Mahamudra and Madhyamika have intellectual positioning. The view is intellectually understood. Intellectual positioning holds on to sounds and words; it is fixating.

The essence is empty, the nature is cognizant, and the capacity is unobstructed. It is like this example: the nature of fire is hot, the nature of water is wet, and the empty is naturally cognizant. The essence of our mind is not something that you can pinpoint at all. It is not made of anything whatsoever. You have heard so many times that the mind is empty, and yet it is not empty like space. It is neither something that is only empty nor something that is only cognizant. There is no blockage or limitation between the two: this is the definition of capacity, tukje, *(thugs rje),* which is the undefined basis for experience. It is not confined to being either a blank emptiness or some conscious entity. The mind is the three kayas of the buddhas.

Please understand, if it were merely empty, like the sky, nothing would be known. Without the cognizance, it would be limited to only being empty. It is the same with being only defined as cognizant; then emptiness would be blocked. It is appearing while being empty, empty while appearing, and in between, nothing is obstructed. Take this example of one thought of anger. If you look into the one who is angry, you recognize the empty essence of anger. Seeing the empty essence, the angry thought falls apart. These two are unified, the empty and cognizant aspects, because if you look into the anger, you see the essence as naturally cognizant. Everything is vividly taking place at the same time; all perceptions and appearances are unblocked. This is the unity of appearances and emptiness, primordially. The knower of the emptiness and the knower of the appearances are in unity. That is the reason why it is possible to think and to have emotions and experiences, because of this unconfined basis for experience, which is the capacity.

These two cannot be separated. They are appearing while being empty, empty while appearing. The empty essence is like space, rootless and baseless. Because of this, everything can be known. When you perceive something, you look into who perceives, and you don't find anything, not even a hair-tip of a thing. There is no thing whatsoever—not even as much as an atom—that experiences.

The great learned ones, the panditas, say in the commentaries: first, you need to know emptiness, truly know the rootless and baselessness aspect. Then you need to know cognizance, which is the knowing quality. The clairvoyances of the Buddha—the five past, the five present, and the five future clairvoyances, totaling fifteen—came from the cognizant aspect. This is also in Guru Rinpoche's life story. This is the knowing side, which is not merely empty, void. Without this, the superknowledges, the mastery of ultimate wisdom, infinite activity, and boundless love and compassion, would not be realized.

The movement of mind is perceiving and empty, empty and perceiving—inseparable. In the moment of knowing the perceiver, the tendency to hold perceiver and perceived simply falls away. Since you see that there is no perceiver in that moment, the empty and cognizant qualities are not two separate entities. You have dismantled the subtle fixation on duality—there's nothing watched and no watcher.

If you do not understand, then it becomes some idea of Dzogchen held in your mind, that this is the view, as the guru is pointing out: "It is empty, empty cognizance; it is rigpa; now there it is; now I got it." Then you put your fork into your steak and hold onto it. That is identifying something or defining the view. But in reality, the view is indefinable, totally inapprehensible. As long as there is something being identified as the view and held in mind, subtle duality is definitely present. However, in the moment of recognizing the empty cognizance as it is, there is no need to form a very subtle concept about the inapprehensible view.

All the extensive teachings are primarily to establish the view. Once the view has been established, it is the authentic, empty cognizance seen. Once this authenticity is seen, delusion is freed. The authentic is free of the watcher and the watched. In Dzogchen, there are the fourfold freely restings, *(cog bzhag bzhi)*.[13] Also, do not meditate outwardly, do not fixate inwardly, and do not place at all; remain completely wide open. These are really precious.

In short, this indivisible empty cognizance has the knowing quality, which is the self-existent wisdom or wakefulness, rangjung yeshe, *(rang byung ye shes)*. That is most important. The essence is empty from the beginning. It is dharmakaya, not altered in any way whatsoever. The essence is primordially empty, free of root, and cognizant, which means that everything can be known. This cognizance is the sambhogakaya. Indivisible self-arisen wakefulness is the unity of the two, emptiness and cognizance. The empty essence and cognizant nature, the knowing aspect, indivisible, is the unconfined capacity. This quality of knowing its own nature is the source or the wellspring of all enlightened qualities. This knowing has the qualities of buddhahood, the compassion for all beings, just as a mother has for her only child. It has the wisdom of knowing whatever exists in the nature of all this, the capability to act for the welfare of others, and infinite activity—the pacifying, increasing, magnetizing, and subjugating activities. All these countless vajra enlightened qualities are inconceivable. Rigpa is like a jewel.

Once you have established the natural state, you do not fall under the power of mind. When that is not the case, the expression of buddha-nature takes form in subtle and coarse ways. Subtle is the experiences of bliss, clarity, non-thought. Coarser is the three poisons. When you are habituated to one of these three poisons, then desire creates the desire realm, anger creates the form realm, and stupidity creates the formless realms.

Knowing the naked rigpa is, from the beginning, free of attachment, anger, and stupidity. The fruition of recognizing rigpa is that the three poisons have no strength. In the very moment of seeing, of recognizing your nature, which is the moment of rigpa, sems totally loses all power. It is totally lost at that point. It is not even there, because you have either one or the other: Where there is sems, there is no rigpa. When there is rigpa, there is no sems. One is latent when the other is manifest, just as when the sun rises, the darkness is latent. When the sun sets, then the darkness is right there. It is like that. Once you become stable in rigpa, sems does not have a chance. The three kayas of buddhahood are within us, but we are obscured by temporary experiences. Then it becomes coarser, and we are obscured by the three poisons. When the light of the sun and moon shines, there is no darkness in the world.

You need to recognize rigpa. It doesn't help just to practice meditation, where the subtle duality is kept up, as in the state of shamatha. Shamatha is based on accepting and rejecting. You are so happy that your mind is still for a while, and then you are so unhappy when it's not, when it moves around with thoughts. You accept one and you reject the other. This emphasis on accepting and rejecting is definitely not the cause of true liberation. The training in rigpa, on the other hand, is a step beyond accepting and rejecting. The accepting and rejecting tendency is of course dualistic mind.

It all boils down to just one sentence: unfabricated naturalness; present, fresh wakefulness. Leave the knowing aspect unaltered; with no knowing, you are a corpse. An example for natural is the wood on the mountainside. It is not cut yet but once the tree is cut and brought down, it is crafted, shaped into something. That is not the case with the uncut tree on the hillside; there it is unmade, natural. There is the expanse of unfabricated naturalness, not doing anything, naturally remaining in this present, fresh wakefulness—unaltered, unfabricated naturalness. This is our very essence within us. Fabricated mind falls under the power of the three times. Unfabricated naturalness—that is it!

QUESTION: In the moment of recognizing a thought it dissolves automatically, and at that point there is a blissful feeling. Is that only in the beginning or is it always like that?

RINPOCHE: In the moment the thought vanishes, there is nonconceptual wisdom. You should not get attached or fascinated by this blissfulness. This is basically what is meant by the inseparability of bliss and emptiness in the Mahamudra system. It is not the bliss of the male and female together. When the thought has vanished and the nonconceptual wisdom can stand alone, there is not even the word for suffering—that is the bliss. But if one experiences this bliss and gets fascinated by it, then it becomes the bliss in the three experiences called bliss, clarity, and nonthought. If it is not grasped, it is just as it is. The bliss in the emptiness is endowed with all aspects, the supreme unchanging bliss—this is what is meant when we say bliss and emptiness inseparable, (bde stong dbyer med).

There is the nature of bliss inherently, but you should not hold onto it. In fact, the three experiences of bliss, clarity, and nonthought are the adornments of the three kayas; they are like ornaments. When you do not grasp these experiences, they become the ornaments of the three kayas. When you fixate on bliss, clarity, and nonthought, you will stray into the three realms of samsara. The three experiences of grasping mind—bliss, clarity, and nonthought—are called the *khams*, the dispositions of grasping mind. This is similar to when we say people have earth disposition or water disposition and so forth. When you do not grasp these three, they have the qualities of the three kayas, and when you do grasp them, they become, as a result, the three realms of samsara. That's how it is.

But as you said, in the very moment of a thought vanishing—there is a saying, "Within thought I discovered nonthought." When there is changelessness, that is the bliss. When there is not even the word suffering, we should call that bliss. This is what is meant. It is not the physical bliss of a man and a woman making love, which is experienced by the body and wherein there is something experienced. What is mentioned here is bliss free from something experienced, because as long as there is experiencing, there is fixation. Here there is bliss but it's free from experience. Do you understand this, without experience?

QUESTION: Without a thing to be experienced.

RINPOCHE: Yes, without something to be experienced, because as long as there is experiencing, there is the defiling, *(zag bcas)* or conditioned quality.

QUALITIES OF RIGPA

To invigorate, *(hur phyung)*, rigpa is to remain one-pointedly, in a specific way. A cloud-free sky that is perfectly pure benefits the inner space, rigpa. In this one-pointedness of rigpa, you do not fall under the power of delusion or distraction. Rigpa itself is energized; it is an experience wherein, inwardly, rigpa is stable. It is not vulnerable to being carried away by distraction or fixation. It is self-contained and stable. It is like the facial expression of a wrathful heruka. You breathe out slightly, exhaling. That is the example for invigorating, like a stainless sky. These three—eyes, prana, and rigpa—are altogether one-pointedly aware. The yoga mingles inseparably with the pure sky, free of any obscuring conditions, not prey to grasping or fixating from deep within. That is what invigorating means. Mind and space are inseparably mingled, a perfectly cloudless sky.

Mind and space mix completely, without the slightest bit of grasping; the perfectly pure sky is free of any obscuring conditions. It is important to have a pure sky. That also refers to the season of late summer, early fall, not really summer or winter but more the fall. In reference to the four seasons, in the fall, the sky is crystal clear. After the summer, when it has rained, the dust has been cleared away. The sky in fall is very clear, perfect for practice.

The qualities of rigpa include being very awake and bright. These are words that describe rigpa; self-aware rigpa is beyond mind, how amazing. No workings of mind are needed. Rigpa is self-existing; mind is the working of concepts that completely mix with mind. Rigpa is free of mind. It is without any stains; stupidity is a stain, and stains are a great defect. Rigpa is totally free of any elaborations. It is completely awake without any obscurities, naked beyond elaborations. It is beyond any type of blank vacantness, which means not falling into oblivion. It is a great fault to fall into oblivion when practicing. These are words that describe rigpa but the meaning in short is "empty, awake, vividly clear, bright, and steady."

To know the ultimate meaning of rigpa is to practice without giving rise to any grasping and fixation. Mind only functions with grasping and

fixation. Rigpa is not tainted by outer grasping or inner fixating. Knowing rigpa is to be uninfluenced by grasping and fixation. You know this
by yourself. The outer fixating mind follows after appearances and holds
them. The inner grasping mind, for example, has no openness. Openness
is without fixating. If there is fixating, there is no openness. The openness
of rigpa does not, in an outer or inner way, hold onto anything. Mind is the
opposite: both outwardly and inwardly, it holds onto subject and object.
Rigpa is totally without any grasping and fixating. Look for yourself.

For example, let's say that while you remain in rigpa, an outer object
presents itself. Unlike mind, rigpa does not fixate on it. The object
appears in the field of rigpa, but when in rigpa, you do not follow after
it. This is a way to tell if you are in rigpa or not. You can know, why
not? Not following after the outer objects, like the five objects of the
sense consciousnesses, is remaining in rigpa. The classic example is mercury, which does not mix with anything. Of course, the reverse is water
on ashes; they mix immediately and cannot be separated. Water totally
mixes with the ashes, whereas mercury is completely self-contained. Similarly, rigpa does not fall under the power of grasping and fixating.

When remaining in rigpa, you will not encounter any work that
taints it. When staying like that, all jobs are unimpeded. No work can
cover rigpa. If that were not the case, then you could not truly practice
deity, mantra, and samadhi, which unfold from rigpa. This all happens
when resting in samadhi.

There is no increase or decrease of the essence of rigpa, once you
are stable in it. All the different activities of pacifying, increasing, magnetizing, and subjugating can be carried out without flaw. Without the
completion stage, there really is no development stage. The perfect development stage arises from the completion stage. When in rigpa, you can
engage as long as you do not lose the continuity. A lot can be projected,
such as the four intents of recitation, which are forms of rigpa.

Those are the qualities of rigpa, being completely unblemished. While
remaining in rigpa, not moving away from it, you can carry out activities
that do not harm rigpa. Working from mind, you have no recognition
of the essence. The essence does not grasp yesterday or today. When you
work from within mind, there are imperfections. This is a way to know
the difference between the two. Checking like this, you can know if you
are in rigpa or not.

From the expression of rigpa, many things take place when your rigpa is stable. Once you have stability, the expression of rigpa—like deity, mantra, and other—can happen. Self-knowing, self-cognizance, is the natural quality of rigpa, like fire being hot and water being wet. Rigpa is naturally self-luminous and clear, *(rang lhang nge)*. Within the essence, all the activities can be accomplished. This is the real strength of development and completion: the power of the deity gets stronger. Without being in the essence, there really is not deity or samadhi.

Lines from *Chöying Dzöd* describe this as well:

> Awakened mind can be compared to the sun.
> It is utterly lucid by nature and forever uncompounded.
> With nothing to obscure it, it is unobstructed and spontaneously
> present.
> Without elaboration, it is the scope of the true nature of
> phenomena, which does not entail concepts.

Within the essence, there is no thought. The expression of awareness has a knowing quality that is unobstructed. If rigpa were unable to work, then it would be obstructed. When we look at rigpa, there is an extraordinary preciousness.

The workings of mind do not recognize its essence. The continuity of rigpa has been thrown away. Mind just grinds on. The yogi who has been introduced to rigpa has gotten the smell of it. With this smell, when the yogi recognizes the essence and remains in it undistractedly, then various things can occur. This is not mind. It is the seeming movement that is not movement. If there is no movement, you have not lost the essence; it has not been thrown away. Once you have thrown away the essence, grasping and fixation appear. If you remain in the essence, these cannot carry you away.

Sustaining the continuity means to remain undistracted. Losing the continuity is being distracted from the state of empty cognizance; the continuity slips. To sustain the continuity means simply to remain undistracted, not that you have to sustain the continuity really, because there is no subject to be sustained and there is no object being sustained either. There is no continuity to sustain other than simply remaining undistracted and not losing the continuity. It is beyond sustainer and sustained. That is very important.

QUESTION: Although it is said that in the recognition of awareness, compassion will arise spontaneously, it does not seem to happen. Why is this?

RINPOCHE: It is said in the guide texts of the Great Perfection: in the beginning one has to slightly fabricate the compassion.

QUESTION: How does one fabricate this?

RINPOCHE: "Oh, this very precious and profound self-existing wakefulness, everybody possesses this, but they do not realize it—poor sentient beings." You have to give rise to or slightly fabricate this kind of thought in the beginning. Then, later as you get more and more trained or accustomed to it, you do not need to cultivate it any further; it will arise spontaneously. Compassion does arise spontaneously when resting in awareness. It is said that the expression arises as compassion. Although it is said that compassion should be inartificial, unfabricated, it is necessary to fabricate slightly in the beginning.

There is a saying about this in Kham: "To retain a secret, one should keep one's own mouth shut." Instead of telling other people, "Don't pass this along," it is better to close your own mouth; then the secret will not slip out. If you only tell other people not to tell, it will spread. Although it is said that you need the unfabricated compassion, you should first begin by thinking (generate compassion). As you get more and more stable in awareness, you will know its qualities, right? In awareness, all conflicting emotions are cleared away. You should think, "All sentient beings have this; it is not only me. All sentient beings, as many as the sky is vast, possess this. They have it but they don't know it. Oh, how sad." You should consider like this and by doing so again and again, it naturally becomes a habit. When you have a butter lamp, darkness will be automatically cleared away. It does not have to be cleared away. Likewise, when you attain stability in awareness, (compassion will be automatic).

However, in the beginning, you should fabricate it a little. The way to fabricate it is to think like this, "This profound path, this precious self-existing wakefulness, how sad that all my mother sentient beings don't know this. All my mothers of the past, they are completely wasting their time not knowing this." In order to stop other people from talking, you should shut your own mouth. You should fabricate a little in the beginning. This is the intent of an oral instruction. Otherwise, what is taught is the inartificial, unfabricated compassion, but this inartificial compassion arises automatically from your being accustomed to it. You need to fabricate a little bit.

QUESTION: In the *Neluk Rangjung,* it says that as a sign of successful practice in one of the speech yogas of the Dzogchen preliminaries, the flesh on one's body will raise up into lumps. How is that?

RINPOCHE: It is said that the mind is a jewel treasure. As a sign that the mind is very powerful, the effect will be shown in the physical body. In the past, when one of the Dzogchen Padma Rigdzin incarnations practiced this, all the vessels in the kitchen of the Dzogchen Gompa started to leak. He was staying in the upper retreat above the Dzogchen Monastery in the snow mountains. It was the retreat place where Chokgyur Lingpa established the *Kunzang Tuktig* in writing. When the former incarnation of Dzogchen Padma Rigdzin practiced the HUNG recitation there, it was such that the whole phenomenal world should be pierced through by the HUNGS. Then, in the retreat center, the butter container and the teapot all got holes in them and could not keep water afterward. That was because of his HUNG practice.

Mind is a great treasure of jewels. Since the mind is like a wish-fulfilling jewel, the effect of whatever you think can be shown even on material objects, even though the mind is immaterial. It is entirely possible that, as a sign and effect of practice, the flesh and skin of your body can hurt and itch and so forth. This is probably entirely correct; it is a sign of practice, because the mind is quite powerful. Also, the ejection of consciousness, *phowa,* is done mentally, not by legs and arms. Only by your attention can the consciousness be ejected. Likewise, the HUNG practice can show some effect.

There is also what is called the transference of consciousness, *('pho ba grong 'jug).* It was known before in India, where one could transfer one's consciousness into a dead body. The practitioner sends his own consciousness into another person's dead body, after which his own body becomes like a corpse and the other body suddenly gets up and walks around. This happened in the past; it is the result of realized mind. It is not through some material substance.

This is not entirely the case, because in the beginning, when practicing, you should have a skull cup with nectar. You pour the amrita in the skull cup, cover it with a mirror, and draw a letter with sindhura powder. When you practice again and again, then finally the nectar will start to boil as the sign. When this sign has appeared, it is said that you have accomplished the practice. You are then able to eject consciousness into a corpse. In the beginning, you need a support for the concentration. It is said, "There is no big or small size for the support. There is no up and down where the mustard seeds fall. There is no distance that is too close or far away for the trö[15] of the mother goddesses." It is said that when the mantrikas throw the mustard seeds, it is not the case that some don't go up or down. They will hit wherever they are directed to go. There is no uphill and downhill for where the mustard seeds fall. There is no close or far for the trö of the mother goddesses. After having invoked the mother goddesses, when you throw the trö, it can even land all the way in America from Nagi Gompa. These are said to be the qualities of wrathful mantras, subjugating mantras.

For sure there will be signs of practice. Furthermore, it is said, "For the herukas there is no difficulty or ease." It is not that they say, "This is very easy for me. I can easily free that being." or "This is too difficult for me. I can't do it." There are none of those things. For the actions of the wrathful ones, there is no difficulty or ease. It is not that it is too difficult, and they can't do it or that it is very easy, and they will free by wrathful means. It is said that once they are enjoined to an action, there is no distance or difficulty. Even without being enjoined, they will liberate the enemy of the mantrika.

It does happen sometimes that if somebody makes enemies of the practitioner, then immediately they get liberated. There is the story about the first Karmapa, (dus gsum mkhyen pa). When he practiced in a cave, there were seven enemies who wanted to come and kill him. They came outside his cave carrying stones. "We are going to kill him," they said. (As they entered) the roof fell in, killing all seven thieves. They had no chance to harm him. Later when he was asked, he said, "I didn't even have the thought of harming those people." The protectors must have done it. The local people said to him, "You're just talking smart. If you really have such powers, you should be able to plant a dry stick and make it grow." He said, "Okay" and he took a dry stick, put it in the ground, and immediately it got leaves and flowers and was in full bloom. After this, they had confidence in him and said, "Oh, you are a real yogin."

Sometimes it is not even necessary to enjoin or invoke the protectors. There are both those you have to and those you don't have to enjoin, various kinds. But if you have great realization, they will be fighting to be able to help you. But if you have no realization, you can enjoin however long you want, yet there is no certainty it will help. If one is selfish, things will not be successful. If it is for the sake of the teachings, it will be successful.

QUESTION: On the one hand, it seems like it is very easy to recognize the mind essence, as there is no physical work to be done, actually nothing to do. On the other hand, due to habitual patterns, it is easily forgotten; therefore, it seems quite difficult.

RINPOCHE: Yes, of course, this is due to the co-emergent and conceptual ignorances. If these two were purified, we would be a buddha. As long as the conceptual and co-emergent ignorances are not purified, we are sentient beings. To forget is co-emergent ignorance. To follow one thought after another, a long train of thoughts, that is the conceptual ignorance. The conceptual and co-emergent ignorances are the original borderline between buddhas and sentient beings. They make the difference between confusion and nonconfusion. As we have not attained enlightenment, why shouldn't it be difficult? This is the difficulty that everybody has. It does happen. We have to practice continually and gradually, not just for a few months. If this job were something very easy, all sentient beings would have attained enlightenment. It is difficult; this is the thing that is actually giving sentient beings a hard time. Being governed by these two ignorances, we are sentient beings.

METHODS OF LIBERATION

In order to identify what rigpa is, you must recognize your own nature; actually, it means that you should recognize rigpa itself. After that, you must resolve this decisively, without any doubt or wavering about whether or not this is actually rigpa itself. Finally, you must gain confidence in that. Confidence means courage, feeling completely self-assured. This confidence should be liberated.

The sense of liberation here is different from fixation, just as water is different from ice, although they are the same water. During the winter-time in Tibet, water would freeze solid. The same water in the summer is liquid and not rigid. Similarly, sems and rigpa are both your own mind, but they are differentiated according to fixation and attachment.

At first there is fixation on a thing, in the sense of identifying what it is; it is an orange; it is an apple. Discriminating and identifying individual things is called fixation. Attachment means to 'either feel attracted or repelled.' As long as we are involved in fixation and attachment, then our awareness lacks an open quality, zangthal, *(zang thal)*. The vital point of zangthal in awareness is absence of fixation and attachment. When fixation and attachment collapse, awareness is like a pure crystal ball. The ordinary state of shamatha has no openness, no zangthal, because there is too much fascination with the feeling of stillness.

To reiterate, first recognize your nature, then decide on one point, and finally gain confidence in liberation. The meaning of this is that as long as we have not yet attained buddhahood, there seems to be no way to completely avoid conceptual thinking. It never totally vanishes, permanently. First, we may get rid of the coarse thinking and then the subtle thinking. Finally, the subtlest thoughts disappear with the attainment of buddhahood. Even when having attained the state of a bodhisattva, you will still have some remnant of conceptual thinking, just like the lingering smell of musk in a bottle after the musk oil itself has been removed. At the state of complete buddhahood, the last trace of defilement is purified.

We understand the term shardrol, *(shar grol)*. When a thought initially arises, it cannot possibly come from anywhere other than our essence itself. Thoughts never arise from the four outer elements. Thoughts come from our own mind, and the essence of this mind is wisdom, which is primordial purity. Although a thought may arise, it is vital that it be simultaneously liberated. Liberation occurs when awareness remains unmoved; it is like a mirror that never gets disturbed, no matter what kind of image may appear in it. Once you recognize your nature, it is like a mirror. Then thoughts are just like reflected images that can neither bring benefit nor harm. Whether the image is white or black, the mirror itself will never really take on that color. To remain totally unmoved by any possible thought that may arise is called *gaining confidence in liberation*.

In this way, the place a thought arises from is the state of awareness, and the place where it is freed or liberated is also the state of awareness, rigpa. That is exactly what is meant when saying, "Arising and liberation are uninterrupted." In order to practice like that, you must first have recognized rigpa.

Again, first recognize your nature and then decide on one point, totally free from any conceptual hesitation about whether or not it is really so. You must resolve on rigpa itself. Finally, gain confidence in liberation upon arising, shardrol, in the sense that in the state of rigpa, any arising thought is freed just like a drawing on water, without leaving a trace. 'Traceless' is when no fixation is present.

Thoughts cannot be obstructed; they couldn't arise if there were any obstruction. The mind is unobstructed. Thought is only a seeming occurrence. The knowing quality is unceasing; that is actually the capacity, which is unobstructed. Without that, we would have only essence and nature but no capacity. It is due to the unobstructed capacity that the yogi is able to eat and drink and do different things; a yogi does perceive things. For a yogi, thoughts are freed upon arising, just like a drawing on water. That is the vital point of confidence in liberation. For an ordinary person, on the other hand, all thoughts are like carving in stone; they create karma and habitual tendencies. They are completely immersed in grasping and fixation.

For a yogi, the arising of a thought is like a drawing on the surface of water; its arising and its being freed are simultaneous. There is no removing and no thing removed by means of a remedy, because the thought is liberated by itself. That is how the text phrases it.

The principle of a thought being self-liberated is that the instant you recognize the essence in the thought, the thought cannot possibly avoid being freed. You never find a thought that somehow lingers on, remaining somewhere.

In short, you must recognize the essence! When recognizing, there is no need to mentally formulate, "Well, well! That's how it is!" Simply recognize the instant of your unfabricated present wakefulness, in which the past thought has ceased, and the future thought has not yet arisen. Otherwise it is indifferent.

The three types of liberation come about in the moment of recognizing rigpa. Even though there are different words, like freed upon arising and self-freed, they are merely different names describing the same thing. In the moment of recognizing the primordially free rigpa, all are complete, like the one spot in the body, where all the different nadis from the different organs meet together in one juncture. Once we recognize or acknowledge the primordially free state of rigpa, the three or four different ways of freeing are simply different expressions, like different facial *expressions*.

If you cut off the hand at the wrist, all of the fingers are cut off. You don't need to cut each separate finger. Once rigpa is recognized it is the same as cutting off the hand at the wrist: all the expressions are cut too. It is said that during the meditation state itself, you don't need to make these an object of the intellect, because self-awareness is beyond concepts.

Otherwise, we will think, "What is self-liberation? What is self-freed, rangdrol, *(rang grol)*? What is directly freed, *(gcer grol)*? What is free from extremes? What is freed upon arising?" If we actually connect with the primordially free state of rigpa, all are caught simultaneously, because they are simply expressions. People make different expressions and show different moods. They are all contained within one point. There are not different kinds of rigpa. The crux of the matter is the primordially free rigpa. Once that is acknowledged, all the others are complete. Once the water pipe up in the mountain is disconnected in one place, there is no water anywhere below. When recognizing rigpa, the primordially free state, everything is freed.

QUESTION: You know the example of the thief entering an empty house? Does that refer to somebody who is already enlightened, or is that someone still on the path, who has done a lot of training?

RINPOCHE: Since self-aware wisdom is beyond concepts, we do not need to analyze the different ways of liberation during the meditation state. We only need to understand them during the post-meditation. A thief entering an empty house refers to the ultimate liberation. Both delusion and liberation are freed. It is not that it can be lost, after attaining stability. It is the state of buddhahood; there is no distraction. When there is no fixating, thought does not have benefit or harm. It is the expression of rigpa's cognizance.

These three stages of liberation can also be applied to three different degrees of caliber of people. The lower capacity, freed upon arising, is like meeting somebody you already know. The second one is like a knot tied in a snake. It doesn't require anyone else to untie it; it is untied by itself, self-liberated. That is the intermediate, the self-liberation. The third one is like a thief entering an empty house. There is nothing for the thief to gain; there is nothing for the house to lose. It is totally beyond benefit or harm.

There is again the superior of the superior type, of which the foremost in this world was Garab Dorje. It is said that when he sat down and received teachings, he was a sentient being. When he stood up, he was a buddha, and from that point on there was never any distraction or delusion in his mind, ever. He was the first human vidyadhara, Garab Dorje, who received the teachings from Vajrasattva. When he received the pointing-out instructions and his confusion and deluded thinking dissolved into dharmata, delusion never arose again. There was no "second thought" ever coming up. Garab Dorje is the example for the foremost, or top-most, practitioner. Guru Rinpoche is the one a step below that, at the intermediate level among the best. The one of lower capacity among the best was probably Chetsun Senghe Wangchuk. Among the best, there are these three types.

QUESTION: How do these examples refer to the thought? For example, in the first case, best case, it is like no thoughts arise at all, I understand? And in the second case, it is freed upon arising, and in the third case, it is what?

RINPOCHE: Garab Dorje was a human being. He was not like Vajradhara or Samantabhadra, who never strayed into the first thought. The first thought was cut at the moment of arising. Garab Dorje did receive the pointing-out instruction and then attained enlightenment. He must have been thinking before he received the pointing-out instructions. Afterward, thought was completely interrupted. He had no more distraction, ever. But he was not a buddha who had no thought movement. Enlightenment means purified and perfected. Thinking is purified and wisdom wakefulness is perfected.

In freed upon arising, the first, one has not recognized rigpa, because in the arising of the thought, there is no recognition. One needs to try to recognize. It occurs so quickly that it is like simultaneous with the thinking; there is also the recognizing rigpa. But in the second case, self-liberation, there is no need for that. There is no need for the technique of the remedy. It is automatic, just as the snake doesn't need any external helper to untie the knot. The snake unties itself. In the freedom of rigpa, the thought doesn't require a recognizing of its essence artificially; it happens by itself. The third case, the thief in the empty house, is even beyond that. It is not really thinking any more. It is actually the expression of awareness.

We should train in liberating the thought upon arising, as the thought is being thought. As sentient beings, we do have an ample supply of thoughts. When the thought arises, since we have already received the pointing-out instruction in recognizing rigpa, we know the smell of it. We should simply recognize again, then the thinking is liberated as it takes place.

When getting really used to the training in liberating upon arising, the self-liberation will come by itself, gradually. The third one is actually transcending the possibilities of being liberated or not being liberated. It is like arriving on an island where everything is pure gold. An island of pure gold means there is no thought to find anywhere, exactly as on a golden island you cannot find ordinary earth and stone. The difference between freed upon arising and self-liberating is the different types of mindfulness. In the beginning, there is the watchfulness that ensures that the movement is liberated as it arises. But later when the mindfulness becomes innate mindfulness, or natural mindfulness, that corresponds to the self-liberation of thought or thinking. But, the point is, unless the essence of the thinking is recognized, it is not liberated. There is only the chasing after the thinking, but the moment the essence is recognized, there is no following up; it only vanishes.

It is just like what is said in the *Ka Ling Shitro:* "Don't look after the thought; look into the thinker. When looking into the thinker, you don't find a thinker. That is called bringing thinking to exhaustion, exhausting the thinking." *Self-liberation* means that you don't strain into thinking when recognizing rigpa. This (accords with) the famous statement in the *Three Words Striking the Vital Point: Recognize this as the dharmakaya awareness.*

Similarly, one of the Mahamudra songs says, "Within thought, I discovered nonthought. Within complexity, I discovered dharmakaya." This means that, while thinking, if all of a sudden you recognize the thinker, the thinking, as a thought, doesn't remain anywhere as a thing; it simply vanishes. Complex thinking is the same. Within that, you realize the dharmakaya, because the absence of constructs, or dualistic thinking, is itself dharmakaya. That is probably the first among the three ways of liberation. While thinking, it is like meeting somebody you already know, and the thinking dissolves. Once the thinking has dissolved, you can call that simplicity, which is dharmakaya.

The example of a thought arising is like a drawing on water. That is freed upon arising. The thinking makes the drawing, but it doesn't remain anywhere. That is not the case for a normal person. Thinking does create samsara. Unless there is first pointing-out and recognizing of the primordially free rigpa, samsara is continually being created. It is like the stake in the ground for the horse with the rope tied to it. The stake is the example of rigpa and the rope the expression of rigpa. Unless you go by the rope, closer and closer, you won't come to the stake. If you simply let it be on the ground, you will never get to the main point, which is within. It is the buddha-nature's expression that is creating samsara. Unless there is the knowing of that, it merely goes on and on creating samsara, evolving in a progressive order. As soon as you start looking into what thinks, it is called reversing the order. Instead of creating more samsara, you are going to the thoughts link by link of the twelve links of dependent origination. That is called the reverse order of the twelve links of dependent origination. It is the same as getting closer and closer to the stake.

Once you start looking into who is thinking, you discover nonthought within thought, like the example before of Karma Lingpa, who said, "Don't follow the thinking. Look into the thinker." Unless you do that, you will be like a normal person who is happy when happy, and sad when sad, and gets engrossed in that again and again. While being so, it is like this analogy of a child chasing a butterfly and falling into the abyss. Looking at the beautiful butterfly and wanting to catch it, the child does not see what is happening and falls into the abyss and dies. That is the example for the normal state of delusion that does not notice it is creating samsara.

QUESTION: Is the quality of openness, zangthal, primordially so, or does it become so after receiving the pointing-out and recognizing?

RINPOCHE: When we say that awareness is openness, it means that outside is one and inside is the other, which makes two; creating a duality such as this is the case now. When there are two, there is no openness. When the duality has mingled into one, there is openness. Actually, since primordial time, in the context of the wisdom of the empty essence, the wisdom of the cognizant nature, and the wisdom of all-pervasive capacity, the term openness applies to the all-pervasiveness. Without openness, something would be left behind—something that is pervaded, and something that is not pervaded. In this case, there would be something outside and something inside, two. Without such duality, there is the all-pervasiveness. Actually, awareness is primordially open, free. However, when a sentient being is in a body of karmic ripening, being fettered by conceptual thoughts, the openness becomes tied or bound by conceptual mind. It becomes without natural freedom. Openness means naturally free. For the state of not being self-liberated, the example of being tied by a string is used. Whether you are bound by a golden string or a copper wire, either way you are still tied, which means you are having conceptual thoughts. When free from concepts, you have openness. Awareness is primordial openness.

The openness of awareness is free from clinging and attachment to anything whatsoever. To be totally free from clinging and attachment is the openness of rigpa. However, when we say outside and inside, it refers to the outside and the interior of one's body or to the inside and outside of a house. What is outside and inside is just a division made by concepts. When free from concepts, there is no clinging or attachment to anything whatsoever. That is the openness of awareness, which is also what primordially all-pervasive means.

Without openness, there wouldn't be any all-pervasiveness. There would be something that is pervaded and something that isn't. But that is not the case because everything that appears and exists—samsara and nirvana, the vessel and its contents, whatever is good or bad—everything is inseparable: that is openness. The ordinary mundane sense of openness means not obstructed, unimpeded. A wall that obstructs does not exemplify openness. But a glass window pane is openness for the eyes but not for the hand, because it obstructs a hand. When there is no clinging or attachment to anything whatsoever then there is neither something that obstructs nor something obstructed. That is the openness of awareness. There is a great significance in the words, *A blankness that is utterly open. A total openness that is indescribable.*

THE THREEFOLD SKY PRACTICE

The practice is called mingling the three skies, the three spaces, or the threefold sky. What are the three skies? Externally, the outer sky is the empty space, the openness right in front of you. Inner sky is the empty quality of mind, and the secret sky is the empty awareness.

There are three words, but actually it is one meaning, so the last word, mingle, means they are all combined into one. The external sky is called space because it is unimpeded, unblocked. It is not like a wall or something. It is empty and it is open. The inner sky is the empty mind, which all sentient beings have. Otherwise, mind would be like a piece of wood or a stone. Since mind is sentient, that is the mind referenced in the inner sky's empty mind. The secret sky is the empty awareness, which is the essence of mind. Once you recognize the essence, the three skies are unified. Otherwise, without recognizing the essence of mind, you will only have unified two skies, not three.

Awareness is understood to be and defined as the essence of the mind. To understand what is meant by rigpa or the essence of mind, we can use the example of our own body. The heart in the main trunk of the body is like rigpa, and the arms or legs are like mind. From one perspective, it is one thing, but from another, there are two. To see rigpa, you have to look to the main trunk of the body. If you are distracted and in mind, it is like looking outwardly, away from the body. You are following yourself somewhere else, and you have no way to meet the essence. If you look into the origin, the source of where mind is, it is like looking at where the arm attaches to the trunk. You come back to the mind essence, the heart is in the trunk of the body. That is why it says that sentient beings look away, and the Buddha looks toward (the mind's essence). Awareness or rigpa is the trunk of the body; dualistic mind is like an appendage. If you look further out the arm to the hand, will you see your own heart? No. That is the difference between looking away and toward. If I want to see my heart and look further and further away, will I see it?

We do not see through dualistic mind. If you look toward the mind's essence, you will get to the heart of it. That is the example. If you practice mingling the threefold sky, you need to recognize awareness; otherwise, it becomes an instruction in mingling the two skies. Mingling the two is something all sentient beings do. They hold their space outside, and inside they have mind. But in the moment of recognizing awareness, the three skies are automatically mingled, because at that moment there is no fixation on outer objects. There is no holding onto the mind, which perceives. There is no dualistic experience. You can easily teach about the mingled three skies, but it will probably only become the practice to mingle the two skies.

Again, in the mingling of the three skies, the outer sky is the empty space, the inner sky is the empty mind, and the secret sky is the empty rigpa, or awareness. In the secret space of rigpa, grasping and fixating are both gone. The three skies are automatically mingled when you have recognized rigpa. If you have not recognized rigpa, you are trying to construct the mingled three spaces. As long as you try to construct something, it is not rangjung, which means self-existent rigpa or self-existing awareness. The basis of the mingled three skies is rangjung yeshe, self-existing wakefulness. It is self-existing because it doesn't have to be constructed and wakeful because it has cognizance. Without recognizing rigpa, it becomes nonarisen, unknowing.

In the moment of recognizing rigpa, you don't have to mingle the three spaces; they are self-mingled automatically. Otherwise, we usually have the concept that the space is there, and that we are here watching; we have this dualistic setup. But in the moment of rigpa, this fixation falls apart. The difference between sems, dualistic mind, and rigpa is that sems has fixation and rigpa does not.

In short, it is like this: you don't need to take charge of space outside. You don't need to take charge of the space within. Just totally disown all three—outer and inner spaces and the secret space of rigpa—as they are already mingled. They do not need to be mingled.

Your eyes need to connect with space and not look down at the ground. Direct your eyes toward space. For sure, the mind is empty. Leave this empty mind within rigpa. This is called already having mingled the three spaces. It is then possible to be free from fixation. Any attempt to mingle the three spaces is always fixation. If you think of the space outside and the space within and then think, "I should mingle these two and then add rigpa," we should not call this `mingling the threefold space', but instead 'mingling the threefold concepts.' If we call 'three concepts' the state of rigpa, it makes concepts more important than rigpa.

Why should we engage in this practice? Because space is perfectly pure, empty, and totally unconfined. There is no center, no fringe, and no edge in any direction whatsoever. Directing the gaze into the middle of empty space is an aid for allowing rigpa to be similarly unconfined and all-pervasive.

Outer space transcends arising, dwelling, and ceasing. This is the example. The ultimate meaning is that rigpa is all-pervasive and empty, with no end, like space. In the context of means and knowledge, this practice is the means, method. Simply leave rigpa in unconfined external space; there is nothing to arrange. Within this state, there is a shimmering configuration of light and something moving about. Direct your gaze toward this configuration. This is beneficial.

What it comes down to is this: If you have recognized rigpa, it becomes, automatically, the general mingling of the three spaces, the three skies. But if you have to try to mix it together, then it becomes quite difficult. You think, "First, there is the sky, then there is my mind, and finally there is rigpa." It becomes very hard because it is interrupted by concepts.

The starting point is to recognize mind essence. When we talk about recognizing mind, we talk about the pointing-out to the essence of mind, not to mind. Nobody asks the lama to please point out the mind. We say, point out the mind essence; we don't say point out the mind. That is the difference, and we should understand its meaning. We don't have to point out mind, as everybody already has mind. If one is sentient, a sentient being, one automatically has dualistic mind. The student requests to a precious master, "Please show me mind essence." The essence of mind is rigpa, awareness. And what is rigpa? It is self-existent wakefulness, whereas the mind is nonexistent stupor.

In order to practice like this, you first have to recognize the mind essence. Then it is possible to practice mingling the threefold space. Without that, I can tell you words, saying that the eternal sky is empty space, which is free from anything that can obstruct or impede, such as mist, dust, or clouds. That is the example for the external empty sky. Sky is unsupported; there is no focal point in the empty sky. Baseless space doesn't have any reference point that we can focus on. If there is a reference point it is shamatha. Unsupported space completely destroys our sense of shamatha, fixating concentration. That is why it is very beneficial. Best is the sky; second best is an endless ocean. You can go to the ocean bank, shore, and look out; that is the second best.

Space is basically complete openness, unobstructedness. It doesn't mean the blue thing we can see up there. This blueness we see is called the ornament of the sky. It is said according to the scriptures that because of the reflection of the sunlight on the southern slope of Mount Meru, which is made of sapphire, our sky and ocean are blue in appearance. However, if you are higher up, further up, the sky doesn't have any colors; it is black. But if you fly further and further, straight up, you will never find a place where you touch something. There is no end to it. No matter how many billion—or countless—aeons you fly, there is no end. Likewise, if you fly down through the earth to what is called the Golden Base, you will also go endlessly through, without finding any bottom anywhere. If there is no above and no below, then how can there be south, east, west, and north?

To practice this, you should take into experience what is really meant by space—that there is no top, no bottom, and no limit to south, east, west, or north. Space is complete without any limitation in any direction. That is what you focus on to begin with for the three skies. That was about the external sky. Now let's turn to the inner sky of the empty mind. Does mind have a place that it comes from, dwells, or goes to at any point? We find that it does not. The external sky is empty and so is the inner sky, the empty mind; it's empty as well. If something has a place where it arises, a place where it stays, and a place where it ceases, it wouldn't be empty. Since the mind is without any arising, dwelling, or ceasing, it must be empty. That was the second sky.

Now for the secret sky of empty awareness, we should first understand what mind essence is and how it is uncompounded. Dualistic mind has thoughts, thinking. Namtok, *(rnam rtog),* dualistic thought, is nram pa, an appearance, manifestation of the five sense objects, and rtog pa, which means to conceptualize, hold onto that. That is thinking. But the secret space of rigpa is without any thoughts. While being free from thoughts, its essence is empty; its nature is cognizant, or luminous; and its capacity is unobstructed.

Dualistic mind is decorated with thoughts, dualistic thinking.

Thoughts are not something that stay by themselves. Thoughts arise, disappear, arise, and disappear, one after the other. That is what causes all the confusion. We sentient beings run after each thought that arises, which is why we forget the essence. In the secret space of empty rigpa, even though it's devoid of any conceptual thinking, there is still a wakefulness. Dualistic mind is decorated with the conceptual thoughts, and rigpa is decorated or adorned with basic wakefulness. Sems falls under the power of the three times but rigpa does not. Sems is always involved in thoughts about past, present, and future. Rigpa is devoid of these thoughts.

The difference between sems and rigpa is this: while sems is empty and cognizant, it has no awareness of its own essence. It has not taken hold of this empty cognizance. It is like the example of not identifying where the heart is and instead looking away from the body to find it. Having not recognized this empty cognizance, the mind of sentient beings is called the unity of being empty and cognizant with a core of nonawareness or ignorance. On the other hand, the mind of a yogi and a practitioner is the unity of the empty and the cognizant with a core of awareness.

The difference lies in knowing how to look, as in the example of looking toward one's own heart or looking out and away—out the length of the arm to find the heart. If you recognize where the heart is, you meet the heart or the essence of mind, rigpa, which is the essence, nature, and capacity. If, instead, you look away from the heart, the essence evolves into the three or five poisons, and you wander in samsara.

Since you are quite intelligent, you can understand this one point, which is what it all comes down to: recognize your own heart as in this example. Recognizing our mind essence is the main point of every teaching—whether it is samsara, nirvana, or the path. If you look and say, "I am trying to find my heart," but you look down the arm to the hand and further away, you will never find your heart.

Finally, the smart person will look the right way and say, "Oh, here it is." That is the example. Just like the most important part of the body is the heart, likewise, the most important point of the dharma, samsara, nirvana, and the path, is mind essence. You find the essence, the heart, by looking the right way, connecting with it. In so doing, you see nothing; there is nothing to see. Still, everything is vividly seen. It is said that this essence is endowed with the threefold wakefulness of essence, nature, and capacity. Actually, seeing this is not the thing seen—it is seeing that there is nothing seen.

In the Kagyü teachings it says, "Nothing whatsoever, yet everything arises from it." 'Nothing whatsoever' refers to the empty essence, which everything arises from—it is the cognizant nature. That is the same as in the Nyingma terminology: the empty essence, yeshe; the cognizant nature, yeshe; and so on. The essence is empty, cognizant, and unobstructed. This is what one has to touch base with. It is said that in the beginning one should touch what should be touched or connected to. Here there is nothing to connect to. There is not a thing that one gets and reaches, because the essence is without anything to hold or to touch. If you want something to hold, then there are plenty of thoughts to hold on to. Not touching something is called nonaction, which means free from concepts. It is said that one nonaction outshines all activities, because this moment of nonaction destroys the three poisons.

There is actually no other agent than this that can clear away the three poisons. The three poisons always follow after a conceptual thought. If there were no conceptual thoughts to begin with, there would be no three poisons to follow after that. Therefore, it is said that one nonaction outshines all activities or doings. The three poisons are not something that we can kind of prohibit or try to bury, burn, wash away, or flush away. Not even the smartest person in this world can handle the three poisons. If you try to suppress mind poisons, they just come back up again; it is impossible. Of course, you can try to be patient, but that won't uproot the three poisons.

It is only the empty essence and wakefulness that can totally annihilate the three poisons. What is meant by yeshe? The basic word is shepa (shes pa), which means knowing or being awake. There is no sense of being oblivious or not knowing. While it is free from action and concepts, it still knows whatever there is to know. That is how the essence is. You are mistaken if you think, "Oh the essence is nothing whatsoever. It is merely a blank state, like being hit and knocked out with a stick." It is not like that at all. It is unobstructed, being completely empty. It is empty while cognizing, cognizing while being empty. We don't have to manufacture that; it is automatic. People can't make the essence anyway.

It is beyond being cleared and obscured, just like the flame of a butter lamp. It is uninterrupted like the flow of a river. But then the bandits of conceptual thoughts have taken it and tied it up with the sense objects and consciousness. In the past, we wandered endlessly in samsara, and if we don't recognize that, samsara will continue endlessly. There is nothing more essential or important than this. Putting this into practice is like the wish-fulfilling jewel, because when we die, we don't have any free will whatsoever. If we have grown accustomed to rigpa, it means we are free from the fixation of the three poisons, which are the basis for continuing in samsara. Once we attain stability in the essence, being in the three realms of samsara is like playing around.

To reiterate, the threefold sky practice is as follows: Outwardly, there is empty space, which means there is nothing to focus on; there is no focus, nothing to rest the attention on. That is the external space, the outer sky. The inner sky is the empty mind, the emptiness of the mind within. The secret space is the empty rigpa that has been recognized, the knowing of empty mind. These three become mingled into one. If you practice this very well, then when you die you will mingle with primordial purity. The threefold sky practice is the ultimate phowa, for a Dzogchen practitioner.

You sit with the eyes directed toward midair, without focusing on anything and without thinking of space inwardly. It is said, "In unsupported space, place nonfixated rigpa." Do not think about space; leave the inner mind without fixation. Do not form any thought such as, "I am looking into the sky," or anything like that.

The secret space of rigpa is the knowing of this emptiness. Do not direct the mind outwardly but recognize mind essence. That is called the secret sky of rigpa. In this way, you naturally let outer, inner, and secret be undivided. That is called mingling. Without thinking of sky outwardly, and without forming any thought inwardly, you automatically mingle the threefold sky.

The first key point is to recognize the mind essence, rigpa. Once you have done that, repeat that recognition in short moments many times; that is the real way to mingle the three skies. When you are sitting outside, aim into space. It means that your eyes can look toward the open sky. Your eyes can face toward the outer empty sky, but really, your mind faces toward the empty rigpa. If you do not recognize rigpa, then you take outer space as the object and dualistic mind as the subject. Then you create this dualistic setup, but after recognizing rigpa, you have no duality like this.

Sit outside letting the eyes face toward the open sky and the inner mind face toward rigpa. That doesn't mean you have to sit and hold this unity of the three skies. Just look once and then completely relax, let go. Automatically the three skies are mingled. The perfect mingling occurs by itself, automatically. In other words, space or sky means no point of reference. There is no thing to look at, right? In space, is there anything to focus on? Focus on no focus. In unfocused space, abandon awareness unsupported.

QUESTION: When we practice mingling the threefold space, firstly, do we concentrate on space far away for a long time?

RINPOCHE: First look away, then lead toward you; then it becomes all-pervasive. But actually, it is the same. Without fixating outwardly, immediately to do that is okay. You can stay that way outwardly and slowly look towards. Wherever the eyes are placed is space—far away, close, and everything in-between is the same space.

If you leave it out in space, then it turns into a conceptual object. Once brought towards, out and in are the same, no division. There is really no difference; it is just a matter of close or far. This is a method; if you do not do it, it is perfectly all right. Away is empty space; close is empty space. The only reason to pull the space towards is to avoid sitting and watching space as being over there as a focus. There is nothing to think about. Simply rest in the all-pervasiveness. Don't dwell on the appearance; rest in rigpa itself.

EQUALIZE BUDDHAHOOD DURING
THE FOUR TIMES:[16]

A practitioner of the Great Perfection should, by means of the vital points of possessing the oral instructions called *Equalize Buddhahood During the Four Times,* exert him or herself in practicing the continuous river of unceasing dharmata.

To seal appearances at daytime: By not losing the natural stability of awareness throughout the meditation and post-meditation periods, resolve whatever arises in your experience to be the great, unimpeded state of realization, which is nondual and primordially free. When unable to do so, train in perceiving all phenomena as illusory. Without letting your mind run wild, lead them to the space of primordial purity.

To gather the senses naturally at dusk: To assume the nirmanakaya posture, focus your attention on a four-petaled red lotus flower in the navel center of the light red-colored, radiant, and straight central channel within your body. At the level of your navel is the ATUNG, the nature of heat, and at the crown of your head is the white HANG, the nature of bliss. Expel the stale breath and hold the vase-breath or, if you cannot, the medium-breath. Thus, focus your attention on the wisdom of blissful heat generated by the blazing and dripping.

To enter consciousness in the vase at midnight: Keep the posture as before, and in the heart center of the central channel visualized as before, amidst a four-petaled red lotus, focus your attention on a radiant white A. After that, visualize another white a on the top of your head. Then, between the two, visualize twenty-one very fine white A letters like a string and hold the vase-shaped or the soft-breath. On the verge of falling asleep, visualize that all the A letters gradually dissolve into the A in the heart center. Imagine that it is within the closed lotus bud, radiant like the flame of a butter lamp inside a vase. Thus, train in falling asleep while intending to recognize your dreams.

To naturally clarify awareness at dawn: As soon as you awake from sleep, assume the dharmakaya posture, direct your eyes into midair, and

exhale with the HA sound three times. Hence, the lotus in the heart center opens, and the white A shoots out through the aperture of Brahma
and remains vividly in the air about a bow's length above you. Focus your
attention on it and keep your breath slightly exhaled. If your mind gets
agitated, let it descend back to remain within your heart center and focus
your attention on it while lowering your gaze. If you feel dull, practice as
above, as it suits your constitution.

I have been asked to teach what is called *Equalize Buddhahood During
the Four Times*. The idea of that is to not waste any time, but to practice
unceasingly. This is a special Dzogchen teaching of dividing the day and
night, twenty-four hours divided into four periods, resembling the normal four sessions that are used in the approach-accomplishment, *(bsnyen
sgrub)*, practice of recitation, where there are four sessions per day. Here
there are four periods: the daytime, evening, night, and then early morning. The evening can also be called dusk, and the morning, the dawn
period. But the whole day is divided into four periods. You practice
during these four periods so that practice becomes continuous. Then you
unite with the state of all the buddhas and become equal to the state of all
the buddhas. In other words, no time is wasted.

In the first of the four, the sentence is: *To seal appearances at daytime.*
That means you should not fixate on the sense impressions, the sights,
sounds, and so forth. Do not concentrate inwardly on the mind; rather,
leave everything totally without fixation in the state of Trekchö. That is
naturally sealing the appearances during daytime.

The moment you do not fixate on perceptions and the perceiver, naturally, both appearances and mind are sealed with rigpa. Just remain in a
state of Trekchö. Once there is no fixation on appearances or on the perceiver of the appearances—the mind—there is no splitting up into subject and object, appearances and mind. This is called the great equality.
By resting free from fixation, the essence of both perception and perceiver
is rigpa. Simply remaining like that is called unifying with the state of the
buddhas or equalizing buddhahood.

That is the opposite of what a normal person does. There is not even
the mention of great equality. Appearances and mind are split up into
subject and object, so that the mind is always chasing after what is perceived—either with attachment, aversion, or indifference. That is the

opposite of the great equanimity of all the buddhas. The word for meditation here is equanimity, resting evenly. That is the state of rigpa: not fixating on appearances outwardly or concentrating inwardly. Merely leaving the perceived and perceiver is great equality. That is called establishing the great equality of all the buddhas.

The great equality is empty of both fixating and grasping. That means you do not follow after the outer perceived objects or inwardly fixate on what is perceived. Through anger and attachment, we have roamed endlessly in samsara. When we grasp and fixate, we are not leaving the mind in equality. The appearances are the five sense objects, and the mind is the subject. These two have us circling around thought movement. It is the opposite for a buddha, who does not follow after perceptions or hold onto the perceiver. As a buddha remains in equanimity, these two become one. Once fixating has fallen apart, there is the great equality. This is the equanimity of the buddhas.

Leaving the mind in equality is beyond both placing and not placing the mind in equanimity, according to the *Chöying Dzöd*. It says rest in the state that is beyond both placing and not placing. For example, if we want to place the mind in a state of equanimity that is a conceptual idea. Not doing it is also conceptual, but beyond both of these is the state of Trekchö.

To get back to *equalize buddhahood during the four periods:* one is for daytime, *to seal appearances at daytime;* two are for nighttime, *to gather the senses naturally at dusk* and *to enter consciousness in the vase at midnight;* and one is for dawn, *to naturally clarify awareness at dawn.*

To gather the senses naturally at dusk is from when it gets dark, when the sun goes down, until you go to sleep. During that time, you do tummo practice.

To enter consciousness in the vase at midnight is before midnight and is combined with the luminosity practice.

To naturally clarify awareness at dawn is from waking up early until daylight. That dawn practice is to invigorate or to refresh rigpa.

In the second of the four periods, the evening-time practice, the sentence is: *To gather the senses naturally at dusk.* What does that mean? It is actually tummo practice and the basis for that is your physical body, within which the buddha-nature is encapsulated or enveloped right now within the confinement of the aggregates, elements, and sense faculties. The essence or root of all these lies in what are called nadis, pranas, and bindus—channels, energies, and essences. These are of two kinds: the normal ones and the wisdom ones. The normal ones are the channels that we know, the winds or pranas that move in them, and the bindus such as the white and red ones that are the basis for giving others a new birth. Furthermore, these normal ones are the support for what is supported by them; the wisdom channels, the wisdom pranas, and the wisdom essences.

To utilize these in practice is called the completion stage. Completion stage has two aspects: one is with concepts and the other is without concepts. Sometimes they are called with form and formless completion stages. Sometimes they are called with focus and without focus or with concept and without concept. In the Dzogchen practice, tummo is also used. In the Mahamudra system, one of the main practices of the six doctrines of Naropa is called tummo. It is said that tummo is the main pillar of the path and is considered the most important of the six yogas. What is being practiced here as the completion stage involves a slight effort, because the wisdom channels, the wisdom energies, and the wisdom essences are based on the physical; then you use the practice.

It is simply as follows: The physical body we have is made out of the two elements, red and white, from our mother and father. Right now in the practice, the ATUNG, the short a below the navel, is the essence of the red element from our mother. The HANG syllable at the top of the central channel is the essence of the white element obtained from our father. These two are, in essence, heat and bliss. Heat is the red one; bliss is the white one. In this practice, you visualize the central channel and below: four fingers below the navel is the red ATUNG, or the tiny flame. At the top of the central channel but upside down is the white letter HANG. By breathing, you fan the ATUNG flame until it flames up through the central channel. It touches the HANG there, which starts to melt and drip down. That is the main part of the practice called the blazing and dripping.

It is like putting drops of oil on a fire. The more oil you drop, the hotter the flames become. The hotter the flames, the more is melted. So, the HANG syllable is being melted by ATUNG. The warmth and the bliss intermingle and start to fill first the whole central channel and then all the channels in the body. At the same time, as your body is filled with bliss and heat, it also burns away all habitual tendencies and all obscu-

rations. They are totally cleared away. The essence of the heat is emptiness; the essence of the bliss is emptiness too. Emptiness is the state of
Mahamudra, which is also described as "the emptiness endowed with the
supreme of all aspects, inseparable from the supreme unchanging bliss."
That is the definition.

At the end of this practice, you should just rest in this, without focus,
in the state of rigpa. That is the completion stage, free from all concepts.
In the Nyingtig preliminaries, within the refuge it says, "I take refuge
in the nadis, pranas, and bindus, the essence of awakened mind." Bodhichitta is not the physical or relative aspect of nadi, prana, and bindu; it
refers to the wisdom aspect.

The reason is that the physical body we have, the vajra body endowed
with the six elements, is sometimes called Vajravarahi, Vajrayogini, or
Dorje Phagmo, the basic body. It is that the red element obtained from
the mother is in essence the Dorje Phagmo, Vajrayogini, while the white
element obtained from the father is in essence Chakrasamvara.

When doing the tummo practice, there are two ways, adorned and
unadorned. Adorned is to visualize oneself in the form of Vajrayogini
or Dorje Phagmo, and the reason for that was what I just said. The
unadorned way is without imagining your body as anything in particular.

Based on a drawing of the channel, one understands the root sentence,
To gather the senses naturally at dusk, instead of saying senses, it can mean
senses, but let's say faculties, gather the faculties to the key point. Faculties
usually are understood as being the sense faculties, but here the essences
of the sense faculties are the true elements, the white and red. To gather
them together, the key point means to utilize the practice of the material
body of the red and white elements. One can visualize the body in the form
of Vajrayogini or one doesn't have to think of it. But when imagining the
body in the form of Vajryogini, it should be transparent, hollow on the
inside, just like a big tent of light, where the central channel is like the
main tent pole. It is also transparent and hollow, and slightly crystal too. In
a simple way imagine the central channel, or more elaborate if you can. It is
good also to visualize the left and right channels. They are called the *roma*
and *kyangma* in Tibetan. The three of them converge four fingers below
the navel. While the central channel ends at the crown of the head, the left
and right ones curve around above the ears and meet inside of the nostrils.

Also, it is good to imagine the five chakras. First, the chakra at the

crown center has thirty-two spokes. The second one, at the throat, has
sixteen spokes. The chakra at the heart has eight spokes and the one at
the navel has forty-two spokes. There is also a chakra at the secret place,
which has sixty-four spokes. When the blissful heat starts to spread,
imagine that it spreads inside the channels. First it spreads in the central
channel and next in the left and right ones, in the five chakras with all
their nadi spokes, and so forth.

Even though we say that the warmth of the heat is the red element,
the ATUNG, and the bliss is the HANG, each of them has both bliss and heat,
each has both bliss and emptiness. During intercourse, there is not only
bliss, there is also heat. Both are always present. The actual visualizing of
channels and the HANG and ATUNG is not imagining something new; it is
reminding us or clarifying what is already present. That is why tummo
is the chief of the six yogas. It is like the basis. Without tummo practice,
none of the other six yogas has the driving force. The three channels, central, left, and right, are the basis for the three kayas. They are the support
for the three kayas and also for the three experiences of bliss, clarity, and
nonthought. Nonthought pertains to the central channel, while bliss and
clarity relate to the left and right ones.

The ATUNG is called *tummo,* which means fierce female. The hang
is called fierce male. The word *tum,* which means fierce, wrathful, or
ferocious, is used for wrathful deities because they are ablaze with fire
and unassailable; they cannot be overcome and they vanquish all enmity.
These syllables burn away all obscurations and habitual tendencies.

The root of Vajrayana has many methods, few difficulties. Understand that a practice such as this, which is completion stage with attributes, always has three degrees of complexity: detailed, middling,
and very simple. The elaborate way is to go through a lot of different
sequences, visualizing all the chakras, all the channels, and the different
spokes. The intermediate version is to image the three channels, the central, right, and left. The very simple way is to think that your body is
like a tent of light that's hollow in the inside, and the central channel is
like a crystal tube. It's like a (crystal tent pole), whose bottom part is the
ATUNG, like a flame, and whose top part is the HANG. The blissful heat
permeates the whole body and burns away the obscurations. These three
levels roughly correspond to the three inner tantras of Maha, Anu, and
Atiyoga. Whereas Mahayoga is usually very detailed and very elaborate,

Anuyoga is simpler, and Atiyoga is even more simple. Whichever of these three feels more comfortable, do that, knowing that they are called completion stage. Completion stage beyond concepts is the view of Trekchö itself, which is like the driving force of the electricity that powers all machinery; without this, nothing will work at all.

If you are practicing according to the Atiyoga style, all visualization takes place within the state of Trekchö. It is always saturated by the view of Trekchö. Even in Mahayoga, all visualization is opened up within the framework of the samadhi of suchness, without which there is not a proper visualization practice.

The practice of tummo and all the different visualizations are just like the example of machinery: the view of Trekchö, the completion stage beyond concepts, is the electricity that drives the machinery. Both are necessary for the machine to run—the different parts and the power itself. In Dzogchen, all unfolds from rigpa. For example, the body composed of the six elements does feel happy and sad; this permeates the body. The key point is rigpa, but different karmas and conflicting emotions have been latent since beginningless time. These are defiled. However, the basis for the wisdoms is this body. As it is said, "The great wisdom abides in the body."

There can be many degrees of detail but to simply have one thought, "I am Dorje Phagmo, transparent like a tent of light"—that's it—and inside the tent there is a crystal pillar. You do not have to sit rigidly and keep the particulars in mind. There are the two syllables, the ATUNG and the HANG, which are warm and blissful. The heat burns away all the obscurations, habitual tendencies, and negative karmas. We do have plenty of fuel to make this fire blaze with obscurations, habitual tendencies, and negative karmas. Through this practice, they can all be burned away. We do have a material body with all these elements and in order to make use of it, do this practice.

The third point, *To enter consciousness in the vase at midnight,* is about the practice of dreaming and luminosity. As you drift off to sleep, try to remain in rigpa without falling unconscious. The consciousness in the vase refers to mind, the knowing aspect, and the vase refers to the physical body. Visualize that in the heart center, instead of the flesh and blood heart, there is a red four-petaled lotus flower, in the center of which

stands a tiny white a. It is brilliant and shining with white light. It illuminates the whole interior of the body and shines out through the pores in
all directions. All the surroundings are also lit up: your room, the whole
house, and outside the house to the distance that an arrow can fly. That
aspect of the brilliant letter a shining like a bright electric bulb illuminates everywhere, as I just mentioned.

This is the aspect of manifest luminosity. It is still a visualization but
the one visualizing, the mind, recognizes the essence, which is rigpa itself.
Simply rest in rigpa, while the visualization is taking place. That is the
empty luminosity. In this way, there are two aspects to luminosity. When
you lie down to go to sleep, keep the attention focused on these two aspects
of luminosity and rest in rigpa while the visualization is taking place. That
will ensure that dreams are transformed into luminosity. During the dream
state, the real nature of mind, the ground luminosity, is realized.

Concerning the practice of luminosity, there are three types of luminos-
ities: one is a dense or deep luminosity; the next is the light luminosity, the
same as light sleep; and the third one is the luminosity of the experiences.
The first one, the luminosity that is deep, like a deep sleep, is from the very
moment of falling asleep, when rigpa cuts the flow of thought totally. That
state of deep luminosity can last from the moment of falling asleep. There
are no dreams in this state. You remain in a constant, unbroken rigpa,
until waking up in the morning. This is possible because rigpa outshines
or totally sends back all conceptual thinking into the all-ground. Thoughts
have all totally subsided. The light luminosity is when the practitioner—
even lying with closed eyes in the state of sleep but with clear rigpa—is
able to see whatever goes on in the house and the whole surrounding area
as clearly as if it were daytime. Then the third type is the luminosity of
experiences, which here refers to the three experiences of bliss, clarity, and
nonthought. That is a kind of sleeping state, where all different things can
take place, such as traveling to other worlds and so forth. Actually, that is
not really a meditation experience; it is still temporary.

Again, the light or brightness from the syllable a, which shines out
from the heart center and illuminates the whole surrounding area, the
manifest luminosity, is an act of visualizing. The mind is the one visualizing, and when you look into this mind, it is empty; it is not a thing. It all
appears but with no self-nature. Yet that does not prevent or block off the
visualization from unfolding. Recognizing the mind while visualizing is

the unity of appearance and emptiness; it is also the unity of development and completion stages.

For example, the normal sadhana practice of carrying out the four activities of pacifying, increasing, magnetizing, and subjugating, is definitely to be carried out while not leaving the state of rigpa. It is the expression of rigpa that fulfills these four activities. Otherwise, merely thinking conceptually that you need to subjugate so and so or accomplish such and such quality will not succeed. In the same way, just to imagine white light streaming out from your heart center, in the state of luminosity, is conceptual. Instead, look at the one who is visualizing this and recognize the nature of mind. Then for sure it becomes the genuine state of luminosity. That was a short explanation of the line *To enter consciousness in the vase at midnight.*

To naturally clarify awareness at dawn pertains to when you wake up. The very moment you regain consciousness, sit up immediately. The A in the heart center shoots up your central channel and departs through the crown of your head as you forcefully say HA. The HA appears in the space in front of you, floating in the middle of space, and you remain in rigpa, the real one, not the fabricated one, for as long as it lasts. Yeshe or rigpa here mean the same, and it naturally has its own brightness or clarity. We do not have to make the clarity when it says *clarify*. Allow the natural clarity to be present, by imagining the A shooting out and remaining. Simply rest the attention on the HA in midair with undistracted rigpa. During this time, you can see how long the duration of nondistraction is. The practitioner can measure for him or herself at that point. For as long as nondistraction lasts, your attention is on HA and rigpa is taking place; when forgotten, it is forgotten. It is obvious, and like that. This will clear away all the effects of dullness or lethargy; it is a very profound method. But the main point of this practice is to dispel absent-minded dullness. It is most important to get rid of that.

The most vital, of course, is the daytime practice, giving experiences the seal of rigpa. The main point about sustaining rigpa is to keep that pure brightness, which is self-sustained, having some kind of natural stability to it. Giving experiences the seal of rigpa means that rigpa is not distracted by deceptions or whatever occurs. Rigpa does not fall under the power of experiences. That means pretty much remaining in nondistraction during the daytime.

Three of the four appear to be some creation of thought, development stage. But actually, since they take place within undistracted rigpa, they are created by the expression of rigpa, *(rigpa rtsal)*. They are not like normal thinking or imagining something, which is ordinary thought. For the person who has never recognized rigpa, there is no question about the mental activity that takes place; it is nothing but conceptual thinking. If there is sun, naturally there is sunlight. In the same way, if we are in the state of rigpa, there is also its expression, which can be manifested as described in these practices. It is not necessarily like normal thinking. If it is rigpa, what takes place is necessarily the expression of rigpa. If the state of mind is sems, it follows that what takes place is conceptual thinking.

In the Dzogchen teachings, it is said, "For the practitioner who wishes to attain complete enlightenment within this very body and lifetime, do not be distracted in daytime and do not sleep at nighttime." The idea of not sleeping at nighttime means to practice as mentioned here, so that even though it looks like you are sleeping, time is not wasted. It is unbroken practice. Other than that, with nondistraction throughout day and night, there is no way that enlightenment cannot be attained in one life, in this very body. But it doesn't necessarily even take a whole lifetime. The Dzogchen tantras say that if one practices like this, to *equalize buddhahood throughout the four periods,* then it doesn't take more than thirteen years. It is said many times like that. The reason is that practices such as this make it possible.

Of course, the foundation for all of the sutra and Vajrayana teachings is the preliminaries, because those are the practices through which obscurations are purified and the accumulations are gathered, perfected. After that come the other preliminaries of Trekchö and Tögal. The preliminaries for Trekchö consist of the vajra posture; HUNG yogas of speech; and the examining of origin, abiding, and disappearance of mind as well as the nalbab and sorshug. The preliminary for Tögal is the khordey rushan, the separation of samsara and nirvana. The companion or helper for both of these two preliminaries for Trekchö and Tögal is called abandoning the ninefold activities. When you do these practices *to equalize buddhahood during the four periods,* in combination with these preliminaries, definitely it is possible to attain complete enlightenment within thirteen years. One does not waste any time whatsoever.

MINDFULNESS

The method for achieving nondistraction is mindfulness. In the beginning, mindfulness is called deliberately applied mindfulness. Following training, you don't need to put effort into mindfulness any more; effortless mindfulness occurs naturally. After this, follows the dharmata mindfulness. In all, there are six kinds of mindfulness. This, itself, is the method for accomplishing nondistraction. When you have your cattle grazing on the mountainside, looking or watching after them to see whether they have been eaten by wild animals or not or whether they themselves are eating grass or not is called being the watchman. You are keeping an eye on something. To keep an eye on whether (rigpa) is distracted or not, you first need the effortful mindfulness. When you have slowly, slowly become practiced or accustomed to that, it becomes effortless. Finally, you reach dharmata mindfulness and wisdom mindfulness.

The scriptures mention six different kinds of mindfulness. When you reach the stage of exhaustion of dharmas beyond concepts, *(blo 'das chos zad),* recollection occurs as wisdom. This means that mindfulness has turned into wisdom, yeshe. When that takes place, you don't need to be mindful, because there is neither distraction nor confusion, day and night. It is said that mindfulness has become wisdom. There is another quote that says, "When rigpa has reached the natural space, analytical meditation naturally ceases. The watcher, the mindfulness, disperses, vanishing into emptiness. How delightfully free and easy it is in the space of nondual awareness." That's how it becomes in Dzogchen.

Well, if you ask what you need in the meantime, there is no way around being mindful. The main thing here is effortless mindfulness. When effortful mindfulness has become self-sustained, there is vivid, wakeful, natural mindfulness without any need for force or struggle, without any tenseness, just naturally alert. When you have become accustomed to that, there is only undistracted rigpa.

At present, rigpa is totally without any strength. It is completely wild or untamed; that is how mind is right now. Even though dharmakaya permeates all of samsara and nirvana, what appears and exists, if we don't recognize, we continue in this wild habit we have fallen into since beginningless time up until now. That is why it is necessary to apply mindfulness, whether according to Madhyamika, Mahamudra, or Dzogchen. According to Dzogchen, it's called awakeness or wakefulness, *(dran rig),* which means that mindfulness, *(dran pa),* and rigpa are mixed. In Mahamudra, it is called watchfulness, *(dran rtsis).* According to Madhyamika, it is called dran shes, which is a combination of mindfulness, (dran pa), alertness, *(shes bzhin),* and carefulness, *(bag yod).* An example for this is a newly wedded bride. When a newly wedded bride has been taken to the home of her husband, she is very careful. It is said that you should be like a newly wedded bride. She has no anger whatsoever. She speaks very softly. She moves (in a) very gentle way and does everything very nicely and carefully. That is the example of carefulness, *(bag yod pa).* This is *dran shes* and *bag yod* according to the path of Madhyamika. On this path, it is said that you need mindfulness, conscientiousness, and carefulness. Definitely you should not be mindless, thoughtless, and careless. You should have presence of mind, conscientiousness, and carefulness. These are the things that are necessary.

According to the secret mantra tradition of Nyingmapa, sights have the nature of body, sounds have the nature of speech, and thoughts have the nature of mind. These are called the 'three things to do, to carry.' Carry means to bring onto the path, or 'not to abandon.' These are the three things you should bring onto the path. In this state, you should be the watchman of mindfulness. In the beginning, it is necessary to have effortful mindfulness and clear wakefulness with effort. Even though it takes a little effort, slowly it will become spontaneous, like a river that flows constantly. A river does flow slowly sometimes and fast at other times. The placid flow of a river means that it is constant—slowly, peacefully flowing on without stopping. In such a way, you remain in a state of nondistraction. In this there should be nonmeditation.

There are some people who say they are meditating without being distracted. That is fine if they do so without thinking that. Be without distraction, but also be without meditating. (For) *sgom,* you can say meditate or cultivate. You do not say with meditating and distraction, right? It is without being distracted, without wandering, and without cultivating, meditating. There is a nondistraction that is cultivated, where you merely sit and hold onto the idea of being undistracted. There is a certain kind of Tibetan medicine against stomach disorder, which if it is not digested becomes poison in the stomach. This is like the idea of sitting and thinking, "I am not distracted; I am not distracted." It is simply a thought.

Actually, when you say self-existing wakefulness, that means it is not manufactured and that it is wisdom—undeluded, undistracted. In *rang byung ye shes, yeshe* means primordial knowing, *(ye nas ha go ba);* whereas, we are not aware of and do not know what we have since the very beginning. To know what is, since the beginning, is primordial knowing, yeshe *(ye nas shes)*. *Rang byung* means 'that which is in one's being already.' It is not forced or produced through effort. It is neither accepted nor rejected, and it has primordial knowing, yeshe. We do not say 'primordial not knowing.' It is primordially known. If this self-existing wakefulness is mixed with even a hair-tip of meditator and meditated, where the meditated is the self-existing wakefulness and the meditator is thinking, "Oh, I am completely undistracted," there is dualistic fixation. That will tie you down.

If we didn't have this defect, all sentient beings would be buddhas. Why not? All beings do possess the buddha-mind, right? From dharmakaya Samantabhadra down to the smallest insect, the self-existing wakefulness is primordially permeating. It does not say temporarily permeating. It says primordially permeating. If it were merely a temporary permeation, we wouldn't have known about it. We could think, "Oh, it is probably not from the beginning. Maybe it is only some temporary thing. I don't know." If it were just for some time, temporarily permeating, it would be difficult to know. However, that is not said. It is said to be primordially pervading. It has been permeating sentient beings since the very beginning.

If you ask what causes disaster or brings us down, it is the idea of there being a meditator and meditated. That is like taking self-existing wakefulness as something to meditate on and your conceptual mind as the meditator. You gain the intellectual knowledge of this being an empty and cognizant state and hold it in mind, thinking, "Ah, the lama has said there is something empty and cognizant; this must be it. Oh yeah, now I must not lose it through distraction." In this case, the whole thing is a fabrication. Without that, it is said to be unfettered and freed. There was nothing to tie the self-existing wakefulness since the very first. If something were tied again, it would have to be untied. But it is untied without fetter. Something that has never been fettered does not need to be untied; it is free, totally free. Untied, free, naked, fresh—this is not something we need to make. This is where we all have to arrive.

Most people relate to what is self-existing as being temporarily existing. They try to make what is primordially known, yeshe, into something that has to be newly understood, re-known. They make what does not need to be contrived into something artificial. They try to catch what does not need to be held. That is called conceptual delusion, being deluded by thoughts. This is what has happened life after life, lifetime after lifetime. It is said, "It is free from being fettered and beyond being freed also." This is very significant. If something were fettered, we would have to untie it; there would be a job to do. However, as it is primordially unfettered, we don't need to free it again. If it were tied or bound at first, then we would need to free it again. This is concerning the truth. However, right now as sentient beings, we are fettered. We are fettered by dualistic fixation, *(gnyis 'dzin),* and this needs to be freed. Nevertheless, what is to be freed and the one freeing it are the same here.

QUESTION: What is the difference between the mindfulness of effortful attention, *(rtsol bcas 'du byed kyi dran pa),* and the mere thinking that I am seeing the essence?

RINPOCHE: The first one, the mindfulness of effortful attention, is the thought: "Oh I wandered away, I must look again and then watch." The other one is just intellectual understanding. It is thinking, "I am watching. I am not distracted." That is thinking. Just to think "I am not being distracted" is fixation. You do not need to think this. You need to cast away the thoughts of distraction and nondistraction at that time. Simply thinking that you are not distracted doesn't help much. The practice is in the very moment of looking toward, not keeping any ideas that it is like this or it is like that, and so on. If you remain thinking, "I have no distraction," then it is like a person who maybe is not bound by an iron chain but by a golden chain. It is the same in being bound, because he is tied down. The golden chain will tie him down just as the thought "I am undistracted" will. It is like a nice chain made of gold. But if you do not even have the thought "I am not distracted," then it is merely unbridled thoughts, *(rnam rtog rang ga ma),* which is like being tied with an iron chain. If you think "Now there is no distraction. I am undistracted," you have fixation. You need to cast away both the thoughts "I am distracted" as well as "I am not distracted."

When it says in the Dzogchen teachings that one should be free from both accepting and rejecting, this is what it means. The most important thing is to recognize, first of all. First with the mindfulness of effortful attention, you should notice, "I am distracted; I was distracted." The thought "I have wandered" or "I was distracted" is the mindfulness of effortful attention, *(rtsol bcas 'du byed kyi dran pa)*. In the very moment of reminding yourself, you should let be in naturalness; whereas, if you start to think "I am without distraction," that is mere concept. At that time give up both the thought "I am wandering" and the thought "I am not wandering." You should just remain freely, *(cog bzhag)*.

There are three (sometimes four) kinds of freely restings: freely resting mountain, ocean, and rigpa. The first one is the view—like a freely resting mountain. A mountain does not move around, does it? Resting freely means the very immediate moment. If you start to think, "I am without distraction," you are not resting freely. Cast away both thoughts of distraction and nondistraction. Then you are free from both the watcher and what is watched. This is the most crucial point of the view. It is the borderline between buddhas and sentient beings. *(Rinpoche laughs.)* If you think you are undistracted, you are still a sentient being. It is the border between buddhas and sentient beings, like the line between light and darkness.

You might have recognized to begin with, but the important point is to resolve on it. If you have recognized but are unable to decide on it, you are still fettered and unable to be freed. In the first moment of noticing that you are distracted, you think, "Oh I was distracted." It is the occurrence of the mindfulness of effortful attention or simply effortful mindfulness. The mere thought of being distracted is effortful mindfulness. If you first think, "I was distracted. I shouldn't be distracted," these are two thoughts. In the moment of thinking "I was distracted," without either accepting or rejecting, you arrive directly in awareness. It is like the light on the torch (the moment) it is switched on. This is the most important point. You should give up the thought "I am not distracted." You don't need to think that. It is said, "Beyond the clouds of appearance is the sky of absolute meaning."

Give up all thoughts such as, "It is; it is not. I am distracted; I am not distracted." Then there is a clear wakefulness. This is the dharmakaya of profound brilliance, *(gting gsal chos kyi sku)*. You arrive in awareness itself. You do not need to think you are undistracted. Even without thinking that, you arrive in it; whereas, thinking it is like applying a patch. There is a defect. We say the wakefulness free from accepting and rejecting. We never say the wakefulness with keeping and casting away. That would be improper. If you think, "I am undistracted," you are keeping, establishing—fabricating the thought of nondistraction. If you establish the nondistraction and cast away the distraction, it is accepting and rejecting, or keeping and casting away.

The most important point is as Jigme Lingpa said, "The first instant is like one thousand ounces of gold." When there is no thought of being undistracted, it is like not wearing any clothes. It is naked, exposed. On the other hand, the thought "I am undistracted" is like putting on clothes. Isn't it like that? Look for yourself. *(Rinpoche laughs.)*

The correct view is said to be free from fixation, never fixating, right? To think "I am not distracted" is just fixation. It is an experience within conceptual mind, whereas, the self-aware wakefulness is beyond conceptual mind. Self-aware wakefulness is beyond concepts. As long as you think you are not distracted, you are fettered by concepts.

You do not need to do anything to awareness. Simply apply the gaze that is like a flash of lightning. Do like this. *(Rinpoche demonstrates.)* In that first instant, there is no need to think, "I am distracted" or "I am not distracted." If you train in this way, it is first class. That is what is meant by one thousand ounces of gold. It is very precious.

Give up both accepting and rejecting. Never do anything like this, thinking, "Oh now it is correct" or "Now it is not really right." The direct awareness is the first instant, when you are not engaged in even a hair-tip of affirming or denying, accepting or rejecting, keeping or casting away. You are not correcting anything. Although the first instant doesn't last very long, if you try to maintain it longer, you are maintaining it with concepts. Then it is no more cutting through; it is a slow cutting. *(Rinpoche laughs.)*

This is the meaning of Trekchö, cutting through. It is a very important term: cutting through or thoroughly cut. Although you have not cast anything away, if you think that there is still something to keep, you still have not cut through. If you think there is something to establish you still have not cut through. It is said, "Having abandoned the thinker and what is thought of, rest like a thought-free little child." Both what has been thought before and what can be thought of later have to be abandoned. Also, the thinker and what is being thought of, *(bsam dang bsam bya)*, can mean subject and object. Both have to be cast away. Having completely cast away the thinker and what is being thought of, *(bsam dang bsam bya rab tu spang du nas)*, watch like a thought-free little child, *(bsam med bu chung bzhin du blta ba bya)*.

A small child has not fully developed the aggregate of concepts. It doesn't have any ideas or notions like "I am going to do this and that. I am going to eat this and tonight I'm going to have my mother's milk." It is only in the immediate presence. It sees the breast and thinks, "Oh I want" and it sucks; this is the example. If you sit and think, "I am without distraction," you are not like a small child, because a small child never thinks, "I am undistracted." However, a small child hasn't been introduced to the essence.

On the other hand, we have been introduced to the naked present wakefulness. If we start to think, "I am undistracted," we have a concept. Actually, we need to abandon all five skandhas or aggregates. Without casting away the five aggregates, we will not obtain the five buddhas. As long as we are involved in the five skandhas, the five wisdoms remain far away. The skandha of concept should be abandoned. If you are involved or engrossed in concepts, thinking, "I am without distraction," you are conceptualizing. Actually, you do not need to think to be undistracted; simply sit like this. *(Rinpoche demonstrates.)* It is by itself completely awake. It is the unity of cognizance and emptiness, with an essence of awareness. As long as it is not deteriorated or lost, then you do not need to think you should avoid or refrain from being distracted. But when the continuity has been lost, it is finished.

MEDITATION AND
POST-MEDITATION

A true practitioner, who has recognized mind essence and stayed in the mountains in samadhi and is almost free from confusion during the day-time, might think, "Now I am free from confusion during the time of day!" But having descended to the village, he or she will soon think, "Oh no! My meditation is destroyed! I must have left it behind in the mountains! Before, when I stayed in the mountains my meditation was splendid—no delusion at all during the day and no distraction. Now, when I stay in the city, my meditation is lost and gone without a trace left!"

That is how it happens, and this is because of failing to mingle the practice with daily activities. The way to mingle the practice with daily activities is the sustaining freshness practice, or Dzogchen vipashyana, which I taught during the preliminaries. You should remain unmoved from the primordial purity of rigpa, resting in the natural face of aware-ness, the ultimate shamatha.

Awareness has a clarity aspect; without leaving this state, engage in the daily activities and endeavor not to get carried away. It is fixation, in any case, that ruins it for us. Most people, even when they are undis-tracted, are still fixating, like when they say, "This is a carpet; this is a window; this is a so and so." There is continuous fixating or thinking. When distracted, we are completely unaware, not noticing what we are thinking of—we are totally dissipated. It is said that on the path of dis-traction, the robbers of mara lie in ambush.

If you have recognized awareness, there is absolutely no point in being distracted. Once you have recognized awareness, the most import-ant point is to not wander. It does not help anything to think, "Oh, I am undistracted. Why should I look to see whether I am distracted or not? To check is fixation. There is no need to look." If you think like that, then everything is lost. Mindfulness is lost. Without giving in to fixation, rest in awareness.

The sorshug perfects the vipashyana by not moving away from naturalness and mingling it with the daily activities. Vipashyana means seeing clearly, in the sense of not only resting in the stillness (stillness meaning the empty state of shamatha), but also maintaining the clarity and awareness within that state. This is because the mind itself is the unity of being empty and cognizant. This unity is not something you have to make by trying to remain in a still state free from thought. The moment you look into that which is still, you see it clearly and vividly. That is called 'recognizing the vipashyana.' In this way, the view is mingled with the daily activities. Shamatha and vipashyana are a unity. That is why Dzogchen is a very precious oral instruction.

The principle is to mingle the four aspects of daily activities—eating, lying down, walking about, and sitting—with the view. We spend our whole life doing these four activities. In the daytime we sit, in the nighttime we lie down, we eat, and sometimes we move about. The important point is to maintain these four aspects of daily activities with the state of mind remaining in naturalness.

These two practices of the extraordinary shamatha and vipashyana are in fact the method for mingling meditation and post-meditation as inseparable. In the general teachings, it is said that the meditation state is contemplating all phenomena being like space, whereas, the post-meditation is regarding all phenomena as magical apparitions. However, that is made up; it is a fabrication. In the Dzogchen system, meditation and post-meditation are totally indivisible. There is no division between the two, because the post-meditation is the meditation state itself.

From the very beginning, Dzogchen differentiates between sems, mind, and rigpa. In Dzogchen, from the start you are introduced to non-meditation, nondistraction. Once you are introduced, the practice is then unfabricated naturalness. In the view, there is neither watcher nor anything watched. The ultimate is to be free of the watcher and that which is watched—because, primordially, rigpa is the one taste of cognizant emptiness. These two are unified and cannot be separated. With this unity, you do not need a watcher and something watched. To be free of the watcher and the watched is the ultimate. Then you do not have a subject and an object. However, beings have dualistic fixation: the grasped object and the fixating mind. Rigpa is empty of grasping and fixating, like the sky.

Dzogchen has no sessions or breaks. To repeat, these two only apply in the general systems of sutra and tantra. The meditation is like the space, and post-meditation is like a magical apparition, with no true existence. That is what you need to understand. The session is like space: there is no watcher and no act of watching. The post-meditation is like a magical display—all of existence and peace, the world and the beings, are like a magical apparition conjured up by a magician. Everything is nonexistent, yet appearing based on mind. Where everything is thought to be a magical illusion—everything is like a dream, like a reflection in a mirror, and so forth—there are still thoughts superimposed onto daily-life activities. Conversely, in equanimity, there are no thoughts.

In Dzogchen, there is no division between meditation and post-meditation—no sessions, no breaks—just remaining in rigpa only. Not everyone can do this, but the method to facilitate this is to rest for short moments, repeated many times. When you are distracted, that is the post-meditation; when you are undistracted, that is the meditation. Do you understand? It is all a matter of whether you are distracted or not. When distracted and you know it, recognize once more and be undistracted.

The difference between ensuing wakefulness and post-meditation is this: Ensuing wakefulness is when you have mingled rigpa with the path of action. Post-meditation is when you have acknowledged distraction. Wakefulness does not have either distraction or nondistraction. Space is the meditation and post-meditation is knowing the distraction. Post-meditation is when rigpa is lost, when you have been distracted. Ensuing wakefulness is when there is some kind of ongoing wakefulness, where the state of equanimity is not left, even though you interact with other people and do different activities. Every thought that occurs is spontaneously liberated, immediately.

QUESTION: What about Paltrül Rinpoche's lines from *Three Words Striking the Vital Point: However, as long as you have not attained stability... It is essential to practice giving up distractions. Divide your meditation into sessions.*

RINPOCHE: To determine if you are distracted or not, in the meditation session, remain in rigpa, and in the post-meditation, do not lose the continuity of rigpa. That is the result: no session, no breaks. As a beginner, if you do not engage in sessions and breaks, you will fall into carelessness.

Once you have strayed from rigpa onto the ordinary path, you know it. If you are doing a session, you are applying mindfulness. That is why you need sessions to train in the view.

QUESTION: Can you explain the quote from Guru Rinpoche that says: "If you are unable to mingle rigpa with the daily activities, you will not attain stability."

RINPOCHE: That is remaining undistracted. It is true that we fall under the power of distraction. If we are not able to mingle the view with daily activities, we have not established the view. This is because of not knowing nondistraction. We must not lose the continuity. A yogi who cannot mingle rigpa with the daily activities has not stabilized the view. Do not lose the continuity, and if you are unable to do this, given that there are many sicknesses and we have short lives, you cannot destroy confusion.

Honestly, this life is very short and there are so many diseases. So in between being disease-free and having our lives cut short, whenever we are able, we should train and take advantage of the opportunity to recognize rigpa. It is difficult when we fall under the power of sickness. Once rigpa has been stabilized, then whatever occurs, like sickness and suffering, it is all a display in the expression of rigpa. At that stage, we do not lose rigpa. If we are not stable, then it is like a small child before reaching maturity; the child is not independent.

It is like that when you are not stable in rigpa, but once you are stable in rigpa, then no matter what happens, it is only an expression of rigpa, an ornament. No matter where the yogi goes, in crowds of people, amidst a lot of chatter, or into negative circumstances, it is all training in rigpa. During the winter before Samten Gyatso's passing, I talked with him quite a lot, and on one occasion, he revealed some extraordinary secrets about his own practice. One day he told me, "I really have no great qualities, nothing marvelous to boast of, except that my distraction has vanished. The tendency to forget mind essence now seems to have vanished completely from my experience. No matter how much work piles up, no matter who comes in to see me, no matter how many people crowd into my room, the lucid quality only grows. I find that when I stay alone and uninvolved, with no task at hand, the clarity of awareness subsides somewhat, although I am not distracted. But the more people, the more bustle, and the more turmoil I am involved with, the more the strength of the awareness grows, just between you and me."[18] Of course, he recognized at the age of eight and he never gave up recognizing rigpa. There were instances of straying but mostly he did not give up the recognition.

All that is an expression of rigpa. When someone is a realized person, he or she is still able to function while resting continuously in rigpa. He or she is able to write scriptures and give teachings. That does not come about out of ordinary thought activity. This practitioner does not have to forget rigpa in order to act; it is all spontaneous. It is said that treatises overflow from within. All the buddhas and bodhisattvas are able to know and to express freely, even in a more perfect way than otherwise. That is not out of normal thinking. The real source of this is what is called the capacity, which is the unstructured basis for experience. This is how all buddhas can know everything, because they do not go blank and are stable in the state of rigpa. On the contrary, they have no impediment whatsoever. Once you have realized the nature as it is, you will automatically have unimpeded knowledge of all existing things. As a matter of fact, a truly realized being does not need to learn the alphabet and study the different topics of knowledge. It is all spontaneously known, even in one instant.

IT COMES DOWN TO THE VIEW

Having confidence and being without any fear, even at the point of death, are the measures or signs of success in practice. Having true confidence in yourself is very difficult, however. If you can say, "Now I have total trust in myself; whatever happens I will not go to the hells," you have attained stability in dharmata, in the essence of your mind. What we call hell is nothing other than a conditioned dharma, a phenomenon; it is not dharmata, the innate. Rebirth in the hells requires two things: the place and the one who takes rebirth. When dualistic fixation has been destroyed and duality has become oneness, how can there be a place to take birth? The hells have then been emptied. As long as you have the dualistic notion of "I and that," of hell, there is no liberation.

The sutras mention twofold egolessness. When resolving egolessness, you must resolve the nature of grasping and fixation. The lack of a self-entity in the grasped external objects is called egolessness of phenomena. The lack of a self-entity in the inner fixating mind is called the egolessness of person. To resolve that grasping and fixation, object and subject, have no self-nature is to realize the twofold egolessness. Then there is no hell in which to be reborn, because a hell needs both a place and a person. The one who takes rebirth is your mind and the place where it is reborn is the hell. With the realization of egolessness, how can there be rebirth in hell? In awareness, rigpa, the basis for hell has been destroyed. At that time, then, you will have confidence in yourself. You will look at yourself and say, "I have attained egolessness now; I have no grasping and fixation; I have no chance of taking rebirth in hell." You can think like that. (*Rinpoche laughs.*)

Unless at that time you feel sure that you really have destroyed grasping and fixation, then just saying, "Now there are no hells!" is completely useless. To mouth the words is like the pretense of saying, "I have no dualistic fixation!" This is only an intellectual understanding and is ultimately useless. In Kham, we used to put patches, extra pieces of cloth, on top of clothes. They were not the clothing itself. Intellectual understanding differs from the view in that it does not destroy dualistic fixation. The

Kagyü tradition teaches that intellectual understanding is like a patch; it will wear off, fall apart.

Once you have gained experience, having realized the egolessness of the person and destroyed the thought of 'I', how can you go to the hells? The two entities—the hell to be born into and the self who will be born there—arise from thinking 'I'. When grasping and fixation have been destroyed, you will have self-confidence. Otherwise you will think, "Despite all this dharma practice I have done, what will happen later in the bardo? How will it be? Will my practice prove successful? Will the yidam deity practice have been useful? The bardo is full of great fears and overwhelming sounds, colors, and light rays, and incredible difficulties in the hot and cold hells. When I arrive there, what will happen?" Without having resolved the view, you will have this kind of doubt. (*Rinpoche laughs.*) Having real self-confidence is the true measure, the test.

Think about the conditioned nature of life. How can that which is dependent upon other things be permanent and lasting? As it is said, "Life is conditioned, it has no permanence." Were our lives unconditioned to begin with, we could do whatever we want. But where in this life is there permanence? It is said, "Objects are perceptions; they have no true existence." All objects are the unreal, natural forms of emptiness. Perceptions or appearances themselves have no concrete existence. Only when our fixation on appearances has been destroyed will appearances or perceptions be beyond benefit and harm.

What we call a hell is a mere perception, an experience. Everything we experience now is just perception. "Objects are perceptions; they have no true existence." They do not possess even the slightest concrete existence. Think about that. Objects are just experience; they don't really and truly exist.

Furthermore, it is said, "The path is confusion; it has no reality." When you failed to recognize your own essence, which is the primordial purity, you strayed onto the path, where you experience the six realms of sentient beings. That is the path aspect. The path is confusion; it is not real.

It is said, "Mind essence is the natural state; it has no concreteness." This means it is without cause and conditions. The natural state is a synonym for the profound emptiness. The nonarising essence is the same as primordial purity. The Dzogchen teachings say that the essence is primordially pure; in Mahamudra they say that the essence is nonarising, beyond origination. The Kagyüpas recognize the nonarising essence, the essence beyond origination. This is in fact the same as primordial purity, merely a different choice of terminology. Your mind essence is the natural state; it has no concreteness.

Finally, it is said, "Mind is conceptual thinking; it is free from ground and root." What we call mind is just conceptual thinking, concepts moving to the five objects, conceptualizing the five objects. It is merely one thought moving after the other. Without an object, a thought cannot possibly move. Objects are the visible forms for the eyes, sounds for the ears, taste for the tongue, touch for the body, and joy and sorrow are the mental objects. If we do not experience these objects, a thought cannot move. Thought movement depends on objects; thoughts are linked to objects.

Inside is the mind, in between are the five sense organs and their five doors, and externally there are the five sense objects. These three components are continuously linked together. Once we realize egolessness, the link breaks; as long as it is not cut, we are connected to samsara.

How can you really trust yourself? Unless you realize the correct view, it is very difficult to have self-confidence. No matter how much you pretend to have self-confidence, without realization it is only intellectual understanding. You might think, "Now it's all right, now it's fine. I'm not going to the hells." This is merely fabricating the thought. Actually, hell exists nowhere apart from you. Once you have realized emptiness, hell has no separate existence, because the hells are deluded experience created by an unvirtuous mind.

Think about what we call hell. It should have a location and should originate from somewhere. The workers who torture sentient beings in the hell realms should have fathers and mothers. All this fire needs to be made; the molten iron must be heated up. The *shamali* tree must be grown by somebody. In the four directions lie the forests of trees with sword-leaves, the swamp of rotten corpses, the great fiery pit of embers, and so forth. All these are created only by the habitual patterns of deluded experience, made by unvirtuous mind. They do not really exist.

Once you realize egolessness, everything is all right. Without having realized egolessness, you cannot make things right. It is taught, "If the understanding of emptiness is all right, everything is all right. If the understanding of emptiness is not all right, nothing is right." Know that once you have become used to emptiness, an emptiness that is not mere intellectual understanding, everything will be all right. Nothing will be incorrect, unpleasant, or unsuccessful. When the understanding of emptiness is not all right, it means that you have not realized the correct emptiness, the true samadhi. Everything will be mere intellectual understanding. You will simply be keeping and perpetuating an intellectual idea.

As I have mentioned before, even if you have recognized mind nature, if you do not attain familiarity with this, then thoughts will arise as enemies and you will be like an infant in a battlefield. As thoughts are inherent, they will arise and make enemies. When the beings of the six realms pass away, they are carried away by thoughts, overpowered by their conceptual thinking. If you have attained stability in nonconceptual original wakefulness, however, there will be no place to go and no one who goes, even if you were thrown down to the lowest vajra hell. There is a saying: "Even if the three thousandfold universe is turned upside down and the monster of the lord of death opens his mouth and the abyss of the hells is opened, not a hair of your body will move." Attaining stability in the truth of dharmata is like this. What it actually comes down to is the view.

When you have realized the view, you will have confidence and trust. This is what self-confidence means: you should act in such a way that you are not ashamed of yourself, never thinking, "I am no good." When you know for sure "I'm good; I'm first class," this is self-confidence. Not despising yourself, "I have no distraction; I have no confusion; I have no fixation; I have attained stability in awareness; there is nobody like me." This should not be mere intellectual understanding. It should be known without any pride or arrogance or conceit. This is the pride of self-confidence. You will think, "Who is superior to me?" (*Rinpoche laughs.*) I am just joking. When Milarepa looked at sentient beings, he thought they were crazy. When sentient beings looked at Milarepa, they thought he was crazy.

THE UNITY OF
TREKCHÖ AND TÖGAL

In Dzogchen, the essence is primordial purity, the nature is spontaneous presence, and the capacity is a unity. You know those words, right? To recognize that your own essence is primordial purity is called Trekchö. To recognize that the nature is spontaneous presence is called Tögal. That these two are indivisible—that the primordially pure essence and spontaneously present nature are indivisible—is called the all-pervasive capacity.

The originally empty, primordially pure essence is dharmakaya. The spontaneously present nature is sambhogakaya. Their indivisibility, the capacity, is nirmanakaya. The unity of essence and nature is the unobstructed basis for arising. The three kayas are your identity. Recognizing them as your own nature is the svabhavikakaya (the essence body). The guru points out the svabhavikakaya. When it is pointed out and you recognize, it is called knowing mind essence.

What is that? Our essence, which is primordially pure wakefulness, is established through Trekchö. Our nature, which is spontaneously present, is established through Tögal. When you recognize this—that your own nature is the indivisibility of these two as a unified capacity and that all three are inseparable—it is called svabhavikakaya. Recognize your essence as being primordially pure, and that the natural expression of this primordial purity is spontaneously present. Finally, recognize that the spontaneous presence is devoid of a self-nature; it is perceived, yet devoid of self-nature, an insubstantial presence. That is called the unity of Trekchö and Tögal.

What is meant by spontaneous presence, lhundrub, *(lhun grub)*? It is the expression of primordial purity. It is rainbow light, major and minor bindus, and bodily forms of the deity. The deities are the manifestation of body, the syllables are the manifestation of speech, and the attributes are the manifestation of mind. All these are devoid of self-nature. No matter what appears as the deities, even though they are visible, can you take hold of them? Are they tangible? Whatever manifests as speech, all the syllables of India and Tibet and elsewhere, can you take hold of them? You cannot. They are immaterial. That is what is meant by insubstantial.

The manifestations of mind are the attributes of the vajra, buddha, ratna, lotus, and karma families. An example would be the vajra. No matter which of these attributes appears, you cannot take hold of any of them, can you? The manifestations of qualities are palaces, thrones, jewels, and so forth. Whatever you experience of these, does it have any concrete nature? It doesn't. The manifestations of activity, such as the swords, the hooks, the vajra crosses, and the flames, are also visible but intangible.

In short, Dzogchen is the unity of kadak, *(ka dag),* and lhundrub. All other teachings of course have the unity of primordial purity and spontaneous presence, but those spontaneously present displays need to be created through visualization. This is like creating your own deity. But actually, the deity is already present as the unity of appearance and emptiness. Because our primordially pure essence is Trekchö, and the spontaneously present nature is Tögal, their unity is the unity of the support and the supported.

All the practices of Kriya, Upa, Yoga, Maha, and Anu are based on the deity as something extraneous to us. But in Atiyoga, the deity is primordially present as our nature without any need to be created. That is the short path. We first acknowledge that this is so, train in that, and attain stability in it. In short, it is the unity of kadak and lhundrub.

One's self is the deity; the deity is oneself. In the *Kar Ling Zhi Khro,* a text of a peaceful and wrathful practice of Karma Lingpa, this is one of the lines: "The deity is one's self; one's self is the deity." It is not some other; it is not somewhere else. The kayas and wisdoms, the support, Trekchö, and the supported, Tögal, are indivisible. This is extremely significant. The body, which is the sole support, is the experience of being the same thing as appearance and emptiness. Completion stage is the emptiness and development stage is the appearance. Primordial purity and spontaneous presence are indivisible. Emptiness and cognizance are indivisible.

According to Dzogchen, you recognize that the kayas and wisdoms are indivisible and that kadak and lhundrub are indivisible. They do not come from elsewhere. You recognize this to be so, train in it, and attain stability in it. That is basically what Dzogchen is about. Concerning kadak, which is Trekchö, it is sufficient to just recognize the moment free from thoughts of the three times, free of concepts. While in the state of Trekchö, the view, you apply the key points of the instructions of Tögal. Then you see the deities. This is not like Maha and Anu, where you have to accomplish a deity that is not already present but is somewhere else. It is not the same. It's also not like the sutra system, which says, regarding the aggregate of form, that everything—from this piece of wood up to and including the state of omniscient enlightenment—is empty and devoid of self-entity. You have to think like that, which is called the yoga of realizing egolessness. But in this case, you practice within awareness, the unity of the primordially pure essence and the spontaneously present nature, the unity of Trekchö and Tögal.

It is claimed everywhere that everything is empty, but everywhere means in the vehicles from Theravada all the way up, in the nine yanas, right? All of them say that everything is empty. There is no way around that, and not just now, but since the beginning. Everywhere it is claimed that everything is empty—but the fact that it is not empty of kayas and wisdoms is the dharma system of the Buddha. If everything were utterly empty, there would be no kayas and wisdoms, which are the qualities, the most precious. Those are not empty. Not empty of the qualities means that appearance and emptiness are a unity. If appearance were substantial, there wouldn't be the empty aspect, and it is not like that.

The sambhogakaya body is like a rainbow you can see, but can you grab it? All the things in this world are visible and also tangible. We can see and grab them, but our essence, which is the unity of being cognizant and empty, is intangible. Our essence cannot be destroyed in fire. Can the kayas and wisdoms be destroyed? That is what is meant by unformed yet spontaneously present. Unformed refers to being empty; spontaneously present refers to the cognizant quality, the perceiving. That is the path of Trekchö and Tögal without need for anything other. Trekchö is established through the four times without three, free from the three conditioned, changing times. The fourth is the unchanging time of dharmata. If you divide them up into four times, past, present, and future all change, right? But the timeless time doesn't change, does it? This is called the great timeless equality, the timeless time of the unceasing state of the view. This is called the fourth time of great equality. This is the ultimate view of Trekchö.

Don't follow the past, invite the future, or analyze the present ordinary mind. As it is said, "Don't follow the past; don't invite the future; then there is the ordinary mind of the present, which is naked, open, and direct." There is nothing other than that. It is free of the three times; the timelessness is called great equality. This time is unceasing. When there is great equality, this great equality is first acknowledged and then realized. If there is such a yogi, he doesn't get distracted; he doesn't get deluded. When caught up in the three times, one is distracted. But when there is the great equality, how can there be any distraction? Everywhere it is claimed that everything is empty. Everyone says that the essence is empty, but it is not empty of kayas and wisdoms. That is what is meant.

In short, when connected to the four empowerments, the kayas and wisdoms are empty appearance, empty luminosity, empty bliss, and empty awareness. This is the intent of the four empowerments. Dharmakaya is the body of space, right? Sambhogakaya is the body of light, rainbow light. Nirmanakaya is the body of the six elements, earth and water, fire and wind, mind and space; that is the vajra body. The mind of the dharmakaya is called rangjung yeshe. The mind of the sambhogakaya is called possessing the fivefold attributes, (mtshan nyid), which are the discriminating, mirror-like, dharmata, equality, and all-accomplishing wisdoms, the five wisdoms. The attributes refer to the colors white, red, and green, etc. The dharmakaya is rangjung yeshe; the sambhogakaya is the five wisdoms; and the nirmanakaya is the wisdom of nature as it is in all that exists.

In short, while dharmakaya is all-pervasive like space, sambhogakaya is distinctly and uniquely present like the sun and moon. Nirmanakaya is like a rainbow acting for the welfare of beings. When we talk in terms of qualities, there are three, but in terms of the reality, there is one identity, which is svabhavikakaya. How do you apply that in practice? The essence is Trekchö. You need to recognize rigpa. The nature is Tögal. When the five kayas, fivefold speech, five wisdoms, five qualities, and five activities are fully manifest that is called reaching fullness. After reaching fullness, there is the exhaustion of phenomena and concepts.

Without a sense of wakefulness, wouldn't we be corpses? Don't project, don't concentrate, don't hold in, don't send out. Just remain free of thought; leave it as it is. In the first and second moment, are there any thoughts? But due to our bad habits, again a thought comes—then gently look toward what thinks. Doesn't the thought vanish by itself? Doesn't it? It vanishes, collapses, becomes empty by itself. Do you need to do anything at all to it? Simply recognize it. In the thought, hasn't it vanished totally without a trace?

Our essence, which is rigpa, cannot really be harmed by thought; it is only that the essence gets caught up in thinking. When not recognizing the essence, as a normal person, awareness is caught up in thought, dragged around within the three realms and the six classes of beings. But the practitioner who recognizes rigpa is likened, at that moment, to a hair put in a flame. Does it have any power left? In this way, when you recognize rigpa, all thoughts lose their power.

The moment you recognize rigpa, any thought, no matter how it is, loses immediately. All thought gets overcome by rigpa; that is the equality of rigpa. For an ordinary person, the thinking, which is the expression of rigpa, overcomes rigpa. It is overtaken by its own expression. Right now, we cannot say that recognizing rigpa lasts for a long time. It is possible to convince ourselves, saying, "This is rigpa. This is rigpa," but that is only imagined. What we need to see is the unimagined. Dharmadhatu is not something that we think of. It is as Vairotsana said:

> Within the inconceivable naked state of dharmadhatu,
> Place ineffable awareness undistractedly.
> If a thought arises, it arises out of yourself and dissolves into
>   yourself.
> There is no basic view, meditation, or instruction superior to this.

Everything is condensed into that. If you want it short, that's it.

The thought moves out of your own awareness, but the moment you recognize what thinks, doesn't it dissolve within your own experience of your own essence? This is the heart of all view, meditation, and conduct. You don't have to imagine rigpa; it is unimaginable:

Once you recognize your own essence, at that moment, none of the thoughts about past, present, and future can remain, right? When there is no thought remaining, how could there be any creation of karma? How can there be any misdeeds and obscurations sticking to them?

Like the empty space in this room, it is not night now, so it is light, right? There is some sunlight. You could say that the light here is the unity of clarity and emptiness. This is the external example. Can the karma and disturbing emotions remain in midair? In short, we should recognize the unity of empty cognizance. We don't need to pinpoint what the empty quality is or what the cognizant quality is.

When recognizing rigpa, you find that you fail to find any word for how it is. It is the ineffable natural face of awareness. It's inexpressible, but you need to see that. The empty and cognizant qualities are not two different entities; they are indivisible. That is why you can recognize your own nature at that moment. It is not that the cognizance needs to look at some other thing and say, "Oh now I see you; there it is." No need to look here or there. At the same time, isn't experience vivid and wide open? Nothing is blocked, right? You are not blacked out?

This is maybe too easy? Since this is so easy, we find it hard to trust that. But it is totally free from pinpointing anything. This is the essence. Beings don't have two minds, one good and one bad, but our mind gets confused into clinging, labeling things, which is called fixation. Directly, you have to recognize your own essence, which is vividly present and not labeled or fixated upon. Right now, don't you vividly see everything before your eyes? However, are you holding or fixating on anything? That is why it is said that a yogi is like a small child in a temple. A small child sees all the things that are there and doesn't form any thoughts about what is what. A yogi should be like that. That is the example, which means 'free of fixation, not holding anything.' It is our holding and clinging that forces us to be in samsara. The cognizant quality is an intrinsic part of rigpa. It is unobstructed. If it is blocked, as when we get knocked out, you don't know anything. It is not like that.

Look around. Isn't everything vividly present? Right now, isn't it like an infant in a temple hall? But a small child doesn't recognize itself. It is only an example for no fixation. The small child feels but has no concepts; for example, it knows that fire is fire, water is water, and so forth, but its concepts are not fully formed yet. There is sensation. If it is pleasant, it laughs; if it is painful, it cries. A child feels. A yogi feels, but it is a feeling that becomes empty feeling. A yogi's mind is unobstructed; everything is known. But actually, the five aggregates need to dissolve. The fixation and the aggregates of form, feeling, perception, formation, and consciousness need to fall apart, collapse—meaning there's no fixation. That doesn't mean that they vanish, but when there is no fixation on them that is sufficient.

It is only the mind that holds onto the objects. The objects don't hold onto the mind. That is what is meant by appearances don't harm. There is only harm once one chases after them. Do the five external objects chase after the mind? It is only the mind that gets caught up in objects. The objects do not get caught up in the mind. It is like Tilopa said, "You are not bound by what you experience; you are bound by your clinging to it. So, cut through your clinging, Naropa."

Rigpa doesn't get caught up in what is experienced, but sems does. Sems has a connotation of being caught up, like being sticky; it sticks to appearances. But rigpa doesn't push you toward tengawhat is experienced. Experiences appear within rigpa, as reflections in a mirror. No matter what appears, white or red and so on, does that influence the mirror in any way? It is like that. The black form doesn't dye the mirror black, does it? Yet it appears. Anything can appear in a mirror, right? To be like a mirror is the analogy for not holding anything. When awareness grabs hold of what is experienced, it loses its own stability, doesn't it?

The ultimate practice in Dzogchen is Trekchö. It is like this: Don't follow the past. Don't follow the future. Don't accept or reject the present moment. That is Trekchö. Don't accept or reject and don't analyze anything about present wakefulness. Right now, all past thoughts are gone, aren't they? Has any thought of the future come yet? Usually we analyze, speculate, and conceptualize. We are reconnecting the present thought to the next thought, but the intent of Trekchö is to not hold onto anything. It cuts through the string of beads. There is nothing to reconnect. The past thought has vanished; the future thought hasn't been formed; and the present thought has not been conceptualized. That is Trekchö. It is a thorough cut.

QUESTION: What is the biggest danger we should try and avoid in Trekchö?

RINPOCHE: The worst pitfall is to imagine emptiness, to think emptiness. Emptiness is supposed to be unimagined naked dharmadhatu. When you don't imagine, you can't describe it either. Actually, the view does not lie within something that can be imagined or described, because the emptiness we have is something that just is, by itself. By itself means that fire is hot by itself, water is naturally wet. In the same way, our mind is, by nature, empty. This is not something we have to imagine. Once we assume or imagine, it becomes a pitfall. Our nature is unimagined naked dharmadhatu; it is already so. That is why all the teachings say that you don't need to accept it or reject it. You don't need to hope or fear. You don't need to do anything.

As this is your nature, the unimagined naked dharmadhatu, you don't need to accept it or reject it. You don't need to hope or fear. You don't need to avoid or doubt, right? It is because it is naturally so. Understand that. The nature of space is emptiness, isn't it? It doesn't have a physical form, a sound, a smell, or some taste, does it? It is not that somebody made it so, is it? It is just naturally like that. That is what is meant by nature. In the same way, the mind of beings is empty by nature. The nature of space is empty, but merely empty; it has no cognizance. Does empty space have the ability to feel pleasure or pain? Our mind is by nature empty cognizance, isn't it? The root error, or pitfall, comes when you start to imagine or think, "Oh, this is how it is." In short, your present wakefulness is not something you need to do anything to; you do not need to improve it, change it, or alter it. Simply let it be as it already is. That is enough.

Isn't it better to train in what is easiest? Otherwise, you have to do the lesser, the medium, and the higher types of one-pointedness, keeping one-pointed. Next, you have to get to the three levels of simplicity; and then to the one taste; and, finally, to the lesser, medium, and highest level of nonmeditation. These are, of course, very precious, but they are meant for the gradual type of person. Dzogchen, on the other hand, is immediately pointing out rigpa. It means that all mental doing has been disbanded at that point. The four times three levels of Mahamudra are different levels of mental effort. In Dzogchen, from the very onset, you connect with four paths without three. You are giving up all mental doing, which is past, present, and future. What is left is the timeless great equality. It doesn't belong to one of the three times. Time is only our thought of time. When the thoughts of past, present, and future do not exist, there is no time. Isn't time merely our thinking? Here we are talking about being free of thought.

It is a naked state of dharmakaya. On the Mahamudra path, first there is one-pointedness, which means that in the beginning, you need to make mind one-pointed. You do this first with shamatha, and then with vipashyana—the lesser degree, the medium degree, and the higher degree, which is called simplicity. Next are the three levels of one taste: lesser, medium, and once you get to the dharmakaya throne of nonmeditation, you have reached the naked state of dharmadhatu. Ultimately, it is the same, identical. This is the reason why Dzogchen is the shorter path. You begin with nonmeditation, because one-pointedness, simplicity, and one taste are actually the doings of mind. In nonmeditation, the naked state of dharmadhatu, you finally connect with the essence itself. That is what is meant here. It is called the unimaginable naked dharmadhatu, not the imaginable. That is the same as the nonmeditation.

QUESTION: What is the biggest pitfall for Tögal?

RINPOCHE: It is to hope that something may happen and to fear that it won't. The key point is to let whatever manifests, manifest, without any hope or fear. Thinking, "This is not so spectacular. Now what should I do about it?" or "Yeah, I do see something, but it is probably not really how it should be"—and, thereafter, being unhappy and suspicious.

As they say in Kham, "If the tulku doesn't screw up, he will naturally be realized." It means if he doesn't get involved in this and that, his realization will naturally bloom. In the same way, simply remain in the Trekchö view, from within, and whatever manifests or appears, let it appear. It will naturally be perfected. That is the key point. That is the saying in Kham: if the tulku doesn't do this and that, he will naturally be able to perform miracles and be clairvoyant. If your view of Trekchö is fine, you don't have to do anything about Tögal at all. As a matter of fact, there is no act of meditating in either the case of Trekchö or Tögal. Not even as much as an atom that needs to be imagined. It is all automatic, as they say in the West.

In Dzogchen, the view is Trekchö, the meditation is Tögal, and both are automatic. The view is Trekchö, primordial purity. The meditation is Tögal, spontaneous presence. It is called meditation, but there is no act of meditating even on as much as an atom. Just do the three postures and the three gazes, apply the key points, and leave the mind in rigpa. Let your attention remain in rigpa. Is there anything to imagine? Nonetheless, while there is no imagining, there should also be no forgetting. You should be without imagining but also without forgetting—because mara lies in ambush when you forget. Remain without imagining, meaning without meditating and also without being distracted. To be undistracted, in the beginning, you need to try your best, but later on it becomes effortless. In the beginning, it isn't automatic. In the beginning, you have to try your best, put your heart into it. After a while, it will be like something you have learned by heart.

If you need to think of it, that is what creates all of samsara. It is our own thinking. The western word automatic is quite a significant, profound word. No need to think of anything if it is automatic. The naked state of dharmadhatu doesn't need to be thought of or imagined.

QUESTION: Someone who has attained accomplishment, like Milarepa, can traverse freely through solid rock and mountains; is that due to his having realized that all phenomena are rainbow lights and bindus?

RINPOCHE: No, it is not. The external phenomena are the four major elements of earth, water, fire, and wind; these are phenomena. In between, we have the flesh, blood, bones, body heat, breath, the aggregates, and sense factors. All phenomena, since the beginning, lack concrete existence. In last night's dream, we experienced joy and sorrow, countries and places, houses and castles, and so forth. We can dream of all these things, but once we awaken, whatever we dreamt no longer exists. Right now, all phenomena definitely exist due to the power of confusion. But when we are not confused, when we have attained stability with the wisdom of all the buddhas, as a sign that they are primordially nonexistent, we can traverse freely through everything. If all these phenomena were primordially existing, the buddhas would have annihilated them in order to traverse freely through them, but it is not like that; that is not the case.

Phenomena do not even possess an atom of concrete existence; however, due to the unvirtuous mind, we feel like they do. For example, to a hell being, their hell seems to have material existence; to the one who has conceptual thoughts, hell truly exists. When one is free from conceptual thoughts, there is no real hell. That is the example we can use. The fact that we can attain rainbow body is due to our having these two: the primordially pure essence and the spontaneously present nature. The empty aspect is unobstructed, and the apparent aspect is the rainbow lights and the major and minor bindus with celestial palaces, buddhafields, and deities. These are the qualities of the primordially pure essence. As its qualities, we cannot say that there are no deities; they certainly appear in the bardo.

When the ground appearance manifested, what we call the 'eight gates of spontaneous presence' (arose)—the seven pure gates and the one impure gate. These can be condensed into two, pure and impure. The impure is the six classes of sentient beings. These gates appear simultaneously and are vividly manifest. When the ground appearance manifested, we became confused and, therefore, are now wandering in samsara. Later on, when awareness arrives at what is called the ground, when we attain stability in that primordial purity, when we take control of our own territory, when we have reassumed the primordial purity, we can manifest as rainbow-colored light and so on. This is called 'attaining mastery of rebirth and exit.' We can manifest the great transformation body. If not, it is said that awareness is established in the inner space. It is liberated in the youthful vase body, wherein mind has dissolved yet is unobscured. That is the state of freedom or liberation.

It is said that first nonexistence is explained, then existence is explained, and finally the union of existence and nonexistence is explained. This concerns talking about mind essence. When we explain nonexistence, we talk about the primordially pure essence. When we explain existence, we talk about the spontaneously present nature. When we explain the union of existence and nonexistence, we discuss primordial purity and spontaneous presence as a unity. They are not separate; they are not apart. The above mentioned are the qualities of rigpa.

When we say space, *(dbyings)*, and wisdom, *(ye shes)*, it means, in this context, that awareness-wisdom is established in the inner space; it has to arrive in the inner space. First, it was lost in the progressive order of straying into samsara. Then, in the reverse order, it has to arrive back in primordial purity. None of the phenomena of appearance and existence, grasping and fixation, possesses even a hair-tip of concrete existence. Primordial purity does not have any concreteness, right? From the space of primordial purity, all the phenomena of samsara and nirvana appear. A dream appears while not existing and all the various phenomena of the waking state are within the framework of grasping mind. When you are free from grasping mind, when you are established in awareness-wisdom, it is like a movie that has collapsed. Right now, we can produce images with a movie, and we can hear sounds from a tape recorder. Through these we can create the third world war, but if the movie falls apart, there is no third world war. That is the meaning of the collapse of confusion.

The reason why Milarepa could traverse freely through rocks and mountains is that he had attained stability in primordial purity, in his own self-existing wakefulness. It was not necessary for him to use force to pierce his body through solid matter. The collapse of confusion is quite an amazing thing. (*Rinpoche laughs.*) Samsara is created by conceptual thoughts. Once thought has been destroyed, samsara has been destroyed as well. If samsara had begun with some concreteness, it would be impossible to destroy it.

QUESTION: Is there ever any mention of samsaric phenomena being rainbow lights and bindus?

RINPOCHE: No, samsaric phenomena are not rainbow lights and bindus, rather, earth and rocks and so forth, coarse matter. Pure phenomena are the rainbow lights and bindus, especially what are called the sounds, colors, and light rays, *(sgra 'od zer gsum)*. Impure sounds are like the barking of a dog or the sound of knocking on a table. When the pure phenomena of sound, color, and light rays appear, the nature of speech is obscured by our ordinary speech, and the mind, which has the nature of light rays, is obscured by our conceptual thoughts. Among the three, the sound is speech, the colored light is body, and the light rays are mind. There are signs among the three called symbol, meaning, and sign. First the signs appear, then the meaning. In our present impure state, our body obscures the enlightened body. The dharmakaya free from complexities has been obscured by our body, the unceasing sambhogakaya has been obscured by our speech; and the nirmanakaya, which is beyond arising, ceasing, and dwelling has been obscured by our mind.

Our body, speech, and mind are conditioned, and they obscure the unconditioned three kayas. The vajra is unconditioned. It is not born, and it cannot be burnt or washed by water. Our body can be burnt and flushed away. When we talk about vajra body, vajra speech, and vajra mind, we use the word 'vajra' because it means changeless, impossible to destroy or annihilate.

QUESTION: Sometimes it is said that samsaric phenomena are primordially pure; why is that?

RINPOCHE: Samsaric phenomena are impure. Concerning samsaric phenomena, it is as I previously said, "First nonexistence is taught," which means the empty essence is being explained. "Next existence is taught," which means the cognizant nature is being explained. Finally, the unity of existence and nonexistence is taught." This means that the essence and nature, the primordial purity and spontaneous presence, are a unity within awareness. Therefore, it is said that samsaric phenomena appear while being nonexistent. In regard to their essence, they don't exist; in regard to their nature, they are manifest, appearing while not existing. They are primordially appearance and emptiness beyond meeting and parting.

It is impossible to separate the empty and the apparent aspects. Pure phenomena are the unity of primordial purity and spontaneous presence. That kind of phenomenon is devoid of fixation and attachment; it is like a rainbow appearing in the sky. It is visible but it has no self-nature. There is nothing to grasp or hold, right? Therefore, the example of a rainbow is used for pure phenomena; it cannot be caught or taken hold of, whereas our phenomena have become coarser. First, it begins with the world called 'neither being nor nonbeing'. Then, we were deluded into the three realms of samsara. So, we wander into samsara through the apparent aspect.

First, the four formless realms of the four limitless perceptions appear. Then, the seventeen worlds in the realm of form appear. Next are the six worlds of the desire gods in the realm of desire and the rest of the six kinds of sentient beings. As it has been said in the words of the Kagyü masters, "Mind essence co-emergent is dharmakaya; appearances co-emergent are the light of dharmakaya." This refers to pure phenomena. Impure phenomena, on the other hand, have become more and more gross. The four realms of infinite sense factors are without form, right? When it says, 'the realm of form in the seventeen god realms,' it means that they have form, but it is not a form of flesh and blood. It is said that the physical form in the seventeen form realms is made of light. It is also said that 'becoming more and more gross' means that in the six worlds of the desire realm, physical form is made of flesh and blood.

With Tenga Rinpoche

SIGNS OF PRACTICE

Concerning signs of practice, if you have cultivated a deity, you should receive the vision of it. There are the general signs such as lights, smoke, mirage, and so forth. You can actually perceive these signs of blessing with your eyes, in a concrete way. Then there is what we call experiences, which are not actuality and are not dream, but somewhere in-between. We can have the experiences of bliss or emptiness, or we might think, "Today my awareness is really amazing; it is naked and unchanging. It is free from fixation, free from the experiences of bliss, clarity, and nonthought. My awareness is incredible; today my meditation is really good!" Understand that these are merely experiences. Still, they are also signs of practice.

Sometimes we find it impossible to practice, very difficult to sit; we feel depressed and angry, irritated. These are called unpleasant experiences, *(rtsub nyams)*. There are two kinds of experiences, pleasant and unpleasant ones, *(bde nyams)*. These are all signs of practice, of which there are two kinds, good ones and bad ones. It is not sure that all signs of practice are good ones, but no matter what happens, within the sky of primordial purity, all these experiences are like mere clouds. The sky sometimes has clouds and sometimes is free from clouds. Sometimes it rains, storms, and snows, which are the unpleasant experiences. Sometimes there are pleasant experiences with sunshine and rainbows and no clouds. Yet still these are only experiences.

The signs of practice fall into two categories, experience and realization. The true sign of practice is that your mind is without fixation; it is natural, without any difficulty. Another true sign of practice is that your mind is endowed with devotion, faith, and compassion, just as the sky is filled with the warmth of sunlight. When your mind feels such ease, it is a good experience. It is the best sign and the greatest accomplishment. The real accomplishment is to be unharmed by the experiences of bliss, clarity, and nonthought, while being free from the two kinds of hindrances to meditation, which are called drowsiness and agitation. These two are what can temporarily harm your practice.

Drowsiness is divided into three: drowsy, dull, and obscured, *(bying, rmugs,* and *thibs)*. Scatteredness, *('phro ba),* is also divided into three: scattered, agitated, and absent-minded, *('phro, rgod,* and *'thor)*. Each of these two divided into three makes six. When our mind has the slightest, subtlest fixation, for example, we don't even notice that we are obscured and have become oblivious. Conversely, we become excited or agitated, so that our mind feels like it is impossible to be quiet. We feel we cannot cut the thoughts. Cutting the thought should be automatic. Anyhow, this is called agitation, *(rgod pa)*. Drowsiness or dullness, *(bying ba),* is when we don't really know whether or not there is any clarity or sharpness in our awareness. That is called obscured awareness. Once we are free from these two, dullness and agitation, our awareness has no obscuration whatsoever concerning the view. Whether or not this lasts for a long time depends on our habituation, how much we are accustomed to it. The method for this, at this point, is to have devotion upward and compassion toward sentient beings downward. If we have that, then, as it is said, "In the moment of love, the empty nature dawns nakedly."

Upward devotion and downward compassion are both love, *(rtse ba)*. In this love, our body, speech, and mind feel kind of overwhelmed. If, at this moment, you are able to look inwardly, it is like a sun unobscured by clouds. This is the way through which the Kagyü and Nyingma practitioners were able to attain enlightenment without being learned, without having much theoretical understanding; they were able to gain experience. This is known as 'experience as the great adornment of awareness.' In this way, experience adorns awareness. What does that mean? It means that experience should be without fixation. Experience with fixation is without any benefit. It should be without fixation. What does the swift attainment of enlightenment depend upon? It depends on having faith and devotion upwardly to the Three Jewels and having compassion downwardly to our mother sentient beings. You should have these two. Then, "In the moment of love, the empty nature dawns nakedly." The nature of emptiness is manifested nakedly. "This is devoid of errors."

What is the meaning of unity? When not tainted by the two extremes of eternalism and nihilism, there is unity. If you fall into either the view of eternalism or the view of nihilism, you have fallen into limitation and will not progress on the correct path. In the view of the unity of being empty and cognizant, the cognizance clears away the extreme of nihilism and the empty aspect clears away the extreme of eternalism. This unity is what we talk about as being the unity of emptiness and cognizance suffused with awareness. That is the special quality of Buddhism, the unity. Without this unity, one will say it is eternal, another will say it is void. Once you stray into this error, the eternalist and nihilist views will create grasping and fixation, the holder and the held.

What is the supreme method or means? It is devotion and compassion. In the beginning, you need a fabricated devotion; a natural, unfabricated devotion will not happen right away. It is said that uncontrived compassion does not occur immediately. How do you do it? As you get more and more stable in awareness, you will feel, "Sentient beings are unaware of this most precious thing, which is like the Buddha in the palm of my hand." Naturally, you will feel compassion toward sentient beings; that is how it will be. Devotion is like this, where you feel, "How fantastic to be able to cut through the very basis and root of confusion. It is incredible, this perfection of all virtues, exhaustion of all faults. There is nothing superior to this awareness." This is how you gain faith. The devotion and compassion that do not need to be fabricated are present within this awareness, in your own essence.

In order to have natural compassion, you first need the fabricated one. In the Dzogchen teachings, it is said that, externally, only unfabricated natural compassion and devotion are important. However, inwardly, if you look carefully, you will see there is no way around having contrived faith and compassion to begin with. Both need to be fabricated. These are the two greatest techniques or means. These are one hundred times better than meditating on deities and reciting mantras. It is said that upward devotion and downward compassion are worth more than visualizing one hundred deities and reciting mantras.

If you know how to meditate on emptiness, then that alone is completely sufficient. But if not, this kind of compassion is extremely effective. It is the special quality of Buddhism. For the best, you need both emptiness and compassion, which is called emptiness suffused with compassion. However, if you haven't truly recognized emptiness correctly, then you will be able to be guided to emptiness through compassion alone. If you are a person who has this true compassion, then you are like the summer warmth that melts the ice. In the summertime, the rain falls without any hindrance; likewise, there is no obstruction for devotion. If you look into the essence of this devotion, then you directly meet the naked awareness there; that is why devotion is so precious, important. As is said, "There are two kinds of bodhichitta: one is emptiness and the other is compassion." It is said, "Bestow the blessings that emptiness suffused with compassion may dawn within my being."

The main or special quality of Buddhism is, at best, to recognize emptiness, the mind essence; but if not, then you should definitely practice compassion. As I have mentioned before, imagine your mother in front of you and then somebody comes and cuts off her arms and legs and head—how will you feel? That is called compassion. This compassion is an overwhelming feeling. For example, imagine that you are tied down with chains and ropes, or otherwise incapable of moving, and your mother is in front of you. Then the enemy arrives and first they pull out her eyes and strangle her and then take out her heart. How will you feel? You will feel love and compassion, which are called compassion. Anyone can cultivate compassion. Through the blessing or virtue of this compassion, emptiness will dawn within your being.

Why is it never taught that one cannot have emptiness without compassion? It is like having water: it will also be wet, liquid. If you have the understanding of emptiness in your being, you will also have compassion. Why is this? First, there is not a single sentient being who will attain enlightenment without understanding emptiness. Once you realize emptiness, you will think, "Oh, if only all sentient beings could realize that, oh how nice it would be." Anyone would feel like that.

THE ULTIMATE GURU
SADHANA OF SIMPLICITY

The preliminaries:

Ah
Yedröl rigpa dön-gyi kyab
Rigtsal nyingjei semkye do
Marig zungdzin bagchak gek
Rangdröl longdu tsamchey do
Nampar dagpey chötrin kün
Ye she rölpey jinchen phob

Ah
Primordially free awareness is the ultimate refuge.
With the compassionate expression of awareness, I form the
    resolve.
For the obstructers — ignorance, dualistic fixation, and habit —
I draw the boundary within the self-liberated expanse.
With the offering clouds of complete purity,
Let the display of wisdom shower down a great resplendence.

The main part:

Ah
Nangsi zhirzheng kyilkhor dir
Ngowo rangzhin tukje yi
Khordey yongla khyabpar dal
Madag payi mingmey pey

Dechir odi yana dag
Deshek nyingpö rangzhin chen

Chalug jizhin dezhin du
Machö lhugpey tsüldu kye

Nyingkhar rikdü dorje sem
Yeshe sempey ngowor zhug
Tindzin sempa küntu zang
Makye yedzog chenpor sal

Aн
Within this mandala, appearance and existence as the manifest
    ground,
Essence, nature, and capacity
Are present throughout all of samsara and nirvana.
There is not even the word impure.

Therefore, even I, Uddiyana,
Possess the nature of sugatagarbha.
Whatever I wear, that's how I look;
Visualize me in the manner of unfabricated naturalness.

In my heart center is Vajrasattva, the embodiment of all families,
Abiding as the essence of the wisdom being.
The samadhi being is Samantabhadra,
Uncreated and vividly present as the original great perfection.

The invitation:

Ah
Döndam shekzhug mi-nga yang
Nangtsül tsamdu chendren no
Tadey meypar zhugsu sol
Ro-nyam tawey jalchak tsal

Künzang namröl chöpey chö
Dribnyi dagtsang longdu shag
Yangdag nyidu jeyi rang

Dümey döndam chökhor kül
Gyünmi cheypar tagzhug ney
Mikmey getsok drola ngo

Aн
Though ultimately you are not subject to coming and going,
I invite you as mere appearance.
Please remain indivisibly.
Paying homage with the view of equal taste, I bow down
And present you with the offerings of Samantabhadra's display.
I apologize within the expanse of the two purified obscurations
And rejoice in the ultimate nature.
Please turn the true Dharma wheel of timelessness
And remain unceasingly and perpetually.
I dedicate all nonconceptual virtue to sentient beings.

The recitation:

Ah
Nyingkyil tingka kyabchen ü
Tigle tongdrön dangmey kyil
Rigdang lug-gyü a-ru sal
Rangbab drenrig gyünmi chey
Tamchey sangye zhingdu gyur
Ah Ah Ah

Aн
In the center of my heart, amidst the great all-pervasive blue,
In the middle of the lamp of the empty bindu,
The chains of manifest awareness are vividly present as an a.
Through unceasing natural wakefulness,
Everything is a buddhafield.
Aн ан ан

Do the vajra recitation.

The conclusion:

Zhinang tsaldang rölpa nam
Zhiying kadag longdu tim
Düsum dümey getsa kün
Korsum yongsu dagpey ngo
Kyabdag lhün-gyi drubpa yi
Dekho nanyi tashi shog

All expressions and displays of the manifest ground
Dissolve back into the primordially pure expanse of basic space.
By means of the total purity of the three spheres,
I dedicate all roots of virtue, both timeless and throughout the three
    times.
By the spontaneously present all-pervasive sovereign,
May the auspicious thatness be present!

Unable to refuse the person who requested,
This was written by the simple Uddiyana.

COMMENTARY ON THE ULTIMATE GURU SADHANA OF SIMPLICITY

The preliminaries:

> Aн
> Primordially free awareness is the ultimate refuge.
> With the compassionate expression of awareness, I form the
>   resolve.
> For the obstructers — ignorance, dualistic fixation, and habit —
> I draw the boundary within the self-liberated expanse.
> With the offering clouds of complete purity
> Let the display of wisdom shower down a great resplendence.

What I have done here is fiddle around, patching together a guru yoga, but I tried to combine it with the ultimate, the true meaning.

First are the preliminaries. Aн is the syllable representing the ultimate state. *Primordially free awareness* is the ultimate yidam, the ultimate refuge. The *expression of awareness* is supposed to arise as compassion, and that is the ultimate bodhichitta. These two comprise refuge and bodhichitta.

Next, as in all sadhanas, there is the expelling of the obstructing forces. Here, the obstructing forces are *ignorance, dualistic fixation,* and *habitual tendencies.* When resting in the state of self-existing naturalness they are self-liberated. That is the ultimate protection circle.

The offering clouds of complete purity refer to the total purity of everything: All that appears and exists is nothing other than the *display of wisdom.* All sights, forms, sounds, tastes, textures, and so forth are the display of wisdom in their pure nature. These two lines include both the offering and the consecration.

The main part:

Aḥ

Within this mandala, appearance and existence as the manifest
    ground,
Essence, nature, and capacity
Are present throughout all of samsara and nirvana.
There is not even the word impure,

Therefore, even I, Uddiyana,
Possess the nature of sugatagarbha.
Whatever I wear, that's how I look;
Visualize me in the manner of unfabricated naturalness.

In my heart center is Vajrasattva, the embodiment of all families,
Abiding as the essence of the wisdom being.
The samadhi being is Samantabhadra,
Uncreated and vividly present as the original great perfection.

Here the syllable AH is the unity of the nonarising and unceasing
qualities. The unity of the essence, which is nonarising, and the nature,
which is unceasing or unobstructed, is the syllable AH.

All that appears and exists is the unity of primordial purity and spontaneous presence. That is the meaning of *the manifest ground*. The manifest aspect is spontaneous presence, and the ground itself is primordial
purity. That is how everything is, and this is the ultimate *mandala* within
which *essence, nature, and capacity* pervade everything, *all of samsara and
nirvana* without exception. Since this is the way it is already, it is not our
construct or visualization. Everything by nature is already the mandala
of all-encompassing purity; therefore, *there is not even the word* impurity.
That is why I too, quite justifiably, also have buddha-nature myself; so
there is nothing wrong in writing a guru yoga. Since everything is pure,
even I, Uddiyana, possess the nature of sugatagarbha.

Visualize me in whatever clothes I happen to be wearing, just like
that. There is no need to add or subtract anything. Whatever I look like,
however you remember or think of me, is how you should imagine me.
Do it without fabricating anything; freely and easily bring it to mind.

That is the manner of the development stage here.

Now for the recitation, the text says that in the *heart center is Vajra-sattva, the embodiment of all families.* There are three sattvas: first, there is the samayasattva, which is me. Next, there is the wisdom-being, the jnanasattva, which is Vajrasattva. Then, in Vajrasattva's heart center, is the samadhisattva, which is Samantabhadra. These are perfectly and primordially present, without having to be visualized. Just simply imagine that they are already there.

The invitation:

> Aн᠋
> Though ultimately you are not subject to coming and going,
> I invite you as mere appearance,
> Please remain indivisibly.
> Paying homage with the view of equal taste, I bow down
> And present you with the offerings of Samantabhadra's display.
> I apologize within the expanse of the two purified obscurations
> And rejoice in the ultimate nature.
> Please turn the true Dharma wheel of timelessness
> And remain unceasingly and perpetually.
> I dedicate all nonconceptual virtue to sentient beings.

Next is the invitation, which is a substitute for the normal sequence of a sadhana, where you invite the wisdom-being to arrive and dissolve separately from the samaya being. Here, there is a resemblance or imitation of that.

Again, the AH signifies that it is combined with the ultimate. It says that the ultimate state does not possess such attributes as *coming or going,* but still *I invite you as mere appearance.* There are two aspects: how it is and how it appears to be, the real and the apparent. The real is called the *ultimate, (dön dam);* what we call the *apparent, (nang tshül),* is how it seems to be. So, in a mere seeming way, please appear and *please remain* or take a seat in a way that is indivisible, meaning that the nature and the appearance are indivisible.

Next *paying homage* or respect is done by *the view of equal taste.* What is meant by *equal?* This means that there are not two types of buddha-

nature. The buddha-nature that one bows down to and one's own buddha-nature are not two entirely different things. As a sentient being not
recognizing one's buddha-nature, there is a difference. Therefore, while
recognizing the buddha-nature, the one that bows and the one being
bowed to are not separate anymore; they are of *equal taste*. That is the
meaning of paying respect by recognizing buddha-nature.

Samantabhadra's buddha-nature and our buddha-nature are not two
different things. The moment we recognize our own buddha-nature, we
are not different from Samantabhadra; we are of one taste. In all the different aspects of sadhana—refuge, bodhichitta, making offerings, and so
forth—there is a relative and an ultimate way. The ultimate way of paying homage and bowing is by recognizing the view, within which there is
no bower, or anything being bowed to.

The next line, *And present you with the offerings of Samantabhadra's
displays,* is not like the normal case of the vast imagined offerings of
the bodhisattva Samantabhadra. Here it is the dharmakaya buddha
Samantabhadra's display, which encompasses everything from the very
beginning, in the sense that the elements, aggregates, sense factors,
sense objects, and so forth are by their very nature the male and female
buddhas and bodhisattvas. In this way, everything is already the display of the expression, display, and adornment of the dharmakaya buddha Samantabhadra, including all the objects of the five senses of sight,
sound, smell, taste, and texture, which are by nature the offering goddesses. That is the ultimate type of offering, which encompasses all types
of offerings—outer, inner, innermost, and ultimate *thatness* offerings. All
of the following are combined with the ultimate in the same way. It is
a resemblance of the deity emanating the offerings to be offered to the
deity himself. Since everything is from the beginning already the display
of Samantabhadra, it is also an offering to Samantabhadra as well.

I apologize within the expanse of the two purified obscurations. Here there
is a double word for *pure* and *clean, (dag* and *gtsang)*. The *two purified
obscurations* actually encompass all different types of obscurations; they are
the obscuration of disturbing emotions and the cognitive obscuration.

In the next line, *the true nature, (yang dag nyid),* is playing on a quote
from the Buddha Maitreya, who said, "Look truly into the true; when
seeing truly, you are utterly free." The true here is the ultimate, which is
acknowledged by recognizing the state of rigpa. That is called seeing the

true. When truly seeing, then, it is utterly free. That is the basis for one's rejoicing.

In the next line, *timelessness* means beyond the concepts of past, present, and future: the fourth time of the great equality, which is the unceasing perpetual state within which all buddhas' activity takes place. All buddhas' activity is said to be the unceasing wheel of perpetuity, which is another word for timelessness, beyond concepts. It is not that there is a rigpa of the past, a rigpa of the present, and a rigpa of the future. Rigpa itself transcends any notion of time. That is the ultimate dharma wheel.

Within the Seven Branches in a normal practice, there is also the request to remain and not pass into nirvana. As a substitute for that here, there is the request for rigpa to *remain unceasingly and perpetually,* even though rigpa itself is unceasing and unchanging.

Dedicating the mass of nonconceptual virtue to all beings is the dedication. Usually there is the concept of what you dedicate, which is the good you have done; the concept of to whom you are dedicating, which is all sentient beings; and the concept of the practitioner, the one who dedicates. These all involve focus or concepts. Here, however, dedication is without holding any such concepts in mind, and that is the ultimate dedication.

Guru yoga should always contain the Seven Branches. Bowing down is the first branch, the branch of prostrating, of paying homage. Second is the branch of making offerings, followed by confessing. Next is rejoicing and then requesting to turn the wheel of Dharma. The sixth branch is beseeching not to pass into nirvana but to remain, and the seventh is the branch of giving the merit to all sentient beings. As a resemblance of these, all seven of the branches are included here.

The Seven Branches are extremely important in Vajrayana practice. It is said that if one does a short sadhana in which the Seven Branches are complete, it is equal to doing a long puja that lasts a whole day. The purpose of the Seven Branches is to eliminate the seven mind poisons—ignorance, the five general poisons, and greed or avarice. Each of the Seven Branches purifies one of these poisons: rejoicing purifies jealousy, offering purifies greed, bowing down purifies pride, and so forth.

In Vajrayana, the practice of the ultimate Seven Branches is vital, in that it facilitates gathering the accumulations and purifying the obscurations, the fruition of which is accomplishing the three kayas. It brings the state of buddhahood closer, and it is the root of skillful means. In the sutra system, there are the three vajras: the vajra-like samadhi; the samadhi of courageous movement, and the samadhi of illusion. In both sutra and tantra, the Seven Branch practice is extremely important. The samadhi of suchness, the dharmakaya, is the vajra-like samadhi. The second one, resembling sambhogakaya, is the courageous samadhi or the samadhi of courageous movement. The third one, the samadhi of illusion, corresponds to the nirmanakaya level. When combined with the Seven Branches, accomplishing these three samadhis also accomplishes the three vajras. It is said that there is nothing more precious than these when practicing deity yoga.

The recitation:

> Aн
> In the center of my heart, amidst the great all-pervasive blue,
> In the middle of the lamp of the empty bindu,
> The chains of manifest awareness are vividly present as an a.
> Through unceasing natural wakefulness,
> Everything is a buddhafield.
> Aн aн aн

Do the vajra recitation.

Now comes the actual recitation. Preceding this was the practice to accomplish body. Now this is how to accomplish speech.

In the first line, *the great all-pervasive blue,* or all-encompassing blue, is actually the manifestation of space, the lamp of pure space.

> Through unceasing natural wakefulness,
> Everything is a buddhafield.

Here, the vajra chain is *vividly present as an* a. In the general sadhana, we say oм is white, aн is red, and нung is dark blue; but here aн is like the sky. It is also okay to imagine it as white, but why not imagine that it is dark blue, like Samantabhadra? The main thing is its sound; the shape is of aн.

Next the wakefulness is *unceasing*. The natural flow of awareness is unceasing. This means that wakefulness is innately stable and unchanging or unceasing and *everything is a buddhafield*.

Vajra recitation means that when you inhale, it is the sound of AH; when the breath is retained in the body, that too is the sound of AH; and when you exhale, it is also the sound of AH. The seed-syllable of the mantra is combined with inhalation, retention, and exhalation. If you do this for twenty-one breaths, it is said that for the rest of the day, the breath is blessed with the vajra recitation, and it will continue by itself. The main practice here is to imagine it once and then rest in rigpa.

The conclusion:

> All expressions and displays of the manifest ground
> Dissolve back into the primordially pure expanse of basic space.
> By means of the total purity of the three spheres,
> I dedicate all roots of virtue, both timeless and throughout the three
>   times.
> By the spontaneously present all-pervasive sovereign,
> May the auspicious thatness be present!

Finally, comes the conclusion. The first two lines in this verse mean that the manifestations of the ground dissolve back into the ground itself. In the next line, *timeless* means without the notions of past, present, or future. The *three spheres* are that which is dedicated, the one who dedicates, and the one to whom it is dedicated. Transcending these three notions is called *the total purity of the three spheres*. The *all-pervasive sovereign* is Samantabhadra and becoming spontaneously present, may the auspicious goodness of the ultimate *thatness* be present. These last two lines comprise both the aspiration and the line of auspiciousness. May Samantabhadra be present is the aspiration, and the presence of the view is the auspiciousness.

> *Unable to refuse the people who requested,*
> *This was written by the simple Uddiyana.*

I was requested so many times to compose this, and, finally, I wasn't able to refuse. *Uddiyana* is Sanskrit for my name, Urgyen, and I wrote this simply, like someone who is simple-minded and not very clever. This was not written by a human being but a dumb beast.

QUESTION: Does one visualize oneself as the guru or is the guru in front of one?

RINPOCHE: It is a self-visualization, not in front. Most guru yogas and guru sadhanas employ front visualizations. Somebody else is imagined to be out there to whom you pray. But in this guru sadhana of the buddha-nature, there is no duality of one's buddha-nature here and another there; so, there is no real point in having a front visualization.

Actually, this is a good prototype for guru sadhanas of others as well. All you do is change the name in the line: *Therefore, even I, Uddiyana.*

QUESTION: When you do the vajra recitation, do you actually say it out loud or silently?

RINPOCHE: Both ways; you do vajra recitation both with and without sound. The vajra recitation with sound, however, is very subtle, almost whispered.

If you do vajra recitation in the early morning, 21 cycles with sound and 21 resting in rigpa, the 21,670 breathing cycles of the day will be transformed into vajra recitation automatically. The same goes for lying down to sleep at night, if you perform 21 breathes with sound followed by 21 without. The actual number of breaths in a day is 21,670 assuming one is not sick; otherwise, there will be more or less.

The vajra recitation with focus, with sound, involves imagining the seed-syllable and quietly repeating the subtle sound AH ... AH ... while exhaling. Having completed 21 breaths, rest in rigpa for 21 breaths. If you do so, the vajra recitation will continue automatically for the rest of the day or night.

I have turned into a charlatan here, but it is a good prototype for other people's guru yoga; simply change the name.

THE ASPIRATION THAT IS A
POINTING-OUT INSTRUCTION
FOR THE BARDOS

Om ah hung
Chokdü gyalwa malü gongsu sol
Dag gi togmey düney datar bar
Düsum sagdang yöpey gewa dey
Dagzhen malü jangchub tobpar shog

OM AH HUNG
Victorious Ones of all times and directions, pay heed to me!
By the virtue gathered throughout the three times and what I
    possess
From beginningless time till now,
May I and all others attain enlightenment.

Dema tobkyi tserab küntu yang
Lamzab dzogchen nyingpö döntog ney
Chönyi ngönsum gongphel tseypheb ney
Zagchey phungpo ökur drölwar shog

In all my lives before attaining it,
May I realize the profound path of the Great Perfection,
And after Manifest Dharmata, Increased Experience, and Reaching
    Fullness,
May the conditioned body be liberated into the body of light.

Neychö dragpö du ngel mijung zhing
Lama yidam pawo khandrö tsog
Mig gi wangpor ngönsum jönney ni
Wangkur lungtön khachö tripar shog

Avoiding the intense pain of the life-force being broken off,
May the gurus and yidams, dakas, and dakinis
Appear before my very eyes,
And may they grant me empowerment, prediction, and lead me to
    the celestial realms.

> Düjey mitag chiwa jungtsa na
> Gyuwey ugchey bemrig drelwey tse
> Zhenchag trülpey nangwa michar war
> Neylug chökü ngangla neypar shog

When my time has come and impermanence and death have
    caught up with me,
When the breathing stops, and body and mind go apart,
May I not experience delusion, attachment, and clinging,
But remain in the natural state of dharmakaya.

> Gyulü döchey jogpey dübab na
> Nangphung trarag togpa gagpey tse
> Trülmey kyabdal dömey yingchen la
> Bemrig drelma tagtu drölwar shog

The moment the illusory material body is left behind
And appearances and aggregates, gross and subtle thoughts cease,
May I be liberated as soon as body and mind separate
Into the undeluded and all-pervasive primordial space.

> Madag jungwa sosor dengpey tse
> Dagpey ö nga madrey ösal ngang
> Togmey öngey dorje lugu gyü
> Yermey chigdrey chönyi tarchin shog

When the impure elements dissolve, one into another,
In the luminous state of the pure and distinct five-colored lights,
May the nonconceptual vajra chain of the five lights,
Indivisible and unified, be perfected as dharmata.

Hung chen tröpa sinpey zukchen sog
Hung drey tongsum malü gangtsa na
Rigtong hung drey neydu ngoshey ney
Dragtong dragcha tabur togpar shog

When the great HUNG is in the form of wrathful demons
And when the sound of HUNG fills the billion worlds,
May I recognize the vital point that they are the HUNG sound of
    empty awareness
And realize this empty resounding is like an echo.

Shinjey shemey tsogkyi kortsa na
Gyobsö drödey trülpa yingdag ney
Drey ngang trülpey nangwa michar war
Yidam zhi trö kuru tongwar shog

When surrounded by the horde of Yama murderers,
May the confusion of being attacked and slayed, taking flight and
    being chased, naturally dissolve.
Without giving rise to the deluded experience of fear,
May I see them as the forms of the peaceful and wrathful yidams.

Dungkhang barwey dechen zhalyey ney
Trowö tsognam neyney gyepey tse
Jigzuk sinpö kuru michar war
Men ngag nyingtig gongpey döntog shog

When the swarm of wrathful ones burgeons forth
From the Blazing Palace of Great Bliss in the bone mansion,
May I not see them as the forms of horrible demons,
But realize the meaning of the pithy Heart Essence.

Tsitta rinchen gurkhang zhalyey ney
Zhiwey tsognam yingsu yalwey tse
Nangwa rulog ökur sharwey dü
Rigpa ökyi longdu timpar shog

When the multitude of peaceful ones vanishes into space
From the Jewel Dome Palace of the heart,
The moment the experience transposes and manifests as forms of
     light,
May awareness dissolve into the expanse of luminosity.

>   Dringül tsayi khorlo drelwey tse
>   Jigpey geygyang drugtong dirtsa na
>   Ah hung zhi trö dangsu ngoshey ney
>   Rigtong kyemey draru drölwar shog

When the wheel of channels at the throat disintegrates,
With a thousand roaring thunderclaps of terrifying laughter,
May I recognize this as the AH and HUNG song of the peaceful and
     wrathful ones
And liberate it as the unoriginated sound of empty awareness.

>   Sangney dekyong khorlö zhalyey ney
>   Tabshey karmar nying gar treytsa na
>   Detong zagpa meypey neylug dey
>   Lungrig umey nangdu tsüpar shog

When the red and white of means and knowledge converge at the
     heart center
From the Bliss Sustaining Palace of the secret place,
May this natural state of undefiled bliss and emptiness
Cause prana and mind to enter the central channel.

>   Chönyi bardö ngangla neypey tse
>   Sherig lungma tendu masong war
>   Rangdröl kadag chenpö döntog tey
>   Zhentong chözey ngangla neypar shog

When dwelling in the state of the bardo of dharmata,
May consciousness not stray into oblivion.
But realizing the meaning of self-liberated great primordial purity,
May I remain in the other-empty state of exhausted phenomena.

Chönyi ngönsum denpa tongwey tse
Nyenpo drendzin gompey lodrel ney
Kadag zeysar khyölwey döntog tey
Togmey trödrel ngangla neypar shog

When seeing the reality of manifest dharmata,
May I be free from the conceptual remedy of fixated mindfulness.
Realizing the meaning of arriving at primordial purity, the stage of
    exhaustion,
May I remain in the nonconceptual state devoid of constructs.

Jatsön na nga dreypey zhalyey ney
Yeshe ngayi gurkhang gochey tey
Kudang tiley zhingkham gangwey tse
Ku nga yeshe ngadang jalwar shog

When the door to the dome of the five wisdoms opens up
In the celestial palace of intermingled five-colored rainbows,
And the realm is filled with bodily forms and spheres,
May I meet with the five kayas and five wisdoms.

Tigle tongdrön ösal zhalyey su
Ku ngag yeshe ngadang jaltsa na
Nyemjey nyinang tetsam meypa ru
Künzang dömey ngangdu timpar shog

When meeting with the five kayas and five wisdoms
In the luminous palace of the lamp of the empty bindu,
May I, free from the doubt of vacillating dualistic experience,
Merge into the primordial state of Samantabhadra.

Semnyi drönma zhidang ngöjal ney
Tigle tongdrön ösal zhalyey su
Lhündrub bubla tenpa tarchin ney
Ying-rig namkhey ngangdu phowar shog

Having met face to face with the four lamps of mind essence
In the luminous palace of the lamp of the empty bindu,
May I reach perfect stability in the sphere of spontaneous presence
And shift to the expansive state of space and awareness.

Chöku tongsal drönmey barwar shog
Tongnyi rigpey chöku tobpar shog
Gagmey nyinang longku tobpar shog
Rangrig tarchin trülku tobpar shog
Kusum tobney zhendön jeypar shog

May the empty and luminous lamp of dharmakaya shine.
May the dharmakaya of knowing emptiness be attained.
May the sambhogakaya of unceasing nondual experience be
    attained.
May the nirmanakaya of perfected self-awareness be attained.
Having attained the three kayas, may I act for the welfare of others.

This aspiration for the bardos of dying and of dharmata, which liberates through hearing, was composed by Omniscient Longchen Rabjam.

COMMENTARY ON LONGCHENPA'S BARDO ASPIRATION

This small text by Longchenpa is an aspiration as well as a pointing-out instruction as to what should happen in the bardo. First one makes the wish to quickly attain enlightenment, both for oneself and for all other beings. Until that happens, when my time is up, and this material body dies and I arrive at the moment when mind and body separate, may I be able to attain liberation in that very moment. As the text states:

> Victorious Ones of all times and directions, pay heed to me!
> By the virtue gathered throughout the three times and what I
>   possess
> From beginningless time till now,
> May I and all others attain enlightenment.

> May the gurus and yidams, the dakas, and dakinis
> Appear before my very eyes,
> And may they grant me empowerment, prediction, and lead me to
>   the celestial realms.

If I do not attain the rainbow body in the bardo, may the gurus, yidams, dakas, and dakinis please appear before my eyes and lead me to the celestial realms. That is the prayer. Since all conditioned things are impermanent, at the time of death, when my rigpa and body have separated:

> May I not experience delusion, attachment, and clinging,
> But remain in the natural state of dharmakaya.

Through the kindness of having practiced the dharma, may I not be outwardly attached to the objects of this world or to my own material body. Not falling into grasping, may I realize my own inherent nature, my buddha-nature. Recognizing this and remaining, may I attain stability.

Longchenpa starts going into the details of exactly what happens the moment the different elements dissolve one by one. There are many types of dissolution stages: coarse, subtle, and extremely subtle. He prays to not get confused and to be liberated into the all-pervasive primordial space. The foremost is to be liberated into dharmakaya:

> When the impure elements dissolve, one into another,

Our bodies possess the six elements of earth, water, fire, wind, consciousness, and space. These impure elements dissolve:

> In the luminous state of the pure and distinct five-colored lights,

At the beginning of samsara and nirvana, we became deluded by the five-colored lights. The impure elements of earth, water, fire, wind, and space manifested. Later, inwardly, they became the substance of our bodies. The five elements are, in essence, these five-colored lights. These pure elements do not dissolve. At death:

> May the nonconceptual vajra chain of the five lights,
> Indivisible and unified, be perfected as dharmata.

Thus, may rigpa and its expression be inseparable in the state of dharmata.

> When the great HUNG is in the form of wrathful demons
> And when the sound of HUNG fills the billion worlds,
> May I recognize the vital point that they are the HUNG sound of
>   empty awareness
> And realize this empty resounding is like an echo.

The impure elements dissolve into us. Next the pure ones, the five-colored lights, and the vajra chain appear in the sky, and we can be liberated into primordial purity.

> When the great HUNG is in the form of wrathful demons

Of the three syllables, HUNG appears in the form of the wrathful demons. Among the three syllables representing body, speech, and mind, OM is body, AH is speech, and HUNG is mind. The great HUNG emanates the wrathful deities. When the experience of the great HUNG happens—wherein HUNG manifests as the demonic forms of the wrathful deities—may I not be struck with terror and:

> May I recognize the vital point that they are the HUNG sound of
> empty awareness

The sound of HUNG appears as the roaring thunderclaps of a thousandfold thunders roaring simultaneously, like great laughter. At this time, may I recognize this as empty awareness. May I realize that this HUNG syllable is the expression of my own awareness.

And realize this empty resounding is like an echo.

No matter how much an echo resounds, it is not a real sound.

> When surrounded by the horde of Yama murderers,
> May the confusion of being attacked and slayed, taking flight and
> being chased, naturally dissolve.

May I know all that manifests as my own expression. When the Yama murderers, the messengers of the lord of death, surround me, may I not give rise to any dualistic concepts, such as being attacked, being slain, or trying to escape.

> Without giving rise to the deluded experience of fear,
> May I see them as the forms of the peaceful and wrathful yidams.

Recognizing these manifestations as my own self-expression, may I see them as the natural expression of the peaceful and wrathful deities.

> When the swarm of wrathful ones burgeons forth
> From the Blazing Palace of Great Bliss in the bone mansion,
> May I not see them as the forms of horrible demons,

The bone mansion is the skull, where the wrathful deities are residing at present. They swarm out at the moment when mind and body separate. When they are large, they are the size of Mt. Sumeru, and when small, they are the size of a mustard seed. When the mind and body separate, the swarming of the wrathful deities is like a gathering in the main hall when there is a pee break; everyone comes out. When that happens, may I:

Realize the meaning of the pithy *Heart Essence*.

The *Heart Essence* instructions reveal that the essence is primordial purity and the nature is spontaneously present. These deities are our own spontaneously present nature. Thus, if we have not become petrified, may we realize the vital point of these pith instructions of the *Heart Essence:* that all manifestations are spontaneous presence, appearing naturally from primordial purity. In the future, when we experience the ultimate Tögal, these hundred peaceful and wrathful deities will appear.

When the multitude of peaceful ones vanishes into space
From the Jewel Dome Palace of the heart,
The moment the experience transposes and manifests as forms of
    light,
May awareness dissolve into the expanse of luminosity.

When the peaceful deities emerge from the heart center, from the jeweled dome palace of the heart, all the peaceful deities vanish into the space of dharmadhatu. It is the spontaneous presence dissolving back into primordial purity. When that happens, may I abide free from constructs in the primordially pure state.

Now all of these deities are abiding in our aggregates and sense faculties in our body. When they manifest outwardly, they dissolve back inwardly. They appear in front of us, and we can actually see them. They are bodies of light, and we make the aspiration that we can dissolve into the expanse of rigpa and remain in rigpa.

When the wheel of channels at the throat disintegrates
With a thousand roaring thunderclaps of terrifying laughter,

May I recognize this as the ah and hung song of the peaceful and
   wrathful ones
And liberate it as the unoriginated sound of empty awareness.

When the throat center disintegrates, that's the pure vidyadharas,
the knowledge holders. When they manifest as great laughter, the great
song of AH HUNG fills the billionfold worlds. At that time, may we not be
struck by fear but recognize this as the natural melody of the peaceful
and wrathful deities and as empty, unborn awareness. May I thus remain
in equanimity.

To reiterate, the wrathful deities emerge from the skull, the peaceful
ones from the heart center, and the vidyadharas from the throat center.

When the red and white of means and knowledge converge at the
   heart center
From the Bliss Sustaining Palace of the secret place,
May this natural state of undefiled bliss and emptiness
Cause prana and mind to enter the central channel.

When we die, the red element rises from the secret place and the
white element descends. These white and red elements of method and
wisdom converge in the heart center. When that happens, may we not
fall unconscious and oblivious, but naturally let the prana and mind enter
the central channel, which is the wisdom element. It is called the central
channel here, but actually it's the wisdom space, undefiled bliss and emptiness, which is the realization arrived at through the practice connected
to the third empowerment. May I rest free from concepts.

When dwelling in the state of the bardo of dharmata,
May consciousness not stray into oblivion.
But realizing the meaning of self-liberated great primordial purity,

After the mind has left the body, the manifestations of wisdoms and
kayas arise; these are the support and what is supported. Now the consciousness has entered the bardo of dharmata. *Shes rig* is the knowing,
(shes pa), and rigpa; these two, in Dzogchen talk, are of one meaning. In
this state of knowing and rigpa, may we not fall into oblivion. Oblivion

is nonrecognition. We need to recognize and not stray into this. Instead, may we realize the self-liberated great primordial purity. If we recognize, self-liberation will happen. The essence is primordial purity, and the unity of knowing and rigpa prevents falling into oblivion. May I realize this primordial purity:

> May I remain in the other-empty state of exhausted phenomena.

There is a mention here of shentong, *(shen stong),* empty of other. It is not really a matter of empty of self and empty of other. All phenomena of samsara and nirvana are complete within empty cognizance. After having recognized the dharmakaya of the natural awareness, may shentong be realized to the stage of exhaustion of phenomena. Usually it's perceived from below as self-awareness as empty, while all phenomena, not self-awareness, are not really decided. That's the lower point of view of rang stong, empty of self. But in the shentong, it is realized definitively that all other phenomena are empty, but self-awareness is not empty; that's the main difference. By realizing the meaning of self-liberated great primordial purity, may I remain in the other-empty state of exhausted phenomena. It is decided that all phenomena are emptiness.

> When seeing the reality of manifest dharmata,

> This is attaining stability in manifest dharmata.

> May I be free from the conceptual remedy of fixated mindfulness.

> Conceptual remedy is movement, thought; may I be free of that.

> Realizing the meaning of arriving at primordial purity, the stage of exhaustion,

The four experiences are being referred to: manifest dharmata; increased experience; awareness reaching fullness; and the final one, the exhaustion of dharmata.

May I remain in the nonconceptual state devoid of constructs.

This is the aspiration to remain in primordial purity.

When the door to the dome of the five wisdoms opens up
In the celestial palace of intermingled five-colored rainbows,
And the realm is filled with bodily forms and spheres,
May I meet with the five kayas and five wisdoms.

Now we reach spontaneous presence, the five lights, and the five wisdoms. The five wisdoms are mirror-like wisdom, the wisdom of equality, the wisdom of dharmata, discerning wisdom, and all-accomplishing wisdom. The basis is the wisdom; what is based on it, the kayas, are the ultimate fruition.

When meeting with the five kayas and five wisdoms
In the luminous palace of the lamp of the empty bindu,

There are three outer lamps: the lamp of the empty space; the lamp of the empty bindu; and the lamp of self-existing rigpa, the vajra chain.

Once meeting the five kayas and five wisdoms,

May I, free from the doubt of vacillating dualistic experience,

May I be free of the cognitive obscuration.

Merge into the primordial state of Samantabhadra.

All phenomena are exhausted in the expanse of dharmata. Attaining stability in the experiences of manifest dharmata, may I merge into the primordial state of Samantabhadra.

Having met face to face with the four lamps of mind essence

The four lamps are the lamp of the flesh heart, the lamp of the smooth nadi, the lamp of the distance water pullers, and the lamp of pure space.

In the luminous palace of the lamp of the empty bindu,
May I reach perfect stability in the sphere of spontaneous presence

The spontaneous presence manifests from the expanse of primordial purity.

And shift to the expansive state of space and awareness.

The king of phowas, transference of consciousness at the time of death, is during the dissolution. First there is the dissolution of consciousness into space, then space into luminosity, luminosity into wisdom, wisdom into union, union into spontaneous presence, and spontaneous presence into full attainment. May we realize the transference into space and awareness. This is the ultimate phowa. At death, when consciousness dissolves into space, if we have been introduced and have recognized rigpa and can mingle, that is the king of phowas.

May the empty and luminous lamp of dharmakaya shine.

This line refers to kayas and wisdoms, the undefiled emptiness and luminous rigpa.

May the sambhogakaya of unceasing nondual experience be
    attained.

May the unceasing nondualistic experience become the sambhogakaya. As long as dualistic experience is retained, there is no enlightenment. Attaining sambhogakaya signifies that duality has fallen apart. There was no space for Longchenpa to put more syllables in the line. If we could put in two more words, they would be *free from:* May I attain the sambhogakaya free from dual experience. If those extra words had been added, it would have been too long to sing. Free of all fixating in the ultimate is the sambhogakaya.

May the nirmanakaya of perfected self-awareness be attained.
Having attained the three kayas, may I act for the welfare of others.

What is most important is how we can apply this to our own practice. The present moment of recognizing rigpa is of vital importance at the moment of death. The previous lines about the red and white experiences refer in a more detailed way to the four experiences: appearance, increase, attainment, and full attainment. For normal people, there are only three; for practitioners there are four.

The first one, the appearance, is called the white experience, where the white element obtained from the father starts to descend from the crown of the head down to the heart center. This is accompanied by the dissolution of the thirty-three types of aggressive thought states. Then the next one is the increase, which takes place when the red element obtained from the mother starts to ascend from below the navel up to the heart center. This is accompanied by the dissolution of the forty states of attachment. Their meeting point is called the experience of blackness, which occurs through the dissolution of the seven thought-states of stupidity.

Usually normal people, who have never recognized rigpa, have no experience or familiarity with the state that is free from thought yet awake. When the red and white elements converge at the heart center, all thought-states cease. If there is no familiarity with the absence of thought, there is just a blackout; it becomes blank. This unconscious state lasts for three and a half days, after which the mind wakes up and is suddenly in the bardo state.

For the practitioner who is familiar with the fourth state—called the ground luminosity of full attainment, which occurs at the end of the dissolution of the eighty innate thought-states—what is left over is a state of no-thought, which is, nonetheless, not oblivious. This is the same as the rigpa that is recognized right now. This is also called the mother ground luminosity and the child path luminosity.

When we recognize the rigpa at present, it is not thinking of anything and yet there is not oblivion either. Attaining familiarity and stability in that right now will ensure that enlightenment takes place easily at the moment of death—the fourth moment, called the ground luminosity of full attainment. A practitioner does not fall unconsciousness when the ground luminosity manifests. Instead he or she recognizes rigpa, attains stability, and becomes enlightened as quickly as flapping a Tibetan sleeve three times. It doesn't take longer than that. That is what is mentioned in the quote from *Chanting the Names of*

Manjushri: "One moment makes the difference—in one moment, complete enlightenment."

Therefore, the vitally important aspect that Longchenpa mentions in the context of the two elements, means and knowledge, converging in the heart center, is the experience of the fourth moment, which is rigpa, indicated by the experience arrived at in the third empowerment, the unity of bliss and emptiness. That is the experience when the white and red elements join together. It is also the same experience that grabbed the consciousness out of the bardo and into this life to begin with, when the mother's and father's red and white elements joined together, and we were conceived in the womb. In that moment of bliss and emptiness, the consciousness faints and it is conceived. Therefore, it's extremely important to be able to not fall oblivious and to not grasp.

QUESTION: When a person dies, it is said that his consciousness will continue through the bardo and take rebirth, but since the mind is uncompounded, to what will his karmas and habitual patterns adhere?

RINPOCHE: What is it like when you have a dream? Even though your body lies comfortably in the bed, your mind goes through the deluded experiences. It is governed by these experiences. By examining what these experiences adhere to, you can use this example to understand that in the same way.

QUESTION: The mind is connected to the body at that time. When the mind and body separate, do these experiences occur?

RINPOCHE: When we dream at night, the mind experiences joy and sorrow and so forth. While dreaming, there is no link between the world and the mind. But when we wake up, body, mind, and sense objects are all linked together; our body, speech, and mind are connected. At night we still have a body, but it is lying very comfortably in our bed, whereas the mind is completely deluded, roaming around, terrified or blissed out. There are different kinds of fears and so forth at night. Right now, we have a direct link or contact (with the world), but in the state of dreams, there is no direct link because our body is lying asleep. What we call the habitual patterns are within the mind.

QUESTION: Habitual patterns don't have any concrete substance, right?

RINPOCHE: No, they don't have any material substance at all. If they did, then in the intermediate state there should also be a physical body, but it has died and is left behind, right? So, if that were the case, there should be a physical body in the bardo, since the experiences are the same as when dreaming. Right now, we do have a physical body, but after death, we don't. While dreaming, we have a body that is lying in bed, but in the bardo after dying the body has been cremated. Although the body has been burned, habitual patterns are still with the mind and cause us to feel like we have a body. That body is called the mental body, *(yid lus)*; we do not have what is called the illusory body, *(sgyu lus)*, made of aggregates and elements, nor do we have a body of flesh and blood. It is a mental body.

When we have attained the state of enlightenment, then all the karmas, habitual patterns, and evil deeds, all of these, have been cast away. We do not have to follow karma; we are not governed by karma. Right now, we are propelled by karma and habitual patterns. In the bardo, we will have a lot of trouble, just as we do in dreams, facing the sounds, colors, and lights, with many terrors and fears. Although we don't have a body, it feels like we do. When we don't have a body, we shouldn't feel thirsty and hungry, right? But due to our habitual patterns that have not been dissolved, we have to undergo pain and misery in the bardo.

Right now, the teachings say recognize mind essence, recognize mind essence. Once you get familiar with that essence, it will conquer all the karmas, habitual patterns, and deluded experiences. It is sufficient unto itself. For example, when you feel angry, look into the essence of the anger. Once you feel angry, if in the second moment you look into the essence, the anger will not remain, right? If anger does not stay, habitual patterns and deluded experience will not remain either. Your body feels cold, hungry, and thirsty, right? If you don't have a body, the mind should not feel cold, hungry, or thirsty, right? But, due to habitual patterns, it doesn't seem to help. *(Rinpoche laughs.)* That gives us a lot of trouble. Otherwise, once we have abandoned the body, we wouldn't need to eat anything. Food has to be eaten through the mouth, right? When feeling cold, it is the body that freezes, not the mind. Also, the body feels hot and cold. If we imagine ourselves in a mass of fire, our mind doesn't burn, does it? If you think of yourself in cold water, do you feel cold? No? It is due to habitual patterns. Habitual patterns and deluded experiences are actually the worst thing. Unless we are able to destroy them right now, later on, after death, it will not be possible to do so, because our karmas and kleshas are too powerful.

As it is said, "One is scared by one's own tail." In the bardo, when the deceased is terrified by his own deities, the dead person gets terrified by the deities from his own body, thinking that they are going to kill him. The deities shout, "HUNG HUNG PHAT PHAT!" and so forth, "Yamantaka has come to kill me." And the thunder feels like your mind is splitting into pieces from the terror. Actually, these are the deities in your own body. Therefore, it says that the deceased is terrified by the deities of his body. But in fact, they are the deities of your own body. When it is said that, "The deceased runs away from the deities of his body," it means that when a person sees a wild animal thinking that it will eat him, he will run away, right? That is called fleeing.

For example, when a donkey is in a meadow where there is a lot of grass, sometimes a great gust of wind will make all the blades of grass move fiercely. The donkey will think that something outside arrived and he will run away. That's what they say anyway, but actually the grass is just something that can be eaten. When the grass is moved by the wind, the donkey becomes scared. The deities in one's body are the expression of primordial purity, the spontaneous presence. These deities are within us. When they appear to someone who has a vision of them, that person thinks that they are the messengers of the Lord of Death and becomes so terrified that it feels like his or her heart is splitting into pieces. In fact, all of these are merely imagined to be such, without really existing at all.

For instance, everything has to be grouped into relative and ultimate, into conditioned and unconditioned. The conditioned is relative, and the unconditioned is the ultimate. When talking about these two, what is conditioned and what is unconditioned, the conditioned is what is conceivable. It is possible to talk about it, to explain it, like flying in the sky and so forth, all that is being conditioned. The unconditioned is inconceivable. When explaining the inconceivable mind, one can get some rough idea about it. Whatever we can understand theoretically, for example, like an idea of all these different kinds of machinery that fly here and drive there and so forth, is only conditioned. Whatever we can conceive of or comprehend by mind is conditioned. The unconditioned is inconceivable, whereas, that which can be told and understood is conceivable. When we say inconceivable it means that it cannot be thought of; it is impossible to envision or formulate. That is the mind of emptiness, the meaning of emptiness. It is inconceivable.

Slowly, slowly, as we progress further, as when arriving at awareness, reaching fullness, *(rig pa tshad pheb),* you can see freely, through everything within and without, even the details inside your body. At this time, when you have attained stability in samadhi, you can resolve everything, just like standing at the top of Shivapuri. But if you have not attained stability in samadhi, it is like still being in the valley or at the base of Shivapuri. When looking in one direction, you cannot see in the other, such as when looking north, you cannot see south. One direction will obscure the other; you cannot see everywhere in a single glance.

Likewise, we can only partially or fractionally hint at the inconceivable truth through words or talking. We can only indicate the words such as primordial purity and spontaneous presence, and so forth, but, actually, we have to experience the inconceivable through practice. When, like Longchen Rabjam, we realize the nature of all things, it becomes inconceivable. Those who have mastered the conceivable are the western scientists. They have realized the conceivable, mastered the conditioned. As long as there is body, speech, and mind, it is conditioned. Mastering the conditioned can benefit a present situation. However, when we arrive in the bardo, and the aggregates and elements collapse, since we have lost the link connecting body, speech, and mind, there is nothing other than the unconditioned that can help us. As long as the conditioned habitual patterns obscure the unconditioned, we do not experience that which is inconceivable. Now we have to get used to it. There is no other way [than practice]. It is the inconceivable wisdom, not the conceivable wisdom.

APPENDIX

THE DROP OF NECTAR

The Smaller Commentary on the Guru Yoga of Simplicity

Nyoshul Khen Rinpoche

I pay homage at the feet of the sublime guru, who is indivisible from the transcendent, perfect conqueror, glorious Samantabhadra.

Previously, I have explained the precious lord guru's mind treasure, *The Ultimate Guru Sadhana of Simplicity,* in my commentary *Cloudbank of Nectar.* Here, for the sake of beginners, I shall clarify it by means of the smaller commentary, entitled, *The Drop of Nectar.* This contains three headings: the meaning of the title, the meaning of the main text, and the concluding description of the colophon.

THE MEANING OF THE TITLE

First, the title:

The Ultimate Guru Sadhana of Simplicity

In general, a tantra says:

The guru is the Buddha, the guru is the Dharma,
And likewise, the guru is also the Sangha;
Thus, the guru is the bestower of all.
The guru is the glorious vajra-holder.

It is also said:

The one who imagines the gracious guru
At the crown of his head or in the center of his heart

Or in the palm of his hand
Will retain all the siddhis
Of the buddhas of one thousand aeons.

In this and other ways, all the tantras, statements, and instructions extol endlessly how the guru is the bestower of all siddhis and how he is the root of blessings.

Specifically, it is recognized that the nature of the luminous Great Perfection is realized exclusively by means of your guru. The omniscient Longchenpa, as well, taught us to "pursue nothing but the blessings of the guru." In short, even though there are an untold number of different guru sadhanas, this particular one contains a method for realizing the *ultimate* wisdom within your own stream-of-being. It is an extremely profound instruction in the form of a *guru sadhana* that is free from the elaborations, simplicity without a multitude of words. An alternative meaning is that here is a profound *sadhana* for realizing the *ultimate guru,* the *simplicity* of natural awareness, within your own stream-of-being.

Here is how to apply this sadhana. First of all, bring to mind the qualities of the glorious guru, who is the unexcelled and most eminent refuge in this life, the bardo, and in all lives to come. And, by doing so, engender the benefits of remembering him.

THE MEANING OF THE MAIN TEXT

Second, the main text has three sections: the preliminaries, the main part, and the conclusion.

The first of these, the preliminaries, is of two types, the general and specific.

The Preliminaries

The General Preliminaries

Think in the following way:

This support for the freedoms is extremely difficult to obtain, and even though I have obtained it, it changes from moment to moment, like a waterfall over a steep cliff, and is unstable. The time of my death is uncertain. Unlike materialistic hedonists, who believe that there is nothing whatsoever after death, I know that upon my death, I will follow the tracks of my good or evil actions and helplessly continue circling in samsara, like being on the rim of a waterwheel. Whatever samsaric realm I am born into -- just like being on an island of cannibals, in a nest of vicious vipers, or in a pit of burning coal -- is never beyond having the nature of the three types of suffering. Now, in my present situation, I am free from adverse conditions and possess the perfect, conducive circumstances for practicing the sacred Dharma. Therefore, I and all others must by all means attain the unified state of the original protector Samantabhadra that is liberated from this samsaric ocean of suffering!

To think like this from the bottom of your heart is the general preliminary practice.

The Specific Preliminaries

Second, the specific preliminaries have four parts: refuge, bodhichitta resolve, command and drawing of the boundary, and the showering down of resplendence.

Refuge

AH

Primordially free awareness is the ultimate refuge.

Visualize in the sky before you the glorious, sublime guru with all the lineage masters in tiers, one above the other. All the other ocean-like deities of the all-encompassing Three Roots are present as cloudbanks, as in a market gathering.

Alternatively, you can visualize the glorious protector, the sublime guru to whom you entrust your heart, as the single embodiment of all objects of refuge. In that way, he is the support for the accumulations known as the all-embodying jewel.

In his presence, you and all other sentient beings, with collective body, speech, and mind, from the core of your hearts, take refuge until you realize the unified state of the Original Protector. This is done in the manner of (the Three Jewels as) your teacher, your path, and your companions. That is the relative, causal refuge, which is implicitly stated. What is actually stated is the following:

AH

As indicated by the nonarising dharmadhatu, the very moment your mind's basic nature, *primordially* beyond the limitations of being fettered by or *free* from disturbing emotions, is allowed to remain composed as *awareness,* the ultimate state of the great self-existing wakefulness is like darkness that cannot continue in the light of day. All the suffering of the innumerable thoughts of the three realms is deprived of any chance to occur. Thus, they are safeguarded in the manner of self-liberation. To compose yourself in primordially free awareness is, therefore, the *ultimate refuge* that is the sublime and most eminent refuge of them all.

Bodhichitta Resolve

Second,

> With the compassionate expression of awareness, I form the resolve.§

Even though the unconditioned essence is primordially pure, for the sake of the beings who fail to realize that, *with the compassionate* self-radiance that is the unconfined and natural *expression of awareness,* I direct myself towards sentient beings. Moreover, motivated by the will to liberate them from suffering, *I form* the relative bodhichitta resolve. This resolve is the wish to attain complete enlightenment for the benefit of others, and *the* ultimate *resolve* is to compose myself in the continuity of unfabricated awareness.

Command and Drawing of the Boundary

Third, issuing the command, drawing the boundary line, and establishing the protection circle are stated together in the manner of simplicity:

> For the obstructers—ignorance, dualistic, and habit—§
> I draw the boundary within the self-liberated expanse.§

In actuality, there is no basis for obstructers and evil influences to have an effect within the basic natural state. However, (the following) is for the sentient beings who are ignorant about this. They mistake the expression of dharmata as the perceiving mind and the *perceived* objects. The subsequent solidified *habits* of their three poisons appear in the forms of *obstructers*. The source from which these evil spirits arise is the deluded mind. The very moment I realize that it is devoid of any basis or root, I draw the *boundary* for all these obstructers and evil influences that are primordially nonarising. In such a manner, they are *self-liberated* within the *expanse* of awareness wisdom, beyond focusing on their abode or movement.

This is like the example of our endless fears of ferocious beasts and so forth that may occur during dreams. Nevertheless, immediately upon awakening from the basis of the occurrence, the state of sleep, all such horrors subside effortlessly into themselves. This is the key point mentioned in this quote:

> To be free from protecting something to be protected,
> That is the king of all protection circles.

Thus, you gain confident trust in the 'great sight of no seeing.' (It is also called) 'abiding in the state of nondoing,' 'absence of accepting and rejecting, the 'great meditation of nonmeditation,' the 'samaya beyond observing,' and so forth.

Showering Down of the Resplendence

Fourth is the consecration of offerings and downpour of resplendence:

> With the offering clouds of complete purity,
> Let the display of wisdom shower down a great resplendence.

Take the example of a white conch or snow mountain that someone with jaundice sees as yellow. Similarly, all phenomena, all that appears and exists, are the great purity and equality, as the *cloud* banks of Samantabhadra's outer, inner, and innermost *offerings* that are primordially a *complete purity*. Nevertheless, for those beings who fail to realize that this is so, let the immense *display of wisdom* perform the consecration by manifesting as primordially pure offering clouds or *shower down a great resplendence*. Thus, the consecration of offerings and the downpour of resplendence are stated together.

The Main Part

Next, for the steps of the main part, there are the three yogas of Body, Speech, and Mind.

The Yoga of Body

The first includes the points of visualizing the support for the accumulations, invoking and requesting to remain, and gathering and purifying through the Seven Branches.

> *Visualizing the Support for the Accumulations:*
> Aн:
> Within this mandala, appearance and existence as the manifest
>   ground,:
> Essence, nature, and capacity:
> Are present throughout all of samsara and nirvana.:
> There is not even the word impure,:

Since the magical display of arising must manifest unobstructedly from the nonarising nature of basic space, an Aн is uttered.

These phenomena of samsara and nirvana, all of *appearance and existence,* according to the extraordinary perspective of Ati Yoga, remain or *manifest* exactly as the *ground* of the natural state of the sugata-element-potential. Hence, *within this* (occasion of training) establish that they are the *mandala* of the awakened mind of rigpa—the threefold mandalas of empty *essence,* cognizant *nature,* and all-pervasive *capacity*. They are *present throughout* as the permeating nature of *all of* the conditioned phenomena of *samsara and nirvana,* in the manner of being their unconditioned nature. This being so, even if you were to search for aeons for specific phenomena belonging to *impure* worlds or beings, *there is not even* the chance of finding *the word* impure.

> Therefore, even I, Uddiyana,:
> Possess the nature of sugatagarbha.:
> Whatever I wear, that's how I look;:
> Visualize me in the manner of unfabricated naturalness.:

Since all of samsara and nirvana has the nature of the threefold mandala, *therefore, even I, Uddiyana, possess* the ground, *the nature of sugatagarbha,* which remains as its essence. This is why it is not necessary to visualize him as a deity, by means of changing and improving his appearance, as in the case of the lower tantras. Rather, I simply visualize myself in *whatever I* am seen to *wear,* since *that's how I look* in my present ordinary body. *Visualize me in the manner of* nonfixating, *unfabricated naturalness,* by means of the view that recognizes him as being the original identity of essence, nature, and capacity.

Thus, no matter how the six types of perceptions are experienced, as attractive or repulsive, to 'bind the life-force by planting the stake of unchanging dharmata' —being unmoved from rigpa itself—is the extraordinary perspective of the supreme vehicle. Here it is given as a supplementary instruction.

This sublime master, our glorious protector—no matter how he may be perceived within the experiences of his disciples—is in reality Lord Manjushri. This very form singularly embodies the original wakefulness of all the victorious ones and is displayed in a human body. He is Sangye Yeshe of Nub, the recipient of the mandate for the *Dogyü Semsum*[20] of the Early Translations. Additionally, he is Guru Chökyi Wangchuk and others. He is someone who willfully took rebirth to be the splendor for the teachings and beings of the Dark Age. Thus, he is a sublime being who is an 'incarnation of primordial compassion.'

> In my heart center is Vajrasattva, the embodiment of all families,
> Abiding as the essence of the wisdom being.
> The samadhi being is Samantabhadra,
> Uncreated and vividly present as the original great perfection.

In the heart center of the glorious protector, the sublime guru—visualized as the samaya being—is glorious *Vajrasattva, the* singular *embodiment of all* hundred *families* of the Great Secret. Visualize him as *abiding as the essence of the wisdom being.* In his heart center is *the samadhi being* who *is* the primordial protector, the glorious *Samantabhadra.* (This visualization manifests) without depending on other ways of visualizing, such as the fivefold true enlightenment, as in the systems of the lower tantras; therefore, it is uncreated. Thus, the extraordinary Dzogchen perspective is that they (the deities) are *vividly present as the great* identity that is the *original perfection* in being the essence of the deity.

Though one is inside of the other, these deities are such that they do not obstruct or touch one another. Rather, you should visualize them as being of a mutually transparent nature: bodies of pure light endowed with an essence of original wakefulness.

Invoking and Requesting to Remain

Ah⁞

Though ultimately you are not subject to coming and going,⁞

I invite you merely in a seeming way.⁞

Please remain indivisibly.⁞

The Ah is as mentioned above. *Though ultimately* means that within the nonarising continuity of the basic space of phenomena (dharmad-hatu), *you are not subject to* as much as a hair-tip of *coming and going* in the sense of something being invited. Nevertheless, in order to influence me and other sentient beings, who have deluded concepts, *merely in a* relative, *seeming way, I invite you*—the sublime guru and glorious pro-tector—to this place. You manifest in the unobstructed manner of being the natural radiance of compassion, together with your retinue of all the victorious deities of the all-encompassing Three Roots.

While I invoke with a yearning melody, *please* arrive in actuality—your vajra bodies moving in dance motions, your vajra voices resounding with mantra songs, and your vajra minds delighting in immense lumi-nous wakefulness. Just as when water is poured into water, please *remain* as samaya being and wisdom being indivisibly.

Gathering and Purifying Through the Seven Branches

Next follows the Seven Branches, which combine into one the vital points of every type of accumulation and purification.

First, paying homage:

> Paying homage through facing the view of equal taste, I bow
> down⁞

Within the expanse of dharmata, all the phenomena of samsara and nirvana have no separate taste to be distinguished as better or worse. They remain as the identity of Samantabhadra, the ever-excellent great purity and *equality*. *Facing* or realizing this, in actuality, in the manner of uncontrived naturalness *through the view of* self-knowing, that is the ultimate *paying of homage*.

In this, the literal explanation of homage, *(phyag 'tshal),* is also com-plete. It is *(phyag)* because all obscurations of good and evil concepts are swept away, *(phyags pa)*. (They are done so) in the manner of being self-liberated, when remaining in the continuity of the view of equal taste, and *('tshal)* because of facing, *('tshal ba),* or acknowledging, the ultimate wakefulness of self-knowing, exactly as it is.

Second, the offerings:

> And present you with the offerings of Samantabhadra's displays.⁞

By knowing that the subject and object of offering are nondual, *And present you with the* infinite outer, inner, and innermost *offerings,* filling the limits of space. The cloudbanks of *displays* of primordially perfect kayas and wisdom arrays manifest from *Samantabhadra's* expanse, the originally pure dharmadhatu of your mind.

Third, apologizing for misdeeds:

> I apologize within the expanse of the two purified obscurations,
> purity, ⁞

I apologize without the need to depend upon rejection, transmutation, utilizing, and so forth—deliberately producing an antidote—as in the case of the lower vehicles. The apology is made in the very same moment of remaining composed *within the* dharmakaya *expanse of* Samantabhadra's mind, the great original *purity* or pureness of mind-essence. It is like (the darkness that) is utterly vanquished when the sun simply rises. *I apologize* for, or purify, the dense darkness of *the two* emotional and cognitive *obscurations* that prevent recognition of the natural state of the ground. This is, therefore, the king of all types of apology, as is said:

> *The one who wishes to apologize,*
> *Should sit up straight and truly look.*
> *By truly seeing, he is utterly free.*
> *This is the most eminent reparation.*

Fourth, rejoicing:

> And rejoice in the ultimate nature.⁞

And in the manner of uncontrived naturalness, I *rejoice,* or compose myself, *in* the very *nature* of *the ultimate* natural state of all things, the Great Perfection. Not only is this the most eminent, being the ultimate way of rejoicing, but, moreover, it is rejoicing in the true nature with confident trust, the source of unsurpassable merit. As is said:

The ultimate is realized through trust.

Fifth, requesting to turn the wheel of Dharma:

Please turn the Dharma wheel of timelessness,§

Please, *I request you to turn* for all other disciples and myself *the Dharma wheel of* the Great Perfection that is the ultimate wakefulness of the 'four parts without three,' the *timelessness* beyond the three times.

Sixth, beseeching not to pass into nirvana:

And remain unceasingly and perpetually.§

The sublime guru, the glorious protector, has already realized dharmakaya from the perspective of the original wakefulness of his individual experience. Therefore, he is free from the constructs of arriving and remaining. Still, from the perspective of the compassion for others' experience, I beseech you to *remain* by manifesting *unceasingly and perpetually* the hundred thousand displays of your rupakaya to tame beings. (Let them appear), like reflections of the moon within the lakes of your disciples' inclinations and abilities, so as to overturn the depths of samsara for the welfare of all beings.

Seventh, dedication:

I dedicate all nonconceptual virtue to sentient beings.§

I dedicate the mass of conceptual merit created throughout the three times and *all* of the accumulation of wisdom *virtue* that does *not conceptualize* the three spheres, however much there may be. (I offer this) *to* all the *sentient beings* filling space for their temporary, high rebirth and ultimate goodness of being liberated into inner space, the expanse of the Youthful Vase Body.

This is the way of directly emphasizing the Seven Branches from the perspective of ultimate wisdom. Through it, you should implicitly understand the Seven Branches that are of the identity of relative means. This is because it is essential to never separate the two levels of truth, no matter which approach you take.

Furthermore, to cause the extraordinary wisdom of realization to take birth within your stream-of-being and to vastly increase the two accumulations, if you prefer a more elaborate style, you can line up thousands of various offerings—amrita, rakta, torma, feast articles, incense, lamps, and so forth. Arrange them in a way that is more splendid than the planets and stars in the sky. Using as the framework other guru sadhanas, of any suitable length and detail, the *Ngakso,* and such, recite the extensive *Narak Kongshak* or other corresponding chants.

In particular, you should invoke the heart-samaya of the precious master, by singing repeatedly any long or short supplication to him. Do so in a yearning tone of voice that is as melodious as the flutes of the gandharvas.

The Yogas of Speech and Mind

Second, for the recitation of the yoga for Speech and Mind, the Sanskrit word jap has the connotation of recitation, (bzlas pa) in Tibetan because it means to recite a particular mantra repeatedly and unceasingly.

> Aḥ
> In the center of the heart, amidst the great all-pervasive blue,
> In the middle of the pure lamp of the empty bindu,
> The chains of manifest awareness are vividly present as A.
> Through the unceasing awareness of natural presence
> Everything is a buddha realm.
> Aḥ Aḥ Aḥ
>
> A; A; A

Aḥ, thus visualize the nondual samaya being and wisdom being in the threefold way. *In the center of the heart* of Samantabhadra, who is the samadhi being, *amidst* the natural manifestation of the great ultimate wisdom, is *the great all-pervasive blue* of pure basic space that is vividly present as the radiance of purified lapis lazuli. *In the middle of the pure* great luminosity, the *lamp of the empty bindu* is the natural radiance of the five wisdoms. Here is that which in identity is the lamp of self-existing insight but in its forms are *the* vajra *chains* of the natural *manifestations* of self-existing awareness-wisdom that *are vividly present as* the white syllable A, as bright as the globe of the moon.

Through remaining or sustaining *unceasingly* the self-cognizing naked state of empty *awareness,* the unconditioned *natural presence, everything* in samsara and nirvana is purified and perfected 'buddha' as the spontaneously present, all-encompassing purity of equality. It is thus the *realm* of the three mandalas. This was the Mind yoga of luminosity.

While exerting yourself in keeping this in mind, recite the vowel syllables AH$^{\circ}_{\breve{}}$ AH$^{\circ}_{\breve{}}$ AH$^{\circ}_{\breve{}}$. The syllables A manifest in the form of mantra as a magical display arising from the expanse of nonarising dharmata. (Recite) in a way that is gentle and not forced but rather like a natural flow. That was the recitation that is the vajra yoga of Speech.

By training in this way, you will perfect the four visions, at best in three years, second best in five, or at least in seven years. You will awaken to true enlightenment in the expanse of the Youthful Vase Body.

Conclusion

The three concluding activities include the dissolution.

The Dissolution Phase:

All expressions and displays manifest from the ground,$^{\circ}_{\breve{}}$
Dissolve back into the primordially pure expanse of basic space.$^{\circ}_{\breve{}}$

Take the example of dreams that dissolve when awakening from sleep, or a magical show that fades away. When composing yourself evenly within the state of rigpa—the basic space of *the ground,* the primordially pure essence that is beyond meeting with or parting from the three kayas—*all* the attributes that are *expressions and displays manifest therefrom dissolve back*—simply. It is so phrased because (the displays) are no longer observable. (They have dissolved) *into the primordially pure expanse of* the *basic space* of luminosity.

Here, unlike in the case of the lower tantras that take dualistic mind as the path, there is no elaborate dissolution phase that involves the dissolving of the world and beings into the celestial palace and the deity. This is because those styles of dissolution phase are for the purpose of eliminating the limited belief in permanence. In this case, because we take wisdom as the path, self-existing awareness is primordially free from the limitations of eternalism and nihilism.

The Dedication:

I dedicate all roots of virtue, timeless and throughout the three
    times,§
By means of the total purity of the three spheres.§

As indicated by the virtuous roots of doing the practice of the glorious
protector and guru, *I dedicate all* possible *roots of virtue*. Thus, the *timeless*
accumulation of wisdom embraced by the view of natural knowing—the
great primordial purity of the four parts without three—*and* the accumulation of conceptual merit created *throughout the three times* of past, present, and future (are dedicated). This is done *by means of the total purity of*
not clinging to *the three spheres*—the sentient beings, who are the objects
to whom the dedication is made; the dedicator, who is making the dedication; and the virtue that is being dedicated. I make the dedication to be
liberated within the expanse of the original protector Samantabhadra.

The Auspiciousness:

By the spontaneously present all-pervasive sovereign,§
May the auspicious thatness be present!§

By the power of having practiced this utterly profound guru yoga, by
means of the glorious guru's compassionate blessings, *may the sovereign*
ground wisdom of the *spontaneously present* three kayas— that is *pervasive*
throughout *all* of samsara and nirvana, and which abides, in actuality,
within yourself—the *auspicious* splendor of perfection, blazing with thousandfold lights of virtuous marks, *be present* and manifest. May this occur
throughout all directions and times, so as to overturn from their depths
the realms of beings with the effulgence of the rupakaya displays—manifesting to tame whoever needs them—out of the dharmakaya expanse of
the realized *thatness* wisdom of the fruition, which is the purification of
the temporary obscurations.

THE CONCLUDING COLOPHON:

Unable to refuse the people who requested,§
This was written by the simple Uddiyana.§

Unable to refuse the people who requested—his son Chökyi Nyima

Rinpoche, a disciple of unchanging trust and samaya, and his Western disciple Ösel Dorje from Germany, and others—*this was written* in the manner of his own sadhana *by* the very hands of *the simple Uddiyana*.

Guru (Padmasambhava) has said:

I, Padmasambhava,
Personally wrote my own sadhanas.

This *Drop of Nectar, The Smaller Commentary on the Guru Yoga,* was requested by his own son Chökyi Nyima and by the other sons, along with the Chakdzö (the general secretary). Accordingly, I, Khenpo Jamyang Dorje, wrote this for beginners in a way that is easy to read, condensing my earlier commentary, *Cloudbank of Nectar,* to the most essential. May this be a cause for everyone to receive the blessings of the sublime guru and glorious protector in their stream-of-being.

> *Compared to approaching countless buddhas for hundreds of aeons,*
> *By simply recalling the name of the guru, the glorious protector,*
> *You receive the supreme and common siddhis, and your wishes are*
>   *fulfilled;*
> *This is praised hundreds of times in the ocean of sutras, tantras, and*
>   *instructions.*

> *Therefore, this guru sadhana that condenses to the quintessential*
> *The key points of the six million tantras,*
> *I deeply venerated on my mind's lotus flower of threefold trust,*
> *And completed* The Drop of Nectar, *the smaller commentary, so that*
>   *beginners might easily understand.*

> *May the cloudbanks of goodness resulting from this,*
> *Cause a gentle rain*
> *Of the blessings of the glorious guru, the primordial protector,*
> *To fall on the fields of the sugata-essence of all beings.*

> *May the basic space, the essential state of primordial purity and*
>   *spontaneous presence,*
> *An uncontrived vast expanse, beyond removing or adding,*
> *Be sustained as it is in the continuity of natural meditation,*
> And may the state of luminous dharmakaya be realized.

May this be auspicious! May it be virtuous!

With the Khenpo's permission, at the sons of Rinpoche's command, and at Danny and Tara's insistent request, this preliminary translation was made on the Full Moon in May, 1999, by Erik Pema Kunsang, for the benefit of Rinpoche's disciples.

Some words in parenthesis are added for clarity by the translator and editor and do not appear in the original text.

With Nyoshul Khen Rinpoche

GLOSSARY OF TRANSLATION EQUIVALENTS

apparent [how it seems to be], *snang tshul*

approach-accomplishment practice, recitation, *bsnyen sgrub*

attributes, *mtshan nyid*

awakeness/wakefulness, *dran rig*

awareness reaching fullness, *rigpa tshad pheb*

brightness of awareness, *rig pa'i dvangs cha*

capacity, *thugs rje*

carefulness, *bag yod*

clear and vivid, *lhang nger*

clear wakefulness/clear and vivid/clear and brilliant, *gsal lhang nge*

cognizant, *gsal ba*

cognizant yet nonconceptual, *gsal la mi rtog pa*

defiled/conditioned, *zag pa*

dharmadhatu experiences, *chos dbyings*

dharmakaya lion posture, *chos sku seng ge'i bzhugs stangs*

direct liberation, *gcer grol*

disposition, *khams*

drowsy, dull and obscured, *bying ba, rmugs* and *thibs*

empty blankness/vacant, empty state, *had de ba*

empty of other, *shen stong*

empty of self, *rang stong*

essence/natural disposition/basic nature, *gshig*

experience vividly, *lhag ger shar ba*

expression, *rtsal*

expression of rigpa, *rigpa rtsal*

four dharmakaya qualities, *chos kyi sku'i khyad chos bzhi*

fourfold freely resting, *cog bzhag bzhi*

ground/basis, *gzhi*

illusory body, *sgyu lus*

innermost, unexcelled cycle of Heart Essence, *yang sang nying tig*

invigorate, *hur phyung*

knowing/cognition, *shes pa*

liberated upon arising, *shar grol*

love, *rtse ba*

mental body, *yid lus*

mind basis of all stored consciousness, *kun gzhi rnam shes* (abbr. of *kun gzhi'i' rnam par shes pa*). Skt. *alayavijnana*.

mindfulness, *dran pa*

mindful and conscientious, *dran shes,* and alertness, *shes bzhin* (combination of)

naked and awake cognizance, *gsal hrig rjen pa*

nonconceptual, *rtog med*

ordinary consciousness, *rnam shes*

pleasant, *bde nyams*

primordial purity, *ka dag*

pure, *dag, gtsang*

radiance/manifestation, *dangs*

relax loosely, *lhod kyis glod de*

remaining in naturalness, *rnal dbab*
remain vividly clear, *gsal lam mer gnas pa*
rishi posture, *drang srong gi'dug stangs*
sambhogakaya mandala of the wrathful ones, *longs sku khro bo'i dkyil 'khor*
scattered, agitated and absent-minded, *'phro, rgod and thor'*
self-existing, *rang byung*
self-liberated, *rang grol*
self-luminous and clear, *rang lhang nge* and *lhame me*
sound, colors and light rays, *sgra' od zer gsum*
space, *dbyings*
spontaneous presence, *lhun grub*
stage of exhaustion of dharma beyond concepts, *blo' das chos zad*

sustaining the freshness [of the original state], *sor bzhag*
Three Words Striking the Vital Point, Tshig Gsum Gnad Brdeg
transference of consciousness, *'pho ba grong jug'*
transparent, brilliant, bright and wakeful, *sang nge, sa le, wa le, hrig ge*
true nature, *yang dag nyid*
ultimate, *don dam*
unconfined cognizant radiance, *gsal mdangs 'gags pa med pa*
unpleasant experiences, *rtsub nyams*
utterly open, *zang thal*
watchfulness, *dran rtsis*
wide awake, *hrig ge*

ENDNOTES

1   Tulku Urgyen Rinpoche, *Blazing Splendor,* eds. Erik Pema Kunsang and Marcia Binder Schmidt (Hong Kong: Rangjung Yeshe Publications, 2005).

2   Vidyadhara Jigmed Lingpa, *Yeshe Lama,* trans. Light of Berotsana Translation Group (Ithaca: Snow Lion Publications, 2008).

3   The four speech yogas: *rgyas gdab pa,* sealing; *rtsal sbyang ba,* developing strength; *nyen btsal ba,* making pliant; *lam du gzhug pa,* taking to the road.

4   Padmasambhava, *Lamrim Yeshe Nyingpo,* trans. Erik Pema Kunsang, (Rangjung Yeshe Publications, 2016), pages 6–7.

5   Karmapa Rangjung Dorje, *Song of Mahamudra.*

6   Karmey Khenpo Rinchen Dargye, *Don sdud rabsel*

7   Ibid.

8   Ibid.

9   Tsele Natsok Rangdröl

10 Ibid.

11 Ibid.

12 Karmapa Rangjung Dorje, *Song of Karmapa,* trans. Erik Pema Kunsang, (Hong Kong: Rangjung Yeshe Publications, 1992) p. 12.

13 Freely resting mountain, freely resting ocean, freely resting awareness/ rigpa, and freely resting experience (Editor).

14 Dudjom Lingpa, *The Vajra Essence: From the Matrix of Appearances and Primordial Consciousness, a Tantra on the Self-Originating Nature of Existence,* trans. B. Alan Wallace (Austin, TX: Palri Parkhang, 2004).

15 Tantric Substance

16 Jamgön Kongtrül, *Sphere of Refined Gold.*

17 Padmasambhava and Jamgön Kongtrül, *Light of Wisdom, Vol III: The Secret Empowerment,* trans. Erik Pema Kunsang, (Hong Kong: Rangjung Yeshe Publications, 2018) pp 30–32.

18 Tulku Urgyen Rinpoche, *Blazing Splendor,* eds. Erik Pema Kunsang and Marcia Binder Schmidt (Hong Kong: Rangjung Yeshe Publications, 2005) p. 233.

19 In English I put the non in front of dual to convey the meaning. (Editor).

20 *Dogyü Semsum* — Scripture, Tantra, and Mind — refers to the Scripture of Anuyoga, the Tantra of Mahayoga, and the Mind Section of Atiyoga.

For information regarding video and audio recordings, published teachings and programs in the lineage of Tulku Urgyen Rinpoche, please access the following websites:

www.lotustreasure.com
www.rangjung.com

Rangjung Yeshe Publications and Translations

www.shedrub.org
Shedrub Development Mandala

www.CGLF.org
Chokgyur Lingpa Foundation

www.tsoknyirinpoche.org
Tsoknyi Rinpoche and Pundarika Foundation

www.all-otr.org
Teachings of Orgyen Tobgyal Rinpoche

Tergar.org
Yongey Mingyur Rinpoche

www.erikpemakunsang.com
Works of Erik Pema Kunsang